Although John Cage has been almost universally recognized as the leading figure of the post-war musical avant-garde, this is the first book to present a complete and coherent picture of Cage the composer. Providing a historical account of Cage's musical concerns and changing style, James Pritchett describes just what it was Cage did and why and how he did it. The book is centered around extensive descriptions of the most important works and compositional techniques, including in-depth explanations of the role of chance and indeterminacy in Cage's music. Dr. Pritchett also considers the relationship of Cage's musical thought to his interests in such diverse subjects as Eastern philosophy and religion, Marshall McLuhan, and anarchism (among many others). This book thus makes the essential introduction to Cage's musical world.

Music in the Twentieth Century

GENERAL EDITOR Arnold Whittall

The music of John Cage

Music in the Twentieth Century

GENERAL EDITOR Arnold Whittall

This series offers a wide perspective on music and musical life in the twentieth century.

Books included will range from historical and biographical studies concentrating particularly on the context and circumstances in which composers were writing, to analytical and critical studies concerned with the nature of musical language and questions of compositional process. The importance given to context will also be reflected in studies dealing with, for example, the patronage, publishing, and promotion of new music, and in accounts of the musical life of particular countries.

PUBLISHED TITLES

Robert Orledge *Satie the composer*
Kathryn Bailey *The twelve-note music of Anton Webern*
Silvina Milstein *Arnold Schoenberg: notes, sets, forms*
Christopher Hailey *Franz Schreker, 1878–1934: a cultural biography*

The music of John Cage

JAMES PRITCHETT

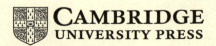
CAMBRIDGE
UNIVERSITY PRESS

Published by the Press Syndicate of the University of Cambridge
The Pitt Building, Trumpington Street, Cambridge CB2 1RP
40 West 20th Street, New York, NY 10011–4211, USA
10 Stamford Road, Oakleigh, Melbourne 3166, Australia

First published 1993

Printed in Great Britain at the University Press, Cambridge

A catalogue record for this book is available from the British Library

Library of Congress cataloguing in publication data
Pritchett, James.
The music of John Cage / James Pritchett.
   p. cm. – (Music in the twentieth century)
Includes bibliographical references.
ISBN 0 521 41621 3 (hardback)
1. Cage, John–Criticism and interpretation   I. Title.
II. Series.
ML410.C24P7   1993
780' . 92–dc20   92–44525 CIP MN

ISBN 0 521 41621 3 hardback

SN

For fw

(the *other* subject of this book)

What is important is to keep our mind high in the world of true understanding, and returning to the world of our daily experience to seek therein the truth of beauty. No matter what we may be doing at a given moment, we must not forget that it has a bearing upon our everlasting self which is poetry.   —Bashō

Contents

Preface   xi

Introduction   1

1 "For more new sounds" (1933–1948)   6
Prelude: Cage's compositional studies   6
Percussion ensembles   10
The prepared piano   22

2 "To sober and quiet the mind . . ." (1946–1951)   36
The sources of a new style   36
Changes in style and aesthetic   45
From choice to chance   60

3 "Throwing sound into silence" (1951–1956)   74
Changes in aesthetic   74
Chart systems   78
Point-drawing systems   92
"The Ten Thousand Things"   95

4 Indeterminacy (1957–1961)   105
Sources of indeterminacy   105
New notations   109
Musical tools   126

5 "Music (not composition)" (1962–1969)   138
Changes in Cage's life and work in the 1960's   138
Process and action   146
Electronics   150
Simultaneity, abundance, and anarchy   154

6 "Joy and bewilderment" (1969–1992)   162

  Return to composition   162
  Work in other media   175
  Program music   189
  Instrumental music   198

  Notes   205
  Sources   215
  Index   220

Preface

My introduction to the work of John Cage was through his extraordinary book *Silence*. In 1978, as a sophomore music major at the University of Maryland, I knew only those things about Cage that every musician "knows" about him: the rumors, the gossip, the hearsay about this possible charlatan who claimed that anything and everything was music. I bought *Silence* as a birthday gift for a friend and then borrowed it to read myself. I remember being taken aback by the brilliance of Cage's thought, its clarity, wit, logic, and power. I went back to the bookstore to buy a copy of his second book, *A Year From Monday*. By this point, I was hooked.

I went to the library to find out more about Cage and his work, but there were no studies of his music, no definitive "life-and-works." Instead, I checked out every score and recording I could lay my hands on. Cage's work became a blueprint for the study of other music: if Cage mentioned a composer in an article, then I sought out that composer's works. I took home stacks of scores and records of music by Morton Feldman, Christian Wolff, Earle Brown, Karlheinz Stockhausen, Pierre Boulez, Sylvano Bussotti, and many others (I recall looking up the piece *Quantitäten* by Bo Nilsson solely because of its appearance as a kind of joke in "Composition as Process: Communication"). I staged performances of some of the indeterminate pieces, enlisting the assistance of other adventurous students. Cage's writing opened up other new worlds for me: I spent hours in dark corners of McKeldin Library reading about Zen Buddhism, Jasper Johns, Meister Eckhart, *Dada*, Marshall McLuhan, Gertrude Stein, the *I Ching*, *Finnegans Wake*, Buckminster Fuller, Robert Rauschenberg, Jackson MacLow, Henry David Thoreau, Marcel Duchamp. The whole process was exhilarating – it changed my life.

All this took place in the late 1970s. Ten years later, I had written a doctoral dissertation on Cage's chance music of the 1950s, and had begun planning this book. I had decided that analytical studies of his works were the most useful approach to Cage's music, and planned to devote my book to this. I prepared extensive outlines of what this study would cover: which works to analyze, which compositional techniques to describe. When I was preparing to write the chapter on the sources of Cage's use of chance, I took a summer to read the books that Cage himself had read in the mid-1940s, most of which I had missed in my earlier explorations: Sri Ramakrishna, Aldous Huxley, Ananda Coomaraswamy, Meister Eckhart. When I told Cage of my plans, he laughed and told me that I should find a nice, large, shady tree to sit under. The daily discoveries and sense of excitement from reading these books were like my undergraduate days all over again. I realized that my plan for the book were all wrong, and the current direction began to take shape. The moral to this story: even after twelve years, the study of Cage's work had the ability to change my mind.

Clearly, I cannot begin to acknowledge what I owe to John Cage. Besides the importance of his work to me personally, I owe him immensely for his assistance in preparing this book. His inability to refuse anything to anyone was legendary; during the course of my studies, he was always completely open, accessible, and helpful in every way. He allowed me unlimited access to his papers, offered much of his time to discuss his work with me, prepared countless delicious lunches, and was the best proofreader I've ever had. I had hoped that I could present this book as a gift to him in return for what he had done for me. After reading drafts of the central portion, he remarked that it "reads like a novel – I'm anxious to see what happens next." Unfortunately, he died shortly before I completed the rest. Cage always distinguished himself from his work, acknowledging that it had to live its life separately from his. He is no longer here to accept my work as a tribute to him; instead I offer it as a tribute to his work – the "everlasting self which is poetry."

Two other people have been exceptionally important to the course of my work. First, Paul van Emmerik: his outstanding thesis *A Cage Documentary* has been my constant companion for the last three years. The amount of time his meticulous bibliography, chronology, and work-list have saved me is incalculable. Second, I am grateful to Frances White, for having read and criticized every page of every draft of this book, helping to guide it to a more composerly end.

I was assisted in my research by a number of people. David Tudor is the current owner of a number of important Cage manuscripts, which he kindly let me examine both at his home in Stony Point and in New York. Michael Hoffmann and Don Gillespie helped me at C.F. Peters; Deborah Campana of the Music Library at Northwestern University guided me through their Cage Archive. Jim Freund was the source of the Cage-Feldman *Radio Happening* tapes.

A number of people read parts of this book and offered their advice and criticism: Scott Burnham, Salwa El-Shawan, Martin Erdmann, Laura Kuhn, Katharine Norman, Joan Retallack, Alistair Riddell, Paul van Emmerik, Alicyn Warren. Thanks also to Kathryn Bailey Puffett at Cambridge University Press, who offered many suggestions that improved the text in various ways.

I am grateful for other resources that were put at my disposal during the work on this book. Paul Lansky of the Music Department at Princeton University was kind enough to allow me the use of their computer equipment for editing, formatting, printing, and archiving the manuscript. The music examples were prepared with *Nightingale*, a music notation program by Don Byrd: I thank him and John Gibson for their assistance with this. The American Council of Learned Societies (with some help from the National Endowment for the Humanities) supported a year's worth of research via their Fellowships for Recent Recipients of the Ph.D. Thanks also go to Kate and Charles Dodge for their advice. Isabel and Agrippina White helped with the typing.

Finally, there are people to whom I owe special debts. Stanley Boorman first put the idea into my head that writing a book on Cage was not just a dream, but a realistic possibility; Penny Souster at Cambridge turned the possibility into a fact. My parents have supported me in this in more ways than I can say. And finally, I owe so much to Professor Shelley Davis of the University of Maryland – above all else, for his sharing my excitement during those two years I spent discovering things in McKeldin Library, never once suggesting that John Cage's music was a silly thing to be taking seriously. Were it not for his permission to explore, and his unwavering faith that I was doing something worthwhile, this book would never have come to be.

All excerpts from Cage's music are © by Henmar Press, New York; the excerpt of Marton Feldman's *Projection 1* is © by C. F. Peters Corp., USA. All of these excerpts are reproduced here by permission of Peters Edition Limited, London.

Introduction

John Cage was a composer: this is the premise from which everything in this book follows. On the face of it, this would not appear to be a statement of much moment. Cage consistently referred to himself as a composer. He studied composition with Henry Cowell, Adolph Weiss, and Arnold Schoenberg. He spoke often of having devoted his life to music. He wrote hundreds of compositions that are published by a prominent music publishing house, have been recorded, and are performed regularly worldwide. He received commissions from major orchestras, chamber ensembles, soloists, and at least one opera company. He is mentioned in every up-to-date history of music. The only monograph devoted to him was in a series of "studies of composers." Of course John Cage was a composer: everything in his life points to this inescapable fact.

And yet, I must begin this book by defending the obvious. For, even though his credentials are clearly those of a composer, Cage has, as often as not, been treated as something else. It has been stated on various occasions by various authorities that Cage was more a philosopher than a composer, that his ideas were more interesting than his music. Cage, says one history of twentieth-century music, "is not to be considered as a creator in the ordinary sense."[1] Another critic wonders whether Cage, after deciding that "he was not going to be one of the world's great composers," refashioned himself into "one of the leading philosophers and wits in twentieth-century music."[2] The degree to which this has become the standard way of dealing with Cage is revealed in a story told by Kyle Gann: a writer for *The New York Times* was told by his editors that he could not refer to Cage as "the most important and influential composer of our time," but rather had to identify him as a "music-philosopher."[3]

For the *Times* editors, as for so many others, the problem with treating Cage as a composer is clearly a problem with his work after 1951. His compositions for percussion and prepared piano written in the 1940s have never been difficult for critics – his *Sonatas and Interludes* of 1948 has even been called a masterwork. In 1951, however, Cage began to use chance operations in the course of his composition, and it is here that things go awry. His adoption of chance techniques is almost always seen as a rejection: a jettisoning of everything traditionally musical. External forces of irrationality (such as Zen Buddhism) are invoked as the cause

1

of this break. Under such influences, it is believed, Cage decided to substitute the throw of dice for his own tastes, so that he could ultimately remove any trace of his personality from the composed work. By 1952, Cage had written *4' 33"*, the silent piece; thus, in the words of one writer, "the authority of the composer [had been] extinguished."[4]

The crux of the problem, then, has been a failure to find some way of dealing with Cage-the-composer, his musical compositions, and his chance operations all at the same time. When faced with music composed using chance, critics have drawn a blank. How can one understand a randomly-made composition? What can one say about such a thing? To criticize it would be to criticize a random act; how does one judge the toss of a coin? The way out of this dilemma has traditionally been to ignore the music and dwell upon "the ideas behind it." For if Cage has left his music to chance, if he has thus extinguished his authority as a composer, then all that remains is an idea – the idea of inviting randomness into his work. The pieces are thus about this idea of chance and are not concerned with anything even remotely musical. These are "conceptual" works in which, as one author writes, "the philosophical underpinnings are clearly more sig-nificant than any mere sound."[5] Cage's importance lies in his having had these ideas, but the results are not music and are not to be evaluated as music. In Cage's work "the issues are all philosophical," says one noted composer, "because composing itself has been entirely devalued."[6] Thus Cage has become "a philoso-pher, not a composer."

The treatment of Cage as a philosopher has had some unfortunate conse-quences. Foremost among these has been the tendency to see all of his work after 1951 – work which presumably shares the same idea about randomness – as an undifferentiated mass of "chance music." The reduction of Cage's music to this one-dimensional approach is made simpler by the nature of chance itself. Critics frequently assume that the compositions are formless and without distinguishing characteristics since they believe them to be, in effect, barely more than random noise. If everything in them is determined by chance, then there can be no stylistic difference between one work and another any more than there can be a difference between one list of random numbers and another. "Instead of a music of definable identity," says one writer, "we have conceptions whose essence is a lack of identity."[7] This failure to see any differences among Cage's chance works has led to their being treated in a superficial fashion; histories of his work tend to pass rapidly over the works composed after 1951, with a few brief descriptions and generalizations. Cage's critics have seemed to take the attitude that if Cage didn't care which sounds became part of his so-called compositions, then why should we bother to listen carefully?

It is this attitude and this approach that I reject in the strongest possible way. In the first place, the claim that Cage's chance pieces do not have distinct identities is complete nonsense. To state that one cannot tell the difference between *Music of Changes*, *Music for Piano*, *Winter Music*, *Cheap Imitation*, and *One –*

all chance-composed works for piano – is an act of either profound ignorance or willful misrepresentation. But beyond such an obvious error, the traditional view of Cage fails to answer the question: Why did he do it? If all that he was left with after 1951 was the idea of chance, then why did he continue to compose? Cage stated on many occasions that he did not like to repeat himself, that he preferred to make a fresh discovery with each new piece. How do we reconcile this with the textbook image of Cage-the-philosopher, pondering the same tired question for forty years? The portrayal of Cage as only a philosopher fails because it cannot serve as the foundation for a believable account of his work. It demeans the composer by presenting a flat, cartoonish version of his life, totally devoid of depth and insight.

Cage-as-philosopher is thus an image that will not bear close scrutiny; we thus must seek a new image, a new role for Cage. It is in this respect that I am, in this book, returning to the obvious: that Cage was a composer. It is not difficult, in fact, to picture him in this role: consider, for example, the story of his composition of *Apartment House 1776*, as told in an interview with David Cope.[8] The work was a commission to commemorate the bicentennial of the American Revolution; Cage thus wanted "to do something with early American music that would let it keep its flavor at the same time that it would lose what was so obnoxious to me: its harmonic tonality." He decided to take forty-four pieces of four-part choral music by William Billings and other early American composers and then to alter them – turn them into new music. In his first version of the pieces, he simply subtracted notes from the originals. For each measure, he used chance to answer the question of how many of the four voices would remain. The results of this process did not suit him: "When I got to a piano and tried them out, they were miserable. No good at all. Not worth the paper they were written on. It was because the question was superficial." He then changed his method by adding silence as a possible answer to his question (in the first version, at least one voice always remained). The results were still "not good." Finally he changed the question itself. He counted the number of notes in a given voice of the piece, and then used chance to select from these. Supposing there were fourteen notes in a line, chance operations might select notes one, seven, eleven, and fourteen. In such a case, he would take the first note from the original and extend it until the seventh note (removing all the intervening notes); all the notes from the seventh to the eleventh would be removed, leaving a silence. Then the eleventh note would be extended to the fourteenth, followed by another silence. Each of the four lines thus became a series of extended single tones and silences. This was the version that Cage settled upon:

> The cadences and everything disappeared; but the flavor remained. You can recognize it as eighteenth century music; but it's suddenly brilliant in a new way. It is because each sound vibrates from itself, not from a theory. . . . The cadences which were the function of the theory, to make syntax and all, all of that is gone, so that you get the most marvelous overlappings.

This is a description of a composer at work. In composing these forty-four pieces for *Apartment House 1776*, Cage had a goal that was clearly defined. His first attempts at making the pieces in accordance with his goal were failures. He evaluated these intermediate results, making refinements and modifications to his way of working. Through this process, he eventually produced a finished product that he judged beautiful, "brilliant," "marvelous." This is Cage, the composer, exercising his craft. The rejection of the first two versions of the pieces was not based on any random factor at all — it was not a matter of one set of random numbers being more beautiful than another. Instead, the focus of his work was on the framework within which chance operated — the questions that he asked. "The principle underlying the results of those chance operations is the questions," he told Cope. "The things which should be criticized, if one wants to criticize, are the questions that are asked."

From his description of his experience in composing *Apartment House 1776*, Cage makes it clear that some questions are better than others, produce better music. Why did he reject those first methods of composition? He tells us that the first two sets of questions were rejected because the individual tones of the original Billings pieces were still locked up by the structure of the tonal harmony — the harmonic structure was antithetical to his musical goals. In the ultimate arrangement, the tones of the four individual voices are extended beyond their original durations, so that they thus break the bonds of the harmony. Each tone is also surrounded on both sides by a silence. Together, these two factors — the breaking up of harmonies and the floating of individual sounds in silences — create the effect of each tone being exactly itself, separate from all the others: "each sound vibrates from itself."

This effect brings to mind the idea of "sounds being themselves," a common theme in Cage's work. What is made crystal clear in the story of his composition of *Apartment House 1776* is that this idea is *musical* and not merely philosophical. That he chose one set of questions over another was purely a matter of taste and style. The frameworks for Cage's chance systems were crafted with an ear towards what sorts of results they would produce, so that the questions he asked form the basis of his own distinctive musical style. If either of the first two chance systems that he derived for this work had been used, the resulting forty-four pieces would still be valid chance compositions — they would still adhere to Cage's supposed "philosophy." But it was only the third and final set of questions that could produce music that was Cage's, that had his style. John Cage evaluated his compositional questions on a strictly musical basis, and so should we.

To understand the music of John Cage, then, one not only needs to know something of the mechanics of his work, but one also needs an image of John Cage the composer — his sensibility, his musical style. As with any composer, this style changed over the years, and not just in 1951 (in this book, I suggest 1946, 1951, 1957, 1962, and 1969 as major years of change in Cage's career, but there are others, and these suggestions are not meant to imply a hard division of his work into periods). But constant throughout, from the earliest works to the last, was his joy in composing: his exercising of his musical imagination, whether through the expressive "considered improvisation" of works such as the *Sonatas and Interludes*, or through the design of elaborate chance-driven systems as in *Music of Changes*, or through the simpler methods of his last works, the "number" pieces. These compositions are the works of a man with a unique and very beautiful sense of musical style.

This book aims to present a coherent picture of this John Cage, the composing Cage. I have asked myself these questions: Who was John Cage? What was his identity as a composer? Who was the man for whom this work was necessary? I do not present this as a biography, nor as a study of his compositions in themselves. Instead, the focus of this book is on John Cage's life as a composer, with what it was that he did and why he did it. In this way, one may say that I have written about something in between Cage and his works: the act of composing rather than the composer or the compositions.

This study is by no means comprehensive. Some of the compositions I mention only briefly, and others I do not mention at all. Similarly, there are some ideas and trends in Cage's work that I do not pursue at any great length. This is in part due to necessity – Cage wrote an enormous amount of music and his work touches on an astonishing range of other subjects. However, this book is also very much my own personal view of his work, shaped by my own attempt to put the pieces of his life together into a coherent picture. In each chapter, I have tried to bring the various disparate materials together into some believable portrait of a composer's life, dispensing with everything but those compositions, techniques, experiences, ideas, and writings that I feel contribute to a satisfying and enlightening account of how and why Cage did what he did.

Cage once indicated that he wished critics would be "introducers": people who could take music and, by writing about it, turn it "into something you can deal with." This has been the model I have tried to follow in this book. I hope that by focusing on the image of Cage composing, I can make his music into something that a listener can deal with *as music*. In the end, there is no substitute for the direct experience of Cage's music itself: this book should be seen as opening a door into that work rather than presenting the final word on it. If you feel it necessary to listen to one or more of the pieces I discuss in the course of this study, then I will consider myself a success. Certainly nothing pleased Cage more than for others to enter along with him into his musical world.

1

"For more new sounds"
(1933–1948)

Prelude: Cage's compositional studies

John Cage's professional career as a composer really did not begin until 1938 – the year he organized a percussion ensemble at the Cornish School in Seattle. However, he had been composing for about six years prior to this, most of that time as a student of various teachers. While these early compositions are only of passing interest, the story of how Cage came to be a composer needs to be presented here, if only briefly.

John Cage's introduction to music was similar to that of so many Americans: as a child he took piano lessons with the local neighborhood teacher. He played the typical literature (Beethoven's *Für Elise* and so forth) and, after gaining sufficient proficiency, sight-read music checked out from the public library. He loved playing the piano, and daydreamed about becoming a concert pianist – perhaps devoting himself to the works of Grieg "for they did not seem to me to be too difficult, and I loved them."[1]

After having been a brilliant student in high school, Cage was confused about what to pursue as his life's career. In 1930, he dropped out of college and traveled to Europe. He arrived in Paris with somewhat unfocused artistic ambitions. The original purpose of the trip was to accumulate "experience" for his goal of being a writer, but he soon began to pursue other interests: architecture, painting, and music. While in Paris, he began going to concerts and visiting galleries; he had his first tastes of modern music and painting there.

It was while wandering in Europe that Cage made his first attempts at composition:

> I remember very little about my first efforts at composition, except that they had no sensual appeal and no expressive power. They were derived from calculations of a mathematical nature, and these calculations were so difficult to make that the musical results were always extremely short. My next pieces used texts and no mathematics; my inspiration was carried along on the wings of Aeschylus and Gertrude Stein. I improvised at the piano and attempted to write down what I played before I forgot it.

Cage returned to California in 1931 and began performing various odd jobs to

6

make a living in depression-era Los Angeles. Among his money-making ideas was to give lectures (for a small fee) to housewives on the subjects of modern art and music. Each week he would present works of a particular artist or composer to his subscribers. Eventually he had to give a talk about the music of Arnold Schoenberg and decided to use the Op. 11 piano pieces as an example. He could not play the pieces himself, nor was he able to find a recording of them. He decided to contact the pianist Richard Buhlig, the only person in Los Angeles he knew of who could perform them. Cage had never met Buhlig, but simply looked him up in the telephone directory and called him without any introduction. Buhlig refused to play for Cage's lecture, but they became friends and Cage began studying piano with him.

Cage showed Buhlig his compositions. Even though he was a pianist and not a composer, Buhlig was glad to offer his criticisms of Cage's work. He encouraged Cage to be more methodical and careful: "He conveyed to me the idea that composition is putting sounds together in such a way that they fit, that is, that they subserve an overall plan." More important than any specific directions, however, was Buhlig's encouragement for Cage's musical efforts; he was Cage's first independent professional musical contact. Cage soon gave up painting and writing and devoted more and more of his time to music.

The compositions that date from the time after Cage's contact with Buhlig are entirely contrapuntal, and perhaps show the indirect influence of the style of Schoenberg. In the United States in the 1930s, many composers, Cage included, felt that they had to choose between the neo-classicism of Igor Stravinsky and the atonal, predominantly contrapuntal style of Schoenberg. His earliest surviving works show Cage clearly leaning in the Schoenberg direction, perhaps as a result of his sessions with Buhlig. The Sonata for Clarinet (1933) is a typical early example: the style is chromatic, rhythmically complex, and unmetrical. In all three movements, Cage makes a free use of short motives, repeating and varying them throughout. In the second movement, this approach leads to an almost serial arrangement of the pitches, but the work is clearly not conceived in serial terms.

Buhlig had criticized the formlessness of Cage's very earliest works, and beginning with his clarinet sonata Cage introduced various organizational methods to make his sounds "subserve an overall plan." In the sonata, for example, the third movement is an exact pitch retrograde of the first movement (although they are completely different rhythmically). A more durable method was the one he devised for a number of works: *Sonata for Two Voices* (1933), *Composition for Three Voices* (1934), and *Solo with Obbligato Accompaniment of Two Voices in Canon, and Six Short Inventions on the Subject of the Solo* (1933–34). In these pieces, each voice is limited to a specific two-octave range (that is, a range of twenty-five notes). In all three works, these ranges overlap: for example, in the *Sonata for Two Voices*, the two ranges have one octave in common. Each voice in these pieces then proceeds to sound all twenty-five notes of its range without repetitions. Once all twenty-five notes have appeared, another presentation begins, and so on, throughout the piece. This is not a serial method, however: there is no specific ordering of the notes. The voices proceed more or less independently, with the following restriction: repetitions of the notes in the overlapping pitch areas are kept as far apart as possible.

The twenty-five-note system supplied a certain structure to Cage's free atonal counterpoint without significantly altering its musical effects. The use of varied motives and complex rhythms continued in all three of these works, unaffected by the twenty-five-note method. Cage added other structuring devices to enhance the method. In *Composition for Three Voices* there is a "theme" with specific rhythmic and pitch contours that repeats over and over throughout the piece (the three parts of this theme are marked in the opening of the score). The *Solo and Six Inventions* has a more convincing overall structure. The solo itself consists of a number of expositions of its theme interleaved with episodic sections. The ensuing six inventions are pieces of a type familiar to all students of counterpoint: each takes a brief fragment of the opening solo and develops it in free three-voice counterpoint, all within the confines of the twenty-five-note method.

It would be a mistake to ascribe too much importance to these pieces, however. They appear to be studies in counterpoint, completely concerned with pitch and rhythmic arrangements – they bear no instrumentation, no dynamic markings, no phrasings or expressive marks. They are also quite impractical, and were probably not performed at the time. The rhythmic complexities are bewildering, and the parts are full of difficult wide leaps. The counterpoint is unrelentingly dissonant; it seems as if all the vertical combinations of voices are arranged in seconds and sevenths. "What I wrote," Cage remembers, "though it sounded organized, was not pleasant to listen to."

In 1933, the time came when Buhlig was no longer able to help Cage with his compositions. He directed him to Henry Cowell, who was active at that time in San Francisco. Cage sent his works to Cowell, who scheduled a performance of the Sonata for Clarinet as part of one of his New Music Workshops. The performance was an experience that would be familiar to any young composer: the hired clarinetist had never looked at the score and could not play it, and Cage wound up having to play it himself at the piano.[2] Despite the performance problems, Cowell took an interest in Cage's work, and recommended that he go to New York to study with Adolph Weiss, a student of Arnold Schoenberg's, with the idea that ultimately Cage would be able to study with Schoenberg himself. This was perhaps the decisive moment for Cage, the moment at which he ceased to compose only for himself, and began to see a future for himself as a professional composer. "I was now anxious to study composition," he recalled later, "for working by myself and developing my own ideas had left me with a sense of separation from the mainstream of music, and thus of loneliness."

During the period from 1934 to 1937 Cage was occupied with his compositional studies, which can be summarized briefly here. Calvin Tomkins describes Cage's routine in New York:

He studied harmony and composition with Weiss for two hours after work each day, and usually spent his evenings playing bridge with Mr. and Mrs. Weiss and Henry Cowell, who was then teaching at the New School for Social Research on 12th Street. No matter how late the previous evening's bridge game had lasted, he got up at four a.m. every day and composed for four hours.[3]

While in New York, Cage also took Cowell's classes in world music at the New School. In 1935 he returned to California to study with Schoenberg. His studies, which lasted for two years, consisted of small group sessions in composition held at Schoenberg's home, and in counterpoint classes that Schoenberg taught at the University of Southern California and the University of California at Los Angeles. By 1938, Cage was hired as a "composer, instructor of percussion, and accompanist to the dance department" at the Cornish School in Seattle; his formal studies were completed.

Of his various composition teachers, Arnold Schoenberg looms largest as a figure of lasting importance for Cage. In 1980, when Cage was nearing his seventieth birthday, Schoenberg still figured in his list of the fifteen men who were most important to his work.[4] But on the surface Schoenberg's importance to Cage is difficult to fathom. Cage could not be called a follower of Schoenberg: he only studied with him for a relatively brief period, and, after 1938, did not write a work that was even remotely like Schoenberg's. A clue to the nature of John Cage's relation to Arnold Schoenberg is found in the following story, here taken from Calvin Tomkins' profile of Cage, but which Cage told and retold throughout his life:

> Schoenberg questioned whether Cage could afford to study with him. "I told him," Cage has said, "that there wasn't any question of affording it, because I couldn't pay him anything at all. He then asked me whether I was willing to devote my life to music, and I said I was. 'In that case,' he said, 'I will teach you free of charge.'"[5]

Schoenberg was a model for Cage – almost a hero. Cage admitted that he was in awe of Schoenberg – he worshipped him, and at the same time, was terrified of him:

> In all the time I studied with Schoenberg he never once led me to believe that my work was distinguished in any way. He never praised my compositions, and when I commented on other students' work in class he held my comments up to ridicule. And yet I worshipped him like a god.[6]

Schoenberg's devotion to music was inspirational for Cage. He offered Cage an example of how to live one's life as a composer, and in the process made Cage feel more and more like a composer himself. Although Schoenberg may not have had a lasting influence on his style of composition, he changed Cage's life. When Cage had entered college, he had thought of becoming a minister; after dropping out of school, he sought to be some sort of artist. Schoenberg, by towering as an almost religious figure, perhaps brought these two aspirations together for Cage, inspiring a permanent devotion to art. Throughout his life, when asked why he composed music, Cage would speak of his vow to Schoenberg.

Cage never studied serial methods with Schoenberg. He did, however, develop his own approach to composition using rows. He would break the row up into short motives or cells, each with a particular rhythmic profile, and these cells would then be repeated and transposed following a few simple rules. This technique was first used in the *Two Pieces for Piano* composed sometime around 1935. Here, it appears in an austere presentation reminiscent of the twenty-five-note pieces, suggesting that these pieces, too, were exercises and experiments rather than full-fledged compositions. Three larger works from 1938, composed after Cage's move to Seattle, are more successful, and show the results of his widened musical experiences of the mid-1930s. These compositions – *Metamorphosis* for piano, *Five Songs for Contralto*, and *Music for Wind Instruments* – all use the cellular-serial idea, but in expanded, freer treatments. In these compositions, one gets less a sense of the cells being simply strung along one after another, or of being piled up on top of each other. Instead, the cells are used expressively and musically. But even though these compositions come the closest to being mature and substantial works, they represent a dead end in Cage's development as a composer. The serial and contrapuntal ideas that occupied him throughout his student years were never again to appear in his work after 1938.

Percussion ensembles

Origins of Cage's work with percussion

> I believe that the use of noise to make music will continue and increase until we reach a music produced through the aid of electrical instruments which will make available for musical purposes any and all sounds that can be heard. Photoelectric, film, and mechanical mediums for the synthetic production of music will be explored. Whereas, in the past, the point of disagreement has been between dissonance and consonance, it will be, in the immediate future, between noise and so-called musical sounds.

This statement forms the core of a lecture, "The Future of Music: Credo," given by Cage in Seattle in 1937 or 1938. In its published form, this "credo" is interrupted at various points by expansions of the ideas set forth. For example, after the phrase "to make music" in the first sentence, Cage discusses the definition of the term "music": "If this word, music, is sacred . . . we can substitute a more meaningful term: organization of sound."

This sweeping statement gives a good sense of the role Cage saw himself as playing in the musical world of the late 1930s. Rather than align himself with either Schoenberg or Stravinsky, in this manifesto he placed himself squarely in the "experimental" camp; allied with composers such as Henry Cowell, Cage saw himself as forging ahead amid the new musical possibilities opened up by new technology. His use of the definition of music as "organized sound" suggests a parallel to Edgard Varèse, and the emphasis on noise as the primary material for new music indicates his awareness of the Futurist writings of Luigi Russolo. Cage's model for the composer was the inventor of new sounds and new instruments, and, along with that, the necessary invention of new forms and methods for composition. Where Henry Cowell had written of "New Musical Resources," Cage wrote "For More New Sounds." In the 1942 article of that title, Cage calls for no less than "the finding and invention of further instrumental resources, the development of an occidental theory of rhythm, and the establishing of another valid form of musical expression."

Above all else, Cage saw the advocacy of percussion music – the musical reclamation of noise – as his primary task as a composer. This was the first musical role that he could take on with gusto, confidence, and flair, and which led to his first successes as a composer. He started by organizing a percussion ensemble at the Cornish School, made up largely of dance students (including Merce Cunningham). Their first concert was held in December of 1938, and by the following year, they were touring other colleges in the area, including trips to San Francisco and Oakland. Cage sent out a call for percussion scores from any interested composers, thus building up the repertory for his ensemble. He met Lou Harrison, a composer with similar interests and tastes, and the two began collaborating on concerts, giving joint performances up and down the west coast.

As his work reached larger and larger audiences, his activities widened and increased. Cage attempted to establish a Center of Experimental Music. This would be:

> A place where the work with percussion could continue, and where it could be supplemented by the results of close collaboration between musicians and sound engineers, so that the musical possibilities might be continually refreshed with new technological instruments.

Cage went so far as to contact officials at the Metro-Goldwyn-Mayer movie studios, but, although he was shown all their sound-manipulation facilities, they would not let him work there. By 1942, he decided to move east: after a short stay in Chicago, he arrived in New York in the summer of 1942. He gave his debut concert of percussion music at the Museum of Modern Art in 1943, garnering mixed reviews in the New York newspapers. From then on, Cage's work was regularly discussed in the New York musical press and in the pages of such journals as *Modern Music*. He became something of a household name in new music circles: in 1947, when Virgil Thomson wrote in the *New York Herald Tribune* that the field of percussion music was "completely occupied by John Cage" he did not feel it necessary to identify Cage any further to his readers.[7]

11

How did Cage become involved in percussion music? How did his preoccupations change from dissonant counterpoint in 1938 to "new sounds" in 1939? One story that he told was of his encounter with Oskar Fischinger, a maker of abstract films. Cage recalled a particular conversation they had in the mid-1930s:

> He spoke to me about what he called the spirit inherent in materials and he claimed that a sound made from wood had a different spirit than one made from glass. The next day I began writing music which was to be played on percussion instruments.

The immediate results of this encounter were the Quartet (1935) and Trio (1936), the former for unspecified percussion instruments, the latter for pieces of wood, tom-toms, bamboo sticks, and bass drum. The Quartet is probably the piece Cage wrote after talking to Fischinger, and was clearly an experiment:

> I had no idea what it would sound like, not even what instruments would be used to play it. However, I persuaded three other people to practice the music with me, and we used whatever was at hand: we tapped on tables, books, chairs, and so forth. When we tired of these sounds, we invaded the kitchen and used pots and pans. Several visits to junkyards and lumberyards yielded more instruments: brake-drums from automobiles, different lengths of pipes, steel rings, hardwood blocks. After experimenting for several weeks, the final scoring of the Quartet was finished: it included the instruments that had been found, supplemented by a pedal tympani and a Chinese gong which lent to the whole a certain traditional aspect and sound.

Cage used rhythmic cells in constructing the Quartet – cells used in much the same way as his serial-cellular pieces of 1935–38. The percussion Trio that followed is similar, but somewhat simpler in construction.

All-percussion music was not an idea completely original in Cage, however. I have already mentioned the importance of Cowell, Varèse, and Russolo as forerunners of Cage's role as experimenter in new sounds; all three had also written music for percussion ensembles (although Russolo's would be known only by reputation). Other composers were attracted to the medium of percussion music in the 1930s, as well. George Antheil's *Ballet mécanique* (1924) and Darius Milhaud's Concerto for Percussion and Orchestra (1930) would be relevant predecessors here. In California William Russell had composed his *Three Dances* (1933) and a fugue (1933). From the Caribbean there was Amadeo Roldán's *Rítmicas V* (1930), and from Indonesia there was the music of the gamelan as explained, transcribed, and re-interpreted by Colin McPhee. Percussion music was a widespread development in the United States in the mid-1930s: Henry Cowell stated in 1933 that he had been offered *fifteen* all-percussion works for publication that year.[8]

Perhaps the single most important factor in Cage's adoption of percussion music as his primary mission as a composer was his work with modern dancers.

Simple percussion accompaniments were common in modern dance classes at the time; dance pioneers such as Mary Wigman saw self-made percussion accompaniments as a kind of non-musical rhythmic accompaniment to dances, thus insuring the primacy of the dance.[9] As a result of this, classes in percussion were common at dance schools and festivals in the 1930s. Cowell taught such classes, and Cage himself took up such work at UCLA in 1937 and later on at the Cornish School. The dancers served as important consumers and performers of his new percussion music. His job at the Cornish School created a demand for his work as accompaniments for dancers, and the dancers in turn served as performers in his percussion ensemble. For a composer whose only prior public performance had been the debacle of the Sonata for Clarinet in 1933, the interest shown in his percussion works and the ease with which he could get them performed must have been a strong incentive, indeed. Composers such as Cowell, Varèse, Russolo, Russell, or Roldán may have provided examples for Cage, but it was his work with dancers that served as the proximate cause for his entry into the percussion field, as explained by Cowell in his 1940 account of Cage and Harrison's work:

> Our newest Pacific coast group . . . have also developed their interest naturally, as composers for the modern concert dance. . . . Composers who work with dancers come to know percussion instruments and their possibilities; daily association with the problem of rhythm forms their background. Having mastered the gamut of the instruments used in the studios, they very naturally proceed to compose for them in larger forms, with enough tone-qualities and rhythms to achieve independent musical compositions.[10]

Rhythmic structure

In "The Future of Music: Credo" Cage mentioned new structures that would be developed for the "all-sound" music he envisioned. In elaborating this point in the talk, he mentions rhythmic structure, but offers no specifics, noting only that such structural methods would ultimately be "crystallized into one or several widely accepted methods." In fact, musical structures based on the relationships of lengths of time – phrase lengths, the lengths of larger sections of music, and so on – became the basis of all Cage's percussion music from 1939 onwards. Rhythmic structure is one of the continuing threads in his work: the conception of compositions or performances as time-structures remained with him for the rest of his life.

In the 1948 autobiographical lecture "A Composer's Confessions" Cage lays out the two reasons that he came to base his music on duration structures. First, there was his work with dancers. In most cases, Cage would write the accompaniment for a dance *after* the choreography was completed. The dancer would give him the "measures" of the dance: so many bars of $\frac{4}{4}$ meter followed by so many bars of $\frac{5}{4}$, and so on. Cage would then write music to fit these phrase lengths. Thus, his compositional structure was completely dictated by the choreography – a situation he found unacceptable. Discovery of a means of organizing and coordinating phrase lengths in a coherent way became his goal: "These counts [of the dancer's choreography] were nearly always, from a musical point of view, totally lacking in organization . . . . I believe this disorder led me to the inception of structural rhythm."

The second cause for Cage's development of rhythmic structures was the very nature of the percussion sounds he worked with. Many of these sounds lack a clear pitch, thus ruling out any musical structures based on harmony or melody. According to "A Composer's Confessions" Cage arrived at duration as the proper basis for structure from an observation about the nature of percussion sounds: that "they are for the most part indefinite as to pitch, but autonomous as to duration. For example: no human power can make the sound of a wood-block last longer than it, by its nature, is going to." Innate duration being the defining component of percussion sounds, it seemed logical to him that duration should form the basis of the structure of percussion music. He concludes his history of rhythmic structure as follows: "Two facts then led me to structural rhythm: the physical nature of the materials with which I was dealing, and the experience I had had in writing within the lengths of time prescribed for me by modern dancers."[11]

Musical structures based on phrase lengths are found in some of Cage's serial pieces of 1938 – even though these are not percussion works. As an example, there is the song "in Just—" from the Five Songs for Contralto. This piece consists of voice and piano phrases in alternation only – the two never play together. In the first half of the composition, these alternating phrases are exactly identical in length and follow an increasing sequence: 5, 14, 18, and 23 beats respectively (see Example 1–1). In the second half of the piece, the four piano phrases have the same lengths, but in reverse order, while the four voice phrases repeat the same sequence of 5, 14, 18, 23. The last two pairs of phrases form a coda to the piece, with identical phrase lengths of 5 and 18 beats. Similar structures based on phrase lengths can be found in *Metamorphosis*.

The first appearance of a clear phrase-length structure in a composition for percussion is in *Imaginary Landscape No. 1* (1939). Here, the overall structure divides into four large sections, defined through the use of contrasting materials, with durations of 16, 17, 18, and 19 measures (see Example 1–2). Each of these four sections is itself subdivided into four phrases: three of five measures each, with the final phrase increasing from one measure in the first section to four measures in the last.

These early pieces show the development of Cage's rhythmic structures from their origin as arbitrary phrase lengths given by dancers, to symmetrical arrangements of phrase lengths, to the grouping of phrases into larger units. This latter principle of a two-level hierarchy of structural rhythm – the phrase and the section – was codified and expanded in what Cage called "micro-macrocosmic" rhythmic structure, a device that was of immense importance to his work.

Example 1–1   Five Songs for Contralto: III ("in Just–"), phrase structure

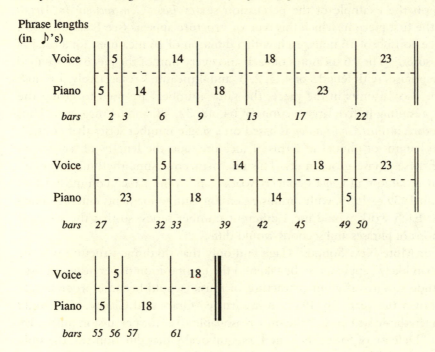

Example 1–2   *Imaginary Landscape No. 1*, phrase structure

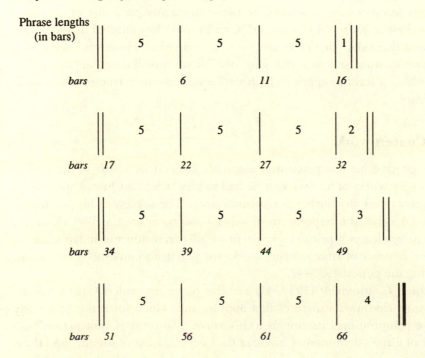

To explain the principle of micro-macrocosmic rhythmic structure, I will draw upon the example of the percussion sextet *First Construction (in Metal)* (1939), the first piece in which this type of structure appears (see Example 1–3). The piece consists of 16 units, each with a duration of 16 measures, for a total of 256 measures.[12] The 16 measures of each and every unit of the piece are divided into five phrases with lengths of 4, 3, 2, 3, and 4 measures respectively. Because there are also 16 units in the piece, the same numbers are used to group the 16 units, resulting in five large sections of 64, 48, 32, 48, and 64 measures. Thus the structure of *First Construction* is based on a single number series that controls both the lengths of phrases in terms of measures and the lengths of sections in terms of these phrase-group units. This micro-macrocosmic rhythmic structure was used in almost all Cage's concert works (and some dance commissions, as well) from 1939 to 1956, with various extensions and refinements entering along the way. Each work would use a different number series, so that the size and proportions of phrases and sections would differ.

In "For More New Sounds" Cage said only that rhythmic structure was the "more than likely" approach to be taken in the composition of percussion music. His attitude towards rhythmic structure in music would become progressively stronger over the years. By 1944, in his article "Grace and Clarity," he would insist on rhythmic structure as the only reasonable basis for percussion music. By 1948, in "Defense of Satie," he stated unequivocally that duration was the only valid basis for any musical structure whatsoever. However, it should be made clear that when Cage made these sorts of statements, he was not speaking of his own micro-macrocosmic structures; he never made any particular or exclusive claims for these at all. In "A Composer's Confessions" he admitted that he could "understand that other rhythmic structures are possible." However, of his own micro-macrocosmic schemes, he said that their "possibilities appear to be inexhaustible," a feeling supported by his adherence to such structures for nearly twenty years.

Concert works

When Cage gave his first percussion ensemble concert in Seattle at the end of 1938, the only works of his own that he had to play were his Quartet and Trio – he had not written any further percussion music. The success of his percussion ensemble concerts, the response from other composers such as Lou Harrison, and his emergence as a primary exponent of all-percussion music led Cage to compose a number of large concert works for percussion ensembles of various sorts during the period 1939–42.

The three *Constructions* (1939–41) are the pieces in which Cage's micro-macrocosmic rhythmic structures first appear, and which form the first really distinctive compositional statements in his *œuvre*. The term "Construction" is a reminder of Cage's definition of music as the "organization of sound," and these

Example 1–3   *First Construction (in Metal)*, micro–macrocosmic structure

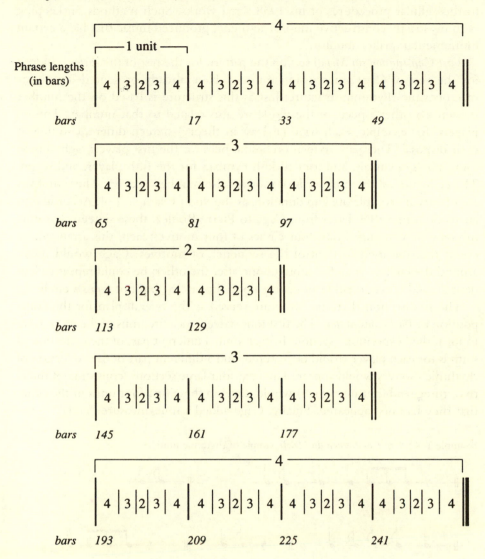

works do have about them the futurist flavor of Varèse or Russolo. We have no real direct access to Cage's aesthetic position of 1939, but he does look back to this time in "A Composer's Confessions":

> It [his aesthetic attitude] had nothing to do with the desire for self-expression, but simply had to do with the organization of materials. I recognized that expression of two kinds, that arising from the personality of the composer and that arising from the nature and context of the materials, was inevitable, but I felt its emanation was stronger and more sensible when not consciously striven for, but simply allowed to arise naturally.

17

All three *Constructions* follow compositional methods that are fairly closely allied to the cellular procedures of his 1938 serial works. Such methods, in keeping with his strictly constructive musical aesthetic, produced music that has a certain monumental quality about it.

First Construction (in Metal) sets up the pattern for the rest of the series – indeed for the rest of Cage's percussion music. I have already presented its micro-macrocosmic rhythmic structure; just as this structure is based on the number sixteen, so other aspects of the work are also related to that number. The six players, for example, each have (at least in theory) sixteen different sounds at their disposal. There are sixteen orchestral bells for the first player; eight anvils, four chinese cymbals, and four turkish cymbals for the fifth player, and so on. The collection of rhythmic cells or motives also numbers sixteen. These motives are of varying complexity and duration, as shown in Example 1–4. According to an account in a 1950 letter from Cage to Pierre Boulez, these sixteen rhythmic motives were arranged into four circles of four motives each; this arrangement could then be used to control the sequence of motives. Cage would move around the circles, using the motives one after the other; he could repeat cells as desired, and move in either direction along the circles, but not *across* a circle.

The five-section rhythmic structure served as the overall plan for the composition of *First Construction*. The first four sixteen-measure units of the piece were to form the "exposition" section. In each unit, a different part of the collection of sounds for each player would be featured, and a different part of the collection of rhythmic motives would appear. The next four large sections (consisting of three, two, three, and four units each) would develop these first four units in the order that they had first appeared. Finally, Cage added a nine-measure "coda" to the

Example 1–4 *First Construction (in Metal)*, sample of rhythmic motives

end of the piece, for reasons that are not clear. This plan is simple enough; it was not followed in a slavishly strict fashion, however. The sounds and rhythmic motives used in the different units of the exposition section are not mutually exclusive: borrowing of motives and sounds from one unit to the next takes place. Still, the plan does function in a general way: there are certainly connections between the first four units and the remaining large sections of the piece. For example, several entire phrases of the second unit of the exposition appear unaltered in the course of the corresponding section of the development, interspersed with new (but related) material.

Several different types of music occur in *First Construction*. The stringing end-to-end of the different rhythmic motives is common, and creates a continuity of irregular patterns with fairly little repetition. At the opposite extreme, a single motive may repeat over and over, or perhaps two or three motives will be grouped into a sequence which is then repeated. Such repetition builds momentum at dramatic points. The long sustained sounds found throughout the piece – thundersheet roars and piano trills – are outside the system of rhythmic motives altogether, supplying a noisy pedal point or a continuous sonic wash.

Cage has used these various techniques of handling the rhythmic motivic materials to create six more or less independent layers of sound – one for each performer – which he then has added together to create differing textures. There is less interest here in the course of events on a note-to-note basis, and more attention paid to the general shapes and textures of the blocks of sound. This approach is a logical outcome of the constructive basis of Cage's micro-macro-cosmic rhythmic structure. In *First Construction*, the individual phrases of the rhythmic structure are defined in almost every case by a change in instrumentation. The sixteen-measure units are marked by more dramatic textural changes, as well as by changes in dynamic level (either sudden or gradual). The five large sections of the piece are marked by tempo changes. The effect of all this is that the listener is aware of a great deal of activity – syncopations, cross-rhythms, and clusters of attacks. There is too much going on to attend to all the details of the music, so that instead the effect of the piece is tied to its rhythmic verve and to the apprehension of the large-scale architecture as it unfolds.

The other percussion works from this period follow similar lines. The remaining *Constructions* are both for quartets of players. *Second Construction* (1940) is of interest only for its closing fugal section, but *Third Construction* (1941) introduces an effective twist on the micro-macrocosmic structural idea. The piece consists of 24 units of 24 measures each, but the phrase structure within each of these units does not follow a single proportion series, as would be expected. Instead, the phrase lengths follow a different number series for each of the four players.[13]

Player 4: {8, 2, 4, 5, 3, 2}
Player 1: {2, 8, 2, 4, 5, 3}
Player 3: {3, 2, 8, 2, 4, 5}
Player 2: {5, 3, 2, 8, 2, 4}

19

As can be seen by the order in which I give them here, these four series of six numbers are in fact simply rotations of the same series. Within individual parts, the phrases are distinguished by dynamics, instrument changes, silences, and the change in rhythmic patterns. As a result of this, *Third Construction* avoids some of the blockiness and predictability of the textural changes found in the earlier *Construction* pieces, since phrase boundaries are rarely aligned among the four players.

The first three *Imaginary Landscapes* (1939–42; the fourth and fifth were written in 1951–52) have in common the use of various electronic devices as instruments. Cage was originally inspired to use electronic instruments while at the Cornish School, which had a recording and broadcasting studio. The electronics battery in *Imaginary Landscape No. 1* consists of devices one would expect to find in such a studio: two record turntables playing recordings of test tones (either constant frequencies or varying ones). The records can be played at either of two speeds – 33⅓ or 78 rpm – the speed changed by a clutch. Rhythms are produced by lifting and lowering the record needle. The effect of the pitch sliding when the turntable speed is changed is striking and eerie, and Cage has heightened this effect by combining the frequency recordings with other ominous sounds: cymbal tremolos, the bass strings of a piano played with a soft gong beater, and three piano notes muted with the fingers. *Imaginary Landscape No. 1* is striking not for any elaborate use of electronic technology, but for the effective and imaginative musical use of these records. Where anyone else would have seen just a utilitarian test-tone recording, Cage saw a new sound to add to his musical palette.

While he was in Chicago, he had access to the CBS radio studios when he was commissioned to compose music for Kenneth Patchen's radio play, *The City Wears a Slouch Hat*; this experience no doubt inspired the second and third entries in the *Imaginary Landscape* series. In *Imaginary Landscape No. 2* (1942), one performer plays a coil of wire that is amplified by attaching it to a phonograph tonearm (this was a sound Cage discovered from his work with radio sound-effects men). The only other unusual instruments are two electric buzzers. The rest of the battery comprises three sets of tin cans, a conch shell horn, a ratchet, drums, gongs, a lion's roar, and a metal wastebasket. *Imaginary Landscape No. 3* (1942) uses the largest collection of electronic devices in the entire series: oscillators, test-tone recordings, a recording of a generator, a buzzer, an amplified coil of wire, and an amplified marimbula.

Besides the *Constructions* and *Imaginary Landscapes*, there are a few other concert percussion works from the period around 1940, most of them shorter or of lesser importance. *Living Room Music* (1940) is, like the 1935 Quartet, for unspecified instruments. The title comes from the suggestions given for sound sources:

> Any household objects or architectural elements may be used as instruments, e.g., 1st player: magazines, newspaper or cardboard; 2nd player: table or other wooden furniture; 3rd player: largish books; 4th player: floor, wall, door or wooden frame of window.

Double Music (1941) was the result of Cage's partnership with Lou Harrison in staging percussion performances. They wrote it collaboratively: Cage composed the parts for two of the four players and Harrison those for the other two. The total duration of 200 measures and the instrumentation (bells, brake drums, sistra, gongs, tam-tams, and thundersheet) were agreed upon in advance; after this, each composer went his own way. Cage chose a rhythmic structure of fourteen units of fourteen measures each, using the number series {4, 3, 2, 5}. This structure covered 196 measures, the closest integer square to 200 (a four-measure coda finishes off the piece). Harrison used a non-hierarchical structure of 21 units of 9½ measures each (the first unit has an extra half-measure to fill out the 200 measures of the whole). When they had finished, the two pairs of independently-composed parts were performed simultaneously.

Example 1–5   *Amores*: II (Trio), bars 21–30

Finally, there are two short pieces written in 1943 (after Cage had moved to New York) which use a different means for controlling rhythmic patterns – what he has called "a method controlling the number of attacks within the small structural divisions."[14] What this means is that rather than creating phrases of music by stringing motives along one after the other, here he used a system that controlled the number of notes to be struck in each phrase unit. The patterns and rhythms were then composed freely to provide the proper number of attacks. This is first seen in the second movement of the suite *Amores* (1943), a trio for tom-toms and rattle. The rhythmic structure here is based on ten-measure units divided {3, 2, 2, 3}. The control of attacks is evident in various places: in the third ten-measure unit, for example, the three players make one, two, and four attacks per measure each, respectively (see Example 1–5). Note that although the number of attacks is the same in each measure, the specific rhythms differ – Cage was free to write whatever rhythms he wished, so long as the required number of attacks was observed. This method was also used in the percussion quartet movement of the unfinished suite of pieces entitled *She Is Asleep* (1943). In both *She Is Asleep* and *Amores*, the effect of the attack-control system is similar to the cellular method of the other percussion works: the musical interest is less at the note-to-note level and more at the larger scale of variations in texture and density.

The prepared piano

Origins of the prepared piano

Cage probably came to write percussion music in large part through his work with dancers; nevertheless, there are only two surviving percussion works for dancers. *Credo in Us* (1942), written for Merce Cunningham and Jean Erdman, is reminiscent of *Imaginary Landscape No. 2* in both its scoring (tin cans, gongs, electric buzzer, tom-toms, piano, and phonograph) and style. The only other dance work involving percussion is *Forever and Sunsmell* (1943), a piece for voice and two percussionists written for a dance by Jean Erdman. Certainly Cage's percussion work with dancers was more extensive than this; it is quite likely that some works were lost or discarded, and some of his percussion accompaniments may very well have been improvised.

Even so, the logistics of percussion music – acquiring and transporting instruments, arranging for multiple performers – made it impractical as an accompaniment for small modern dance recitals. This problem led to the invention of the prepared piano, one of John Cage's best-known innovations. The story, recounted by him in "How the Piano Came to be Prepared," begins in 1940 with the request by Syvilla Fort, a dancer at the Cornish School, for music to accompany her dance *Bacchanale*. The piece needed to reflect the African theme of the dance, and hence Cage wished to use percussion instruments. This plan was foiled, however, when he found out that there was no room in the auditorium for a percussion battery; the only instrument he could use was a piano. He tried to write a serial piano piece in the proper style, but, not surprisingly, found this impossible. Instead, he decided to change the piano itself – to work inside on the strings of the instrument, just as Henry Cowell had done. After much experimenting, he found that screws and pieces of felt weather stripping placed between the strings would stay in place and completely alter the sound of the piano, turning it into a miniature percussion orchestra. As the story concludes, "I wrote the *Bacchanale* quickly and with the excitement continual discovery provided."[15]

The alteration of a piano tone by preparing the strings with various objects is a complicated matter, involving many physical factors, some of which are contradictory. The object adds mass to the vibrating string, thus lowering the pitch; heavier objects (such as large bolts) thus lower the pitch more than light ones (such as small screws). At the same time, the object stretches the strings, thus tending to *raise* the pitch and making the diameter of the object an important variable, as well. The placement of the object along the string is important, in that the muting object will effectively shorten the string; placement at a nodal point will produce a more or less distinct harmonic. Soft objects (such as weather stripping or rubber) will tend to dampen the tone, shortening the decay; at high registers, this effect is less noticeable, since the decay of these notes is already so short. Placing preparations only between the two rightmost strings of a triple-strung note means that the altered sound of these two strings will mix with the unaltered sound of the third string. Thus, such a note will maintain a certain amount of its original pitch, but the altered sonorities of the prepared strings will perhaps conflict with this, causing beating. The *una corda* pedal can be used to silence the unaltered string by shifting the hammers to the right, thus allowing for two different sounds to issue from the same note.[16] All these factors combine to produce sounds that are complex, inharmonic, microtonal, and hence percussion-like.

Cage actually used a fairly small repertoire of objects to prepare his pianos. Both weather stripping (made of a felt-like material) and pieces of rubber mute the string without altering the pitch significantly. The rubber gives a somewhat more resonant sound than the weather stripping, and in the higher registers the effect is similar to that of a resonant wood block. Screws and bolts provide the metallic, complex, gong-like sounds that dominate so many of Cage's prepared piano pieces. In some cases, metal washers or oversized nuts were included in the screw or bolt preparations, so placed that they would rattle against the string when played. This effect is not unlike that of a tambourine or cymbal. Pennies threaded through the triple-strung notes produce a similar gong-like sonority, but mellower, perhaps because of the penny's ability to mute all three strings simultaneously. Other less common preparation materials include pieces of wood, bamboo, and rubber pencil erasers.

Although all the scores include a table of preparations, Cage's practice in notating these changed over the years. In his earliest pieces, he gave only the most general indications of what kind of object to use; in later scores, he became increasingly precise, giving the size of screws and bolts. At the same time, he began specifying the precise position of the preparation on the string, giving measurements from the piano dampers accurate down to a sixteenth of an inch. This precision, he soon found out, was misleading, since different pianos were constructed slightly differently; the same object at the same location on the same string of two different pianos could produce two different sounds. In the table of preparations for *The Perilous Night*, he took this into consideration, and indicated to which specific Steinway models the measurements are applicable. In *Amores*, he approached the problem from a different direction, describing the desired results (e.g., "The screw must be large enough and so positioned on and between the strings as to produce a resonant sound, rich in harmonics") but leaving the precise sizes and locations up to the performer.

Although Cage invented the prepared piano in 1940, he did not compose another piece for it until 1942, after he had moved to New York. It took the place of percussion ensembles in his work, and in the process changed his musical style. In his percussion works, Cage had been reaching for bigger effects – all the *Constructions* have a thunderous moment in them somewhere – and "more new sounds." He was ambitious: he was still attempting to found his center for experimental music, and in composing the score for *The City Wears a Slouch Hat*, he wrote a 250-page score for radio sound effects that was so complex as to be entirely impossible to perform.[17] When he moved to New York, circumstances changed dramatically. He was unable to move his percussion instruments from Chicago; he had no money and no prospects for getting any. Cage's reliance on the prepared piano – a poor man's percussion ensemble – was a product of these hard times. Almost all of his compositions from 1943 to 1945 are for the instrument, and it figures prominently in his work until about 1948.[18]

The shift in medium from percussion ensembles to prepared piano changed Cage's style of composition. In his percussion pieces the music was made up of blocks of sound organized by the rhythmic structure. These blocks were filled up with motivic material strung along in arbitrary sequences, or were just built up of ostinato patterns. The resulting tendency is to hear these masses but not their components, to be aware of architecture and not line. In the works for prepared piano, the solo medium leads to an emphasis on melody, either alone or with simple accompaniment. The rhythms become simpler and more fluid; Cage developed a fondness for ornaments and subtle inflections. Where the percussion pieces strive for large-scale dramatic effects (just think of the six thundersheets roaring in *First Construction*), the new music for prepared piano aims for intimacy and personal expression. Although it may seem strange to use the term "lyrical," it is quite appropriate in describing Cage's prepared piano works and in isolating the essential stylistic difference between these and his percussion compositions.

The 1944 article "Grace and Clarity" represents a statement of Cage's new lyrical aesthetic. In this essay, first published in a magazine devoted to modern dance, Cage presents his prescription for a healthy relationship between music and dance: an emphasis on clarity of phrase structure. He had emphasized rhythmic structure in music and dance before, but whereas then he had spoken of constructions and abstractions, he now associates it more with phrasing – the rhythm of poetry and breathing. By "grace" he seems to mean "content": he sets it up as the antithesis of structure, defining it as "the play with and against the clarity of the rhythmic structure." He follows this with a quotation from Coventry Patmore, which presents the same duality in terms of poetry:

> In the finest specimens of versification, there seems to be a perpetual conflict between the law of the verse and the freedom of the language, and each is incessantly, though insignificantly, violated for the purpose of giving effect to the other. The best poet . . . preserves everywhere the living sense of the metre, not so much by unvarying obedience to, as by innumerable small departures from, its *modulus*.[19]

Cage's citation of Patmore makes clear the effect the medium of the prepared piano had on his compositional thinking. It was only in a soloistic, personal medium like the prepared piano that he could develop a music of "innumerable small departures" from a "living" phrase structure. This turn towards subtler effects would deepen throughout the 1940s and ultimately lead to the almost ascetic sense of quietness found in the *String Quartet in Four Parts* and *4′ 33″*.

Dance works

The majority of the prepared piano works from the 1940s were dance commissions. Of these, works written for Merce Cunningham predominate, Cunningham having moved to New York at about the same time as Cage. As with *Bacchanale*, the prepared piano was Cage's favored medium for dance accompaniments because of its portability (any auditorium would have a piano, so he need only bring his preparations) and its ability to produce a diverse array of percussive timbres without need of additional performers. Also in keeping with *Bacchanale*, these dance works were usually written rather rapidly; as a result they tend to be less distinctive in themselves, and I will limit myself here to a summary of their general style.

Perhaps for practical reasons the dance works are timbrally and texturally fairly simple. Usually only a few notes (a dozen or less) are prepared, and these use only one or two kinds of preparation. In *Totem Ancestor* (1943), for example, eight notes are prepared with screws or bolts, two with weather stripping, and one with a screw and free-rattling nut. Texturally these works are often dominated by a single unaccompanied line, or by a line with a simple accompaniment, such as a trill or ostinato pattern (a trilling accompaniment continues intermittently throughout the first seventy measures of *Bacchanale*, for example). Frequently the pieces fall into a constant eighth- or sixteenth-note motion with regular repeating patterns – a kind of *moto perpetuo* style. Compared to the cross-rhythms, unusual gruppettos, and irregular patterning of the percussion works, the prepared piano dance accompaniments are rhythmically and melodically much simpler. In *Bacchanale*, the music tends to proceed in straight sixteenth notes, with syncopations arising through the use of accents and the occasional changing of pattern lengths. The melodies are built on a limited set of tones – usually no more than five or six.

Most of the dance pieces are workaday affairs. Occasionally, however, Cage could turn the simple dance style to more effective ends. *Tossed As It Is Untroubled* (1944) consists mostly of an energetic unaccompanied line improvised on just five tones (these are prepared with weather stripping, so that their pitch is quite distinct). Only at the end does Cage add a high trill on two notes prepared by screws. The sparkling metallic sound of this accompaniment changes the entire character of the muted middle-range melody in a magical way.[20] *Root of an Unfocus* (1944) is even more limited, relying on only three sonic elements: an irregularly-repeated, indistinct thud (produced by two low notes prepared by bolts and weather stripping), the crashing sound of a cluster of high screw-prepared notes, and a pair of tones prepared with bolts that touch the sounding board of the piano, thus producing a sharp *clack* when struck. The brevity, focus, and effective overall shapes of *Tossed As It Is Untroubled* and *Root of an Unfocus* make them two of the best of the dance works. This style appears in other non-dance and non-prepared piano works, as well: a notable example is *The Wonderful Widow of Eighteen Springs* for voice and piano (1942). The voice part intones a text from James Joyce's *Finnegans Wake* on only a few tones, while the pianist acts as percussionist: the keyboard cover is closed and no notes are played, the voice being accompanied only by the soft knocks of the pianist's fingers and knuckles on the wood of the piano.

It is best to consider the *Music for Marcel Duchamp* (1947) in this context as well. This work, while not a dance commission, was also written as an accompaniment, this time for a portion of Hans Richter's surrealist film *Dreams That Money Can Buy*. The film consists of several unrelated segments designed by different artists, linked together by a somewhat absurd common story line. Cage's music was for the sequence prepared by Marcel Duchamp – hence the title of the composition. It continues in the style of *Tossed As It Is Untroubled*: an improvised line on a few tones muted by weather stripping. A new idea in this piece is the prominent use of silences to punctuate the melodic phrases.[21] The ending of the piece uses this device to great effect, with the seven-fold repetition of a four-bar pattern: a two-bar phrase followed by two bars of rests. These repetitions provide a sense of tension without the rhythmic propulsion of Cage's earlier prepared piano works.

26

The flatness of the materials, set off by silences, creates a taut yet static music; its impassiveness is the perfect accompaniment for Duchamp's film sequence, which consists of a series of purely optical images on rotating disks.

Music for Marcel Duchamp is perhaps the summit of this style of prepared piano composition. Most of the other dance works lack its cohesion and economy. There is a tendency in these pieces towards the use of repeated patterns as "filler" for the phrase lengths required by the choreography. In pieces like *Bacchanale* or *Mysterious Adventure* there can be a great deal of frenetic activity that has no particular direction, or the repetitions can become sing-song and trivial rather than static and grand as in *Music for Marcel Duchamp*. When Cage understates and simplifies he is able to maintain the intensity and drive of his dance accompaniments.

Concert works

Cage learned a great deal about the prepared piano in his dance works, but it was only in the series of concert works written between 1943 and 1948 that the full capabilities of the medium were made apparent. At the same time, the creation of large works for prepared piano – free from the restraints implied by the dance commissions – allowed his style to mature further. By the end of this period, with the *Sonatas and Interludes*, he appears as an accomplished artist in command of his medium.

The first appearance of the prepared piano in a concert setting, rather than as a dance accompaniment, is in the suite *Amores* (1943). Only the opening and closing movements of the suite are for prepared piano; the second movement percussion trio has already been examined, and the third movement is simply a revival of the Waltz movement of the 1936 Trio for percussion. The overall mood of the suite is quiet and intimate, its subject as stated by Cage (and suggested by the title) being "the quietness between lovers." In this sense, it is the antithesis of the noisy, impersonal *Constructions*. The quiet, personal tone of these two movements and the contrast within them between improvisatory, unmetered exclamations and soft but metrically regular accompanied lines are style traits that reappear elsewhere in this period of Cage's work, particularly in the *Sonatas and Interludes*.

Amores is the first concert work to include the prepared piano, but *The Perilous Night* (1943–44) is the first large-scale work for the instrument. For this piece, Cage made use of a more extensive timbral palette than he had used before: twenty-six notes are prepared, using rubber, weather stripping, screws, nuts, bolts, bamboo, wood, and cloth. This suite of six separate pieces, like *Amores*, was composed with a particular subject in mind: "the loneliness and terror that comes to one when love becomes unhappy." In it, Cage gave the devices and styles of his dance works a fuller musical treatment. The opening movement, with its use of tones muted by weather stripping and a propulsive improvised line, reminds one of *Tossed As It Is Untroubled*, but held within a tighter structure. In other

27

movements, the simple dance-style ideas are made more effective simply by keeping them brief. In the second movement, one finds the kinds of syncopated patterns over a regular accompaniment common to so many of the dance pieces, but here restricted to a thirty-six measure miniature, so that they do not have time to lose their freshness. The sixth and last movement is particularly effective. Introduced by a very short, violent fifth movement, the finale is based on an idea common to the dance pieces: that of an improvised line based on a limited number of tones. Here, however, there are two such lines, one based on high muted notes reminiscent of wood-blocks, and the other on lower metallic sonorities. The rhythmic drive and obsessive patterning are kept lively not only by the irregularities in both lines, but by the resulting interaction between their patterns. The ending is quite remarkable: the momentum of these lines dies out suddenly, as if their rhythmic drive had just evaporated completely.

In 1944 and 1945, Cage composed two large pieces – lasting about a half-hour each – for two prepared pianos. These pieces, *A Book of Music* (1944) and *Three Dances* (1945), were written especially for the duo-piano team of Arthur Gold and Robert Fizdale; they were the first commissions Cage had received from professional performers. The duo-piano works are mainly of interest for their rhythmic structures. It will be recalled that in *First Construction*, the different large sections of the structure were marked by tempo changes. Since the units of that work remained a constant sixteen measures long throughout, the changing tempo altered the proportions of the different sections. In *A Book of Music* and *Three Dances*, Cage set out to compose works in which such tempo changes do not destroy the structural proportions. When the tempo changes the phrase lengths change as well, becoming longer as the tempo increases and shorter as it decreases.

The novel structural schemes aside, these are not the most successful of Cage's concert works for prepared piano. The increased resources made available to him here (not just one piano but two, and two virtuosi at that) lured him away from the strengths of his prepared piano compositions – intimacy, flexibility, lyricism – and turned him again towards the ambitions of his percussion works together with their concerns for the impersonal and architectural. This is seen in his choice of subject matter for *A Book of Music*, as explained in "A Composer's Confessions":

> The Book of Music for Two Pianos was less concerned consciously with my personal feelings and more concerned with my idea about Mozart, that his music strictly adheres to three different kinds of scales: the chromatic, the diatonic, and that consisting of the larger steps of thirds and fourths.[22]

The work is formed almost entirely of different types of scales and arpeggios. Although Cage makes use of a wide variety of different patterns, the repetitive motions up and down along the range of each instrument ultimately become taxing. This is the problem with both two-piano works: when Cage tries to take advantage of the virtuosity of his performers, he tends to go against his natural strengths and those of the medium. The third of the *Three Dances* is a clear demonstration of the excess of these pieces: too many notes played at too fast a tempo produce a clangorous blur.

The scale-patterning ideas developed in *A Book of Music* appear in other works in the later 1940s. Of these, nothing could be further from the virtuoso duo-piano pieces than the Suite for Toy Piano (1948), which, although not a work for prepared piano, belongs in this section. Written at Black Mountain College, it was later choreographed by Merce Cunningham. The choice of instrument had a similar effect to the prepared piano medium: it limited Cage to the range of a few tones, in this case only the white keys between E below middle C and the F above. The white-key limitation is the source of the diatonic, modal feel throughout the work. The brightness of the toy piano sound, the clarity of the white-key diatonicism, and the vitality of the rhythms themselves act together to make this one of Cage's most joyous works. Two dance works from 1948, *Dream* and *In a Landscape*, both for unprepared piano, make use of similar scale patterns.

Sonatas and Interludes

In "A Composer's Confessions" Cage mentions many projects he has been working on, and projects he wishes to pursue. Among these is the following:

> Another passing remark, this time by Edwin Denby, to the effect that short pieces can have in them just as much as long pieces can, led me two years ago [1946] to start writing twenty short *Sonatas and Interludes* which I have not yet finished.

The *Sonatas and Interludes*, thus a result of Denby's "passing remark," is the work that has almost universally been acclaimed as Cage's masterwork for the prepared piano; one of his most popular works, it is performed regularly and has been recorded numerous times. Whether or not one considers it a masterwork, it is easily the finest of Cage's compositions for prepared piano, and the crowning achievement of his work of the mid-1940s.

Edwin Denby may have suggested the outward format of the pieces – a set of twenty miniatures – but their content comes from Indian aesthetics. Cage was introduced to the subject through his reading of the works of the art historian and critic Ananda Coomaraswamy. Coomaraswamy was to have a strong impact on Cage's whole approach to music, as I shall describe in the next chapter; his importance for the *Sonatas and Interludes* lay in his presentation of the theory of *rasa* and the "permanent emotions" in his book *The Dance of Shiva*. *Rasa* is defined by Coomaraswamy as "aesthetic quality," and the theory of its operation is developed in various treatises dealing with Sanskrit poetry and drama. Of importance for Cage was the description of the permanent emotions: the moods or different "flavors" of *rasa*. According to the treatises, there are eight permanent emotions: the erotic, the heroic, the odious, anger, mirth, fear, sorrow, and the wondrous. These eight emotions all have a common tendency towards a ninth, tranquillity.[23]

29

According to Cage's own description, the *Sonatas and Interludes* were "an attempt to express in music the [eight] 'permanent emotions' . . . and their common tendency toward tranquillity." The exact plan of this program – how it relates to the cycle of sixteen sonatas and four interludes – is not known. Cage never indicated in the score or in any of his writings what his programmatic scheme was. One possibility that makes a good deal of sense is that each piece expresses a single emotion. This would adhere to the rule in Sanskrit aesthetics that a work should have a single permanent emotion as its master-motif. Lacking any explicit program, we are left with speculation based on hearing the pieces. Some of the sonatas seem clearer in their emotional connotations than others. With its supple, seductive lines, I have always found the third sonata to be a vivid expression of "the erotic," and I also get a strong sense of "fear" from the ninth sonata. But others are much less clear, and the emotional differentiation of the pieces seems to fade in the second half of the work. Cage indicated at the time that the emphasis on ten-bar units in the last four pieces represented tranquillity,[24] and certainly all four of the last sonatas are less emotionally-charged than much of the rest of the work. Perhaps Cage's plan was for the common tendency of tranquillity to develop over the course of the cycle, with the intensely-expressed emotions of the opening sonatas gradually mellowing to the placid, paler tones of the closing.

Sonatas and Interludes consists of twenty short pieces: sixteen sonatas and four interludes. As shown in the following list, the sonatas are gathered into four groups of four, and the work as a whole is divided into halves, with two groups of sonatas and two interludes in each half. In the first half of the piece, the interludes follow the groups of sonatas, while in the second half they precede them, thus producing a symmetrical arrangement. Beyond this symmetry there is no overall controlling musical structure.

Pieces	Forms
Sonatas I–IV	binary
Interlude 1	through-composed
Sonatas V–VIII	binary
Interlude 2	through-composed
Interlude 3	4-part: AABBCCDD
Sonatas IX–XI	ternary: ABBCC, AABBC, AABCC
Sonata XII	binary
Interlude 4	4-part: AABBCCDD
Sonatas XIII–XVI	binary

It can be seen that most of the sonatas (numbers I–VIII and XII–XVI) are in binary form with both halves repeated. The three remaining sonatas (numbers IX–XI) are in ternary forms that consist of two sections marked to be repeated

Example 1–6   *Sonatas and Interludes*: Sonata XI, bars 1–20

and one non-repeated section – that is, a binary form with an "extra" section. Among these three sonatas, all permutations of this ternary plan are present, with the non-repeated section occurring before, after, or in the middle of the basic binary form. The interludes are of two formal types. The first two are through-composed, with no repeated sections, while the last two are four-part forms with all sections repeated.

The use of binary forms has certain effects on the compositions. Since these pieces all make use of the micro-macrocosmic rhythmic structure, the binary forms result in rhythmic structures based on pairs of repeated numbers – in the fourth sonata, for example, the structure is {3, 3, 2, 2}. The repeated numbers are the result of the repeated sections; at the small scale they frequently result in parallel phrases. At the large scale, the use of binary forms suggests the compositional problem of how to handle the transitions from the ends to the beginnings of sections: the same music must lead to two different destinations. In "Composition as Process: Changes," Cage indicates that in these pieces "the formal concern was to make the progress from the end of a section to its beginning seem inevitable." In some pieces, this was done by actually blurring the distinction between the ending and beginning of a section. Example 1–6 shows the opening section of the eleventh sonata. The start of the sonata is occupied entirely by patterns on a handful of tones (measures 1–4). This then swells to a more melodic passage in the following six measures: the notes used in the opening, which have taken on an accompanimental role, disappear entirely by the tenth measure. They reappear at the end of the section (measures 18–20), so that when the return to the opening occurs, the listener does not even realize it. A similar strategy is used in the fourteenth and fifteenth sonatas, but with an added dimension: the second halves of these two pieces are exactly identical, so that the distinction between *pieces* has been blurred as well.

The rhythmic structures of the individual pieces of the *Sonatas and Interludes* are more complex than any Cage had used before, largely as the result of his inclusion of fractions in the structural formulae. The rhythmic structures of all the pieces are shown below.

Piece	Unit size (Measures)	Structural proportions
Sonata I	7	{1¼, ¾, 1¼, ¾, 1½, 1½}
Sonata II	7¾	{1½, 1½, 2⅜, 2⅜}
Sonata III	8½	{1, 1, 3¼, 3¼}
Sonata IV	10	{3, 3, 2, 2}
Interlude 1	10	{1½, 1½, 2, 1½, 1½, 2}
Sonata V	9	{2, 2, 2½, 2½}
Sonata VI	6	{2⅔, 2⅔, ⅓, ⅓}
Sonata VII	6	{2, 2, 1, 1}
Sonata VIII	7	{2, 2, 1½, 1½}

Interlude 2	8	[proportions unclear]
Interlude 3	7	{1¼, 1¼, 1, 1, ¾, ¾, ½, ½}
Sonata IX	8	{1, 2, 2, 1½, 1½}
Sonata X	6	{1, 1, 1, 1, 2}
Sonata XI	10	{2, 2, 3, 1½, 1½}
Sonata XII	9	{2, 2, 2½, 2½}
Interlude 4	8½	{1, 1, 1, 1, 1, 1, 1¼, 1¼}
Sonata XIII	10	{1½, 1½, 3½, 3½}
Sonata XIV	10	{2, 2, 3, 3}
Sonata XV	10	{2, 2, 3, 3}
Sonata XVI	10	{3½, 3½, 1½, 1½}

The fractions cause some changes in the way Cage used his rhythmic structures, and lead to asymmetrical phrase patterns. Example 1–7 is the first half of the fifth sonata; with its structure of {2, 2, 2½, 2½}, it is one of the more interesting pieces from this point of view. The right hand part of the first unit is occupied entirely with a simple undulating scale pattern. The dotted quarter notes at the peaks of the pattern mark the beginnings of phrases. At first this pattern takes up two bars, while at measure 5, the pattern is extended by half a bar. More alterations to the ostinato take place in the following measures: first it is shortened to only one bar, then this shortened version is itself extended by half a bar. The overall pattern of these alterations, then, is 2 + 2 + 2½ + 1 + 1½. In the second unit of the piece, the left hand part is subject to similar procedures. The rhythmic asymmetry of the fifth sonata is caused by the half-bar extension implied by the rhythmic structure based on the numbers 2 and 2½. This idea is developed further in the 1 + 1½ subdivision of some of the 2½-bar phrases. Examining pieces such as this (or the third sonata, which uses similar devices) makes it clear what Cage meant in "Grace and Clarity" when he emphasized the relationship between structure and content in his music: this is a perfect example of the musical content playing with and against the rhythmic structure.

There is much, much more to say about these pieces – more than can be said in such a short space. *Sonatas and Interludes* is a work that repays a prolonged study – new details jump out from every page. Different listeners will have their own favorite pieces, their own compelling experiences. There are the marvelous organic and dramatic shapes of some of the pieces, particularly the fourth, thirteenth, and sixteenth sonatas and the second interlude. I particularly enjoy the way Cage has used repetitive and regularly-pulsed music: a staple in the dance pieces, it is used here not just to fill space, but for dramatic ends (as in the conclusion to the tenth sonata) or as a foil for flexible and irregular rhythms (as in the second interlude). Peter Yates, in his account of the piece, gives a sense of the complexity of the work:

Example 1–7   *Sonatas and Interludes*: Sonata V, bars 1–18

The principle of tonal balance is to the effect that more highly pitched sounds tend to unrest and sounds of lower pitch to rest. Instead of a dominant and tonic pair of final chords, Cage may repeat the same group of simultaneous sounds, emphasizing first the higher registers as a dominant and then the lower as a tonic, a very reasonable and satisfactory ending process. Many variations of this principle enliven the sonatas. Other means of structure are found in the balance between movement and non-movement, between sound and silence, between the hurrying of many tones at one level of sound and the slow fall of single sounds upon another level, the two interpenetrating but never mingling as chords.[25]

As suggested by Yates, there is a breadth to the *Sonatas and Interludes* that is lacking in all of Cage's previous work. Perhaps as a response to the needs of his rather broad "permanent emotion" program, Cage developed a variety of musical styles, techniques, and effects; he appears here as a composer with a broad palette at his disposal and the ability to use it effectively.

But the achievement of *Sonatas and Interludes* goes beyond just the technical aspects; it has a musical and emotional depth that is greater than much of what Cage had composed before. The pieces are vibrant, elusive, and alive. This is the end to which his work since 1939 had been pointing: the development of a broad, satisfying, very personal musical style relying almost entirely on unpitched percussive materials. Cage transcended the obvious musical attributes of noise and rhythm – brutality, vigor, momentum, power – and made music instead by turning these materials towards the expression of intimacy and tranquillity. In the process he himself had changed – from a somewhat bombastic experimenter describing "The Future of Music" to a quiet composer expressing the permanent emotions. Even at its premiere in 1949, the *Sonatas and Interludes* was recognized as a pinnacle in Cage's young career. Said the critic for *The New York Times*, the work "left one with the feeling that Mr. Cage is one of this country's finest composers and that his invention [the prepared piano] has now been vindicated musically."[26]

2

"To sober and quiet the mind . . ." (1946–1951)

The sources of a new style

Interest in Indian philosophy

The period of the middle 1940s was a difficult time in Cage's career. Although his works were well-received in some quarters (particularly by Virgil Thomson and Henry Cowell), the majority of musicians and concert-goers in New York seemed to miss the point of his music; if they were not openly hostile, then they treated the whole thing as some sort of joke. Cage, in describing one such incident involving *The Perilous Night*, gives a sense of the larger doubts these problems raised in his mind:

> I had poured a great deal of emotion into the piece, and obviously I wasn't communicating this at all. Or else, I thought, if I *were* communicating, then all artists must be speaking a different language, and thus speaking only for themselves. The whole musical situation struck me more and more as a Tower of Babel.[1]

It was at this time, while depressed and disillusioned, that Cage began his study of Indian philosophy, with the assistance of an Indian musician, Gita Sarabhai. Sarabhai had come to America to study Western music, and had approached Cage for lessons in counterpoint and contemporary music. Cage in return asked her to teach him about Indian music and aesthetics, which she gladly did. At the end of their time together, Sarabhai gave him a copy of *The Gospel of Sri Ramakrishna*, a book that, in Cage's words, "took the place of psychoanalysis."[2] Ramakrishna's message of living unattached in the world became a sort of therapy for Cage, but beyond this, it served as his introduction to Indian philosophy and led him to further immerse himself in Eastern thought. His interest was broadened by his reading of Aldous Huxley's *The Perennial Philosophy*, which, in addition to suggesting a more general approach to the same spiritual world view, introduced Cage to the literature of Zen Buddhism and to such figures as Meister Eckhart, Chuang Tze, Huang Po, and Lao Tze.

While the works of Ramakrishna and Huxley opened Cage's mind to a more spiritual approach to life, it was his study of the writings of Ananda K.

Coomaraswamy – in particular *The Transformation of Nature in Art* and *The Dance of Shiva* – that had the most influence on his musical thinking. Of particular importance for him was the connection of art and spirituality. Coomaraswamy presents art as the contemplation of the Absolute – a sort of Yoga. He stresses that the forms and images the artist draws upon exist eternally "in God," so that the complete identification with them, either by the artist or the observer, is a form of mystic experience. In *The Transformation of Nature in Art* he states this plainly: "Art is religion, religion art, not related, but the same."[3] This view of art as a form of spiritual discipline is reflected in Cage's new formulation of the purpose of music, given to him by Sarabhai: "To sober and quiet the mind thus rendering it susceptible to divine influences." The religious tone found in Cage's writings starting in the late 1940s can be traced to his reading of Coomaraswamy. An early example of this is found in "A Composer's Confessions." Most of the talk is a fairly straightforward history of Cage's involvement in music from his childhood on, but when talking about contemporary music, he laments that "our culture has its faith not in the peaceful center of the spirit, but in an ever-hopeful projection on to things of our own desire for completion." He closes with a call for a more spiritual approach to music that is strongly reminiscent of Coomaraswamy:

> Each one of us must now look to himself. That which formerly held us together and gave meaning to our occupations was our belief in God. When we transferred this belief first to heroes and then to things, we began to walk our separate paths. That island . . . to which we might have retreated to escape from the impact of the world, lies, as it ever did, within each one of our hearts. Towards that final tranquillity, which today we so desperately need, any integrating occupation – music is only one of them – rightly used can serve as a guide.

Cage's indebtedness to Coomaraswamy was limited largely to the general tone and spiritual outlook, rather than extending to specific concepts – this is not surprising, considering that Coomaraswamy's central concern is with Eastern traditional arts and not with anything remotely resembling the Western avant-garde. One specific idea from Coomaraswamy's writings *is* mentioned repeatedly by Cage, however: that art should "imitate Nature in her manner of operation." This line became a recurring theme in Cage's writings, and its importance suggests that its context in Coomaraswamy's writing should be examined more closely. The phrase occurs in Coomaraswamy's discussion of the Sanskrit term *sadrśya*, which he notes is usually translated as "imitation." Coomaraswamy asserts that this imitation is of eternal forms and not merely of appearances; the key phrase appears in his elaboration of this concept:

> However, if we suppose that all this implies a conception of art as something seeking its perfection in the nearest possible approaches to illusion we shall be greatly mistaken. . . . We shall find that Asiatic art is ideal in the mathematical sense: like Nature (*natura naturans*) not in appearance (viz. that of *ens naturata*), but in operation.

37

He clarifies this point later on: "*sadṛśya* is then 'similitude,' but rather such as is implied by 'simile' than by 'simulacrum.'"[4] Throughout *The Transformation of Nature in Art* (and in much of the rest of Coomaraswamy's writings) he sets this Eastern goal of imitating things "as they are in God" in contradistinction to the post-Renaissance Western ideal of representing things "as they are in themselves."

Cage's interpretation of "the imitation of Nature in her manner of operation" is at first quite close to Coomaraswamy's, as seen in the *Sonatas and Interludes*, with its portrayal of the permanent emotions of Indian aesthetics. Cage's choice of the permanent emotions as a subject was perhaps influenced by Coomaraswamy's warning that the transient (more personal) emotions cannot serve as a basis for a well-made work of art. The permanent emotions are closer to the sense of forms that exist eternally in Nature, and thus Cage's use of them as a subject in *Sonatas and Interludes* can be seen as an early attempt at "imitating Nature in her manner of operation" in the sense that Coomaraswamy uses the phrase.

"Defense of Satie"

Cage's discoveries of Ramakrishna, Huxley, Coomaraswamy, and Indian music were very stimulating to him, and together they acted as a catalyst for new activity in the late 1940s. Among the fruits of his newfound interests was the first full articulation of his own personal view of composition in his lecture "Defense of Satie" (1948). Cage had been interested in Satie's music throughout the 1940s, and came to connect it to his reading of Coomaraswamy: in a 1946 article "The East in the West" he cites Satie as a Western example of the Eastern ideal of "static expression," a term that reflects his knowledge of Coomaraswamy and the Indian permanent emotions. When Cage was asked to teach at Black Mountain College in 1948, he decided to publicize Satie's music (which was poorly-known at that time) by giving a festival of twenty-five concerts of that music, with the explanatory lecture "Defense of Satie" as its centerpiece.

In the lecture Cage states that his purpose is to reconcile the opposing needs of individualism and tradition in music by deciding which elements of music should be held in common and which should be unique for each composer. He divides music into four elements: structure (the division of the whole into parts), form (the continuity of sounds), method (the means of producing continuity), and materials (the sounds of the composition). He then proceeds to analyze these four elements to see which can be agreed upon by all and which must remain individually determined. Form, he says, comes from the heart and hence cannot be made the basis of a universal discipline. He is noncommittal on material and method, indicating that these may or may not be agreed upon. But he finds that it is essential to agree on matters of structure, since "we call whatever diverges from sameness of structure monstrous." He refers to the agreed-upon elements as "law elements" and the rest as "freedom elements," and indicates that music has the ability to bring these contradictory elements together into a harmonious whole. At the conclusion of the lecture, he asserts that this function of music is "a problem parallel to that of the integration of the personality."

The four-fold division of music given in "Defense of Satie" owes a good deal to the duality of structure and content (the latter now called "form") presented in 1944 in "Grace and Clarity." In both writings, structure is associated with the mind and form with the heart. The addition of method and materials in "Defense of Satie" does not detract from this basic dualism: these new elements are not so much on an equal level with structure and form as they are components of form itself. Cage's definitions of these two "new" elements imply that form is actually the result of method operating on materials, thus suggesting that these two newer elements of music are in fact on a different level than the basic dualism of structure and form.[5]

Another point on which "Defense of Satie" is in agreement with "Grace and Clarity" is in its insistence that rhythmic structure is the only correct structure for music. In "Defense of Satie," however, Cage does not merely assert the advantageousness of musical structure based on time, but attempts to prove its absolute necessity. He points out that duration is the only aspect of sound that is common to both sound and silence. From this he concludes that "there can be no right making of music that does not structure itself from the very roots of sound and silence – lengths of time." This is the central failure of harmonic structure in Western music, a failure that Cage asserts has served "to practically shipwreck the art on an island of decadence." He had similarly attacked the Western emphasis on harmony in "The East in the West," where he characterized it as "the tool of Western commercialism," and in "A Composer's Confessions" he calls it "a device to make music impressive, loud, and big, in order to enlarge audiences and increase box-office returns." Cage associated the traditional, nineteenth-century, intensely progressive use of harmony with ego-attachment in art; to "imbue their music with the ineffable," he advised in "The East in the West," composers should turn to music "where harmony is not of the essence." Solving this problem of how to use harmony in a static fashion would occupy Cage for the next few years, and would play an important role in his composition of *The Seasons* and the *String Quartet in Four Parts*.

There is little new ground broken in "Defense of Satie." Instead, the lecture seems to have served as a summary and codification of Cage's past practice: indeed, virtually any of his works of the 1940s could have passed as a demonstration of its principles. While not a path-breaking work, however, "Defense of Satie" did provide Cage with an intellectual and technical framework for the future exploration and expansion of his ideas on composition, one that would persist in his thinking and writings for the next ten years.

Gamut technique: *The Seasons*

"Defense of Satie" reveals the currents that were stirring in Cage's aesthetic thought in the mid-1940s, currents that became more prominent in the crucial period of 1949 to 1951, most notably in his "Forerunners of Modern Music," "Lecture on Nothing," and "Lecture on Something." "Defense of Satie" reflects changes in Cage's compositional practice, as well: with its isolation of material as a separable part of composition, the lecture signals the emergence of a "gamut technique" in his compositions of the later 1940s. In his usage, a gamut is simply a specific collection of musical materials to be used in a piece, defined before the rest of the process of composition continues. Some of his earlier compositional techniques, such as the twenty-five-note and cellular methods of the 1930s, or even the limited melodic ranges of many of his works of the 1940s, can be seen as precursors of this idea. His work with percussion and the prepared piano also played an important role in the development of the notion of a sound gamut: in composing for these instruments, collecting the sounds to be used was a crucial compositional action. Cage's notion of a gamut was affected not only by the *way* in which materials were selected in these pieces, but also by the *kinds* of materials themselves. A gamut in this context is not simply a collection of pitches, themes, motives, or scales, but a collection of *sounds* of varying character and complexity.

While these earlier experiences laid the groundwork for Cage's conception of gamut technique, what brought these new ideas to the forefront of his thinking was his composition in early 1947 of a ballet score, *The Seasons*. Commissioned by The Ballet Society in New York City (with choreography by Merce Cunningham and scenery and costumes by Isamu Noguchi), the work, according to Cage's catalog, "is an attempt to express the traditional Indian view of the seasons as quiescence (winter), creation (spring), preservation (summer), and destruction (fall)." The rhythmic structure of the piece follows from the seasonal program. This structure is in nine parts: {2, 2, 1, 3, 2, 4, 1, 3, 1}. The nine large sections of the work are translated into seasonal movements and preludes as follows:

2	Prelude I
2	Winter
1	Prelude II
3	Spring
2	Prelude III
4	Summer
1	Prelude IV
3	Fall
1	Finale (Prelude I)

The last section is a reprise of the opening prelude, thus emphasizing the cyclical nature of the seasons.[6]

The Seasons was Cage's first piece for orchestra – indeed, the first substantial piece he had composed for pitched instruments in nearly a decade. This posed various compositional problems, but perhaps the most difficult for him was how

Example 2–1   Two Pieces for Piano (1946): II

(a) bars 1–5

to handle harmony in this work, particularly considering his aversion to harmonic progression. The gamut technique, as applied to harmonies, provided a solution to this problem. The basic premise was that he could simplify the use of harmonies by limiting himself to a collection of specific sonorities composed at the outset. This principle was first explored in the *Two Pieces for Piano* composed in 1946, as shown in Example 2–1.[7] In these two passages from the second piece, Cage has used the same sonorities in different permutations and contexts: this is the essence of the gamut technique. In *The Seasons*, the technique tried out in the piano pieces was developed further, using a larger gamut of sonorities. These were voiced in only one specific way, and the harmonies could occur only in these arrangements, although the orchestration could vary. The gamut technique is used more freely in *The Seasons* than in the piano pieces, inasmuch as there are many harmonies that are used only once or twice, in free combination with those of the fixed collection. In addition, melodic lines appear in *The Seasons* independently of the chords from the gamut.

The gamut elements themselves were used quite flexibly. Example 2–2*b* is the first 31 measures of the "Summer" movement of *The Seasons* (in reduction); this can serve as a representative example of the use of gamut elements in the work. This excerpt is focused on two harmonies drawn from the gamut, shown in Example 2–2*a*. These harmonies are fragmented and arpeggiated throughout these measures, as shown by the circled notes. There are also harmonies that

Example 2–1   Two Pieces for Piano (1946): II

(b) bars 15–23

Example 2–2   *The Seasons*: "Summer"

(a) primary sonorities

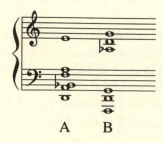

A   B

Example 2–2   *The Seasons*: "Summer"

(b) bars 1–31

43

Example 2–3   *The Seasons*: Prelude IV, bars 1–8

suggest mutations of the gamut elements, such as the A♭/E/G sonority at measure 17; the relation of this sonority to the A♭/D/G of the gamut is made clear in measures 20–21. In other parts of *The Seasons* the harmonies of the gamut are used to produce melodies. Cage does this by extending only one tone of a sonority and keeping the rest very short; the long notes are then perceived as a melodic line. Example 2–3, drawn from the Prelude to the "Fall" movement, is an example of this technique, and the "Fall" movement itself uses it exclusively.

The harmonic world of *The Seasons* produces the effect of weakened harmonic motion – a hint of the static sense of harmony that Cage desired. In parts of the ballet the repetition of harmonies lends a quality of flatness to the music that would have been in keeping with his expressed tastes at that time. In "The East in the West" he had admired the stasis of Satie's music, which he attributed to the use of "musical situations (rather than themes) which recur unaltered." The use of specific sonorities in *The Seasons* may very well have been Cage's attempt to create such "musical situations," but the resulting music did not perfectly reproduce the static quality of Satie's music. The many free elements and the great latitude given in their handling afforded Cage too many possibilities. The system only defined which harmonies were *available*; within this limitation, there was very much a sense of progression from one harmony to the next. In brief, through the use of a gamut of harmonies Cage had restricted his freedom of harmonic movement but had not nullified that sense of movement completely. Nevertheless, the gamut technique was a step in a direction that he found intriguing, and served as the basis of his compositional explorations over the next few years.

Changes in style and aesthetic

"Forerunners of Modern Music"

His immersion in Indian philosophy and aesthetics, the development of his own formal model for composition with the four-fold division of music, the gradual establishment of the gamut technique, particularly in respect to harmony – these developments in Cage's musical thought set the stage for the striking changes that would take place in his work over the three years 1949–51. The first indications that he was taking a new direction appear in the article "Forerunners of Modern Music," published in March of 1949 in *The Tiger's Eye*, a small journal of avant-garde art and poetry.[8] In this original publication, "Forerunners of Modern Music" was characterized by Cage as "a concentration of about all that I am aware of at this time"; clearly he intended for this article to summarize his aesthetic outlook.

The first half of the article presents ideas drawn mostly from "Defense of Satie." The four-fold division of music is described, the law and freedom elements are enumerated, and, once again, Cage indicates that the purpose of music is to integrate these opposites. This is then followed by another attempt to prove the correctness of rhythmic structure and the error of structure based on harmony (this time Cage uses the disintegration of harmonic structure in the twentieth century as proof of its decadence). But while the premises of these first few pages are taken directly from his earlier writings, the language used is new and reflects his commitment to a religious view of art. For example, in stating that music should integrate opposing elements, he uses the following formulation:

> Music is edifying, for from time to time it sets the soul in operation. The soul is the gatherer-together of the disparate elements (Meister Eckhart), and its work fills one with peace and love.

He later returns to this idea with the statement that "activity involving in a single process the many, turning them, even though some seem to be opposites, towards oneness, contributes to a good way of life."

As Cage indicates above, the specific source for much of this new language was Meister Eckhart, the German Christian mystic of the early fourteenth century. Cage was introduced to Eckhart's writings by his reading of Coomaraswamy and Huxley. In *The Transformation of Nature in Art*, Coomaraswamy had drawn parallels between Asian aesthetics and Eckhart's writings, and this perhaps inspired Cage to make similar connections between his own aesthetic theories and Eckhart. "Forerunners of Modern Music" is full of references to Eckhart, and Cage at times quotes from him directly.

The most extensive and prominent of these direct quotations is the one labeled "Interlude" in the text:

> But one must achieve this unselfconsciousness by means of transformed knowledge. This ignorance does not come from lack of knowledge but rather it is from knowledge that one may achieve this ignorance. Then we shall be informed by the divine unconsciousness and in that our ignorance will be ennobled and adorned with supernatural knowledge. It is by reason of this fact that we are made perfect by what happens to us rather than by what we do.[9]

This quotation is given prominence by its central location in the article and by its being set off from the rest of the text, but at the same time, its relevance is unclear, appearing as it does just after the mostly technical discussion of the first half of the article. It is difficult to assess the relevance of this quotation when taken out of its original context, so a brief discussion of Eckhart's notion of "ignorance" and "knowledge" is appropriate here. For Eckhart, an inner emptiness – which he refers to with such words as "silence," "ignorance," "unselfconsciousness," or "unknowing" – is necessary for the realization of God. To be in such a state, Eckhart says, is to have true spiritual poverty, to be completely detached and indifferent to the will, knowledge, and desires of the self. The purpose of this self-mortification is made clear in the following image, which Eckhart is fond of using: "In the middle of the night when all things were in quiet silence there was spoken to me a hidden word."[10] This "quiet silence" is the "ignorance" of the "Interlude" passage quoted by Cage; if we go to the original sermon, the lines immediately preceding this passage make clear the function of this silence as the prerequisite for hearing the "hidden word":

> It is in the stillness, in the silence, that the word of God is to be heard. There is no better avenue of approach to this Work than through stillness, through silence. It is to be heard there as it is . . . for when one is aware of nothing, that word is imparted to him and clearly revealed.[11]

According to Eckhart, once one has attained this state of total emptiness, one then obtains all things: "Purify till thou nor art nor hast not either this or that, then thou art omnipresent, and being neither this nor that thou art all things."[12]

Thus, in the "Interlude" quotation, Eckhart proclaims that through the discipline of self-negation we shall attain a state of such emptiness that we can then freely receive knowledge of the infinite. Cage connects this to his own work in the second half of "Forerunners of Modern Music," in which he describes the implications of rhythmic structure in music. Although the technical basis of rhythmic structure is unchanged, there is much in Cage's discussion that reveals a fundamental change in attitude towards structure. He describes structural rhythm as being the relationships of lengths of time, and uses the analogy of the calendar year and its division into seasons, months, weeks, and days to make this concept clearer. He goes on to describe the relationship of specific events to this structure:

> Other time lengths such as that taken by a fire or the playing of a piece of music occur accidentally or freely without explicit recognition of an all-embracing order, but nevertheless, necessarily within that order.

To elaborate on Cage's analogy, the occurrence of a fire is completely independent of the division of the week into days, and yet by necessity the fire occurs on one of those seven days.

What is new here is the description of rhythmic structure without any mention of measures, phrases, or sections – in other words, without any musical, expressive, or syntactic implications at all. The structure exists in itself, completely without any regard for the events that occur within it. This is a sharp departure from the point of view expressed in "Grace and Clarity," where the musical content is manipulated so as to "now observe and now ignore" the rhythmic structure. In "Forerunners of Modern Music" Cage asserts that the affirmation of structure by content is caused by "coincidences of free events with structural time points": in short, more by accident than by expressive intent or design. In the case of the analogy of the fire and the structure of the days of the week, such a coincidence would happen if the fire began exactly at midnight. In sum, the view of rhythmic structure expressed here is that such a structure is fundamentally empty and void of formal implications. As a result, Cage concludes that any sounds of any sorts, and in any combinations "are natural and conceivable within a rhythmic structure which equally embraces silence."

This, then, is the point of connection with Meister Eckhart: the conception of rhythmic structure as being so empty that it allows for all sounds is quite similar to Eckhart's notion of inner emptiness as the means of attaining the universal ("for by keeping thyself empty and bare, merely tracking and following and giving up thyself to this darkness and ignorance without turning back, thou mayest well win that which is all things"[13]). Just as Eckhart sees the discipline of self-denial as necessary for obtaining the all-encompassing inner silence, so Cage sees rhythmic structure as a discipline that "leads now to self-knowledge through self-denial."

The remainder of "Forerunners of Modern Music" is a comparison of this sense of the all-inclusiveness of rhythmic structure with the similarly boundless possibilities of electronic music. This comparison is unclear, as is much of the article; ideas are neither clearly nor concisely stated. This is perhaps because the ideas were still new and inchoate in Cage's mind (it is revealing that he described it as all that he was "aware of" at the time, and not all that he "knew" or "believed"). His new ideas on matters of structure and form were to be more fully developed later in "Lecture on Nothing," but only after some compositional experiments had made them clearer.

String Quartet in Four Parts

The composition that was to clarify Cage's new musical ideas was the *String Quartet in Four Parts* (1949–50). The quartet was begun while Cage was on a seven-month trip to Europe in the spring and fall of 1949. He traveled to The Netherlands and Italy, but spent most of the time in Paris, where he gave concerts, accompanied Merce Cunningham, and met with French musicians, writers, and artists. It was at this time that he first met Pierre Boulez, and the two composers immediately took a strong interest in each other's work. Cage continued work on the quartet after returning to New York and, after an interruption to write the music for a short film on the artist Alexander Calder, completed the work early in 1950.[14]

The *String Quartet in Four Parts* has an eight-part structure with proportions {2½, 1½; 2, 3; 6, 5; ½, 1½}, for a total of twenty-two units of twenty-two measures each. The eight sections are grouped in pairs into four movements, thus giving movement lengths of four, five, eleven, and two units. The *String Quartet* is based on the same program as *The Seasons*: that of the Indian conception of the four seasons. In this case, the first movement represents Summer, and the remaining movements follow accordingly. The movement titles do not mention the seasons, but rather the first three give what appear to be tempo indications ("Quietly flowing along," "Slowly rocking," "Nearly stationary"), while the last movement is marked "Quodlibet." In reality, the tempo is constant throughout the piece, and the effect of a gradually slowing tempo in the first three movements is produced by doubling the basic rhythmic unit from one movement to the next (quarter note, half note, whole note). In the last movement (the "Spring" movement), the basic pulse is the eighth note, so that a sudden and dramatic increase in tempo is suggested. This plan of tempi is clearly related to the seasonal program: the progression from "Preservation" to "Quiescence" is accompanied by a gradual slowing down, while the return to "Creation" is marked by a sudden increase in activity.

The *String Quartet in Four Parts* represents a further development in Cage's use of the gamut technique. Here, as in *The Seasons*, the gamut is a collection of sonorities to be used in the piece. But where there was a great deal of freedom in the use of the gamut in *The Seasons*, the *String Quartet* uses it in a very restricted way. First, the collection itself is relatively small: only thirty-three elements, as shown in Example 2–4. Secondly, as there are essentially no "free" elements used in the quartet (such as melodic lines or nonce harmonies), the gamut represents the entire musical material present in the work. Finally, the sonorities of the *String Quartet* always appear in only one formation, with no transposition, fragmentation, or arpeggiation. This static quality extends to the scoring of the individual gamut elements, as well: every chord in the gamut has its various tones played by the same instruments (and even on the same strings on those instruments) every time it is heard. This makes the score quite difficult to read and perform, since the voice-leading heard frequently bears little or no relation to the individual instrumental lines.

In *The Seasons*, the gamut technique had arisen in large part as a solution to the problem of how to use harmony in a non-progressive way. In "Forerunners of

Example 2–4 *String Quartet in Four Parts*, gamut of sonorities

Modern Music," Cage continued to ponder this question, suggesting that the solution lay in freeing harmony from structural responsibility, so that it "becomes a formal element (serves expression)." In the *String Quartet in Four Parts*, he attempted to do this by making harmony completely subservient to melody. In fact, in his descriptive catalog of works he described the quartet as "a melodic line without accompaniment," and he told Boulez that in it "there is no counterpoint and no harmony."[15] The technique used is similar to the one used in the "Winter" movement of *The Seasons*, in which harmonies are used to "play" a melody by treating one note of the harmony as its main note. However, where in *The Seasons* the rhythmic profile of the chord was used to emphasize the melody note, in the *String Quartet* it is most often the topmost note of the chord that serves as the melody note. Example 2–5, drawn from the opening of the quartet, gives an example of this technique in operation: 2–5a shows the gamut sonorities used here, while 2–5b gives the melodic line of these twenty-two measures; 2–5c, is the actual music of the passage, showing how the sonorities are used to "play" the melody.

This stricter approach to the handling of the gamut was a revelation for Cage. In *The Seasons*, his use of a harmonic gamut did not lead to a truly static sense of harmony since his use of the gamut elements was based on traditional harmonic and voice-leading concerns. In the *String Quartet in Four Parts*, on the other hand, the technique of subordinating harmonic usage to melodic lines produced an ordering of sonorities that owed nothing to the world of harmonic progression. Through this extension of the gamut technique Cage was able to divorce harmony from voice-leading, and thus produce a succession of harmonies that is truly freed from structural responsibility. The harmonic stasis is highlighted by the relatively slow pacing through the first three movements, by the overall lack of expressive dynamics, and by the indication that the players are to use no vibrato at all in their playing.

That stasis is most prominent in the third movement, whose structure is of particular interest. Cage described it twice in letters to Boulez:

> The third part . . . is a canon (retrograde and inversion, which is quite interesting because of the variations resulting from the rhythmic structure and the asymmetry of the gamut).   [February 1950]

> Such ideas as the following occur [in the canon]: direct duration imitation with retrograde or inverse use of the gamut or vice versa. This gives some interesting results since the gamut to begin with is assymetrical [*sic*].   [May 1951]

These statements raise the question of what Cage meant by the "inverse use of the gamut." In traditional usage, an inversion of a pattern is produced by making a mirror image of it using some arbitrary point on the scale of pitches as a reference point. To adapt this idea for the *String Quartet*, Cage created a "scale" of gamut sonorities, so that inverse relationships could be produced. This scale of sonorities is shown in Example 2–6. He did not produce a traditional scale of pitches, however: as can be seen in the figure, the ordering of the sonorities in his scale follows no particular pattern. As a result, the gamut-wise inversion of a particular series of chords is quite independent of a true pitch inversion (which is what he meant when he described the scale as asymmetrical). In Example 2–6, I have numbered the chords from −5 to 5: chord 0 is the center of the scale around which inversions are measured. Example 2–7 shows a specific inversion from the piece. In the first part of the figure (measures 221–30), the chords used are (2, 3, 2, 0, 5, 0, 2, 3, 4, 5, 4, 3, 4, 5), as marked in the figure. The inversion of this pattern is presented in the second part of the figure (measures 244–53), where the identical pattern is traced on the *left* (or "negative") side of the gamut scale.

The "canon" of this movement, however, is not a canon in the polyphonic sense of the term, but rather in the sense of there being rules for relating one part to another, based on the techniques of imitation, inversion, and retrograde. The combination of these strict rules and the asymmetrical use of the gamut "scale" produce some of the most striking music of the quartet – music that sounds completely different from the rest of the work and which is worlds removed from any piece he had composed before. If the gamut technique of *The Seasons* had been a largely unsuccessful attempt to recapture the effect of Satie's static expressiveness, then the new, stricter use of the gamut in the *String Quartet* hits that mark beautifully. The quartet (particularly its third movement) has that overall mood of austerity and understated beauty found in Satie, but the sense of

Example 2–5   *String Quartet in Four Parts*: I, bars 1–22

(a) gamut sonorities

Example 2–5 *String Quartet in Four Parts*: I, bars 1–22

(c) resulting score

Example 2–6 *String Quartet in Four Parts*: III, gamut "scale"

a single line (rather than a differentiation of melody with accompaniment), the disjunct voice leading, and the fragmentation of the harmonic progression combine to produce a score that is distinctly Cagean.

Example 2–7 *String Quartet in Four Parts*: III

(a) bars 221–30

(b) bars 244–53

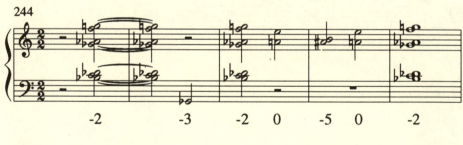

This new style was made possible by Cage's realization here that the sense of a collection of sounds that he had felt in working with the prepared piano was extensible to harmony. The unsatisfactory treatment of harmony in *The Seasons* was corrected in the *String Quartet* by treating the chords as *sounds* rather than as *harmonies*, by treating the gamut of sonorities in exactly the same way a collection of prepared piano tones would be handled. The result is a monophony of harmonies: a "line in rhythmic space," as Cage put it to Boulez, formed by the chords of the gamut, just as dissimilar beads can be strung to form a necklace. The strict use of the gamut of harmonies, especially when combined with the canon rules of the third movement, was the discipline necessary to allow Cage to free himself from the trap of Western harmonic practice.

"Lecture on Nothing"

The *String Quartet in Four Parts* helped Cage clarify the ideas he had hinted at in "Forerunners of Modern Music." His excitement over the composition of the quartet and the ideas that it engendered resulted almost immediately in the "Lecture on Nothing," rightly one of his most renowned and oft-quoted writings. Ideas about the emptiness of rhythmic structure, already encountered in "Forerunners of Modern Music," are presented more clearly and forcefully in this new lecture, and with an eloquence and poetry that exceeds any of Cage's earlier writings.

The lecture was first delivered at The Artists' Club in New York City sometime in 1950. This venue, also known as The Club or The Eighth Street Club, was organized in 1949 by prominent New York abstract expressionist artists such as Willem de Kooning and Franz Kline. Lectures were given regularly, and the list of speakers included such important figures as de Kooning, Jean Arp, Robert Motherwell, Mark Rothko, and Richard Huelsenbeck. Cage was a regular at The Artists' Club, and delivered lectures there on three occasions: "Indian Sand Painting or The Picture that is Valid for One Day" in 1949,[16] "Lecture on Nothing" in 1950, and "Lecture on Something" in 1951.

The "Lecture on Nothing" is the first of Cage's lectures to employ a rather unusual format and performance style. This stems from his treatment of the lecture as a piece of music, thus using the same structure and methods as for a musical composition. Written and delivered in such a fashion, a lecture is no longer just a conduit for information, but is both an explanation and a concrete demonstration of ideas. As Cage said in retrospect:

> My intention has been, often, to say what I had to say in a way that would exemplify it; that would, conceivably, permit the listener to experience what I had to say rather than just hear about it.[17]

This is the model that he was to follow increasingly in future years, becoming less and less interested in plain essaying, and more concerned with writing such musical lectures that would fill his need for poetry.

The "Lecture on Nothing," then, serves as an explanation and demonstration of rhythmic structure by being written within such a structure. The structure used is of five parts with proportions {7, 6, 14, 14, 7}, or a total of forty-eight units of forty-eight measures each. There are four "measures" per line of text, so that twelve lines form one unit of the structure (these divisions are marked in the text). The content of the lecture is based again on the four-fold division of composition first developed in "Defense of Satie," with each section of the rhythmic structure devoted to one element. The first, second, and third sections deal with form, structure, and materials, while the fifth section deals with method. The fourth section is special: it conveys no information at all, and its role in the lecture will be discussed more fully below. The unusual layout of the lecture in print is for performance reasons and is related to the rhythmic structure. The lines of text are divided into four columns, which correspond to the four "measures" of each line. The words are then distributed among these columns, sometimes with large gaps representing silences. The measurement of the text presented by this layout serves only as a means of loosely regulating the timing of delivery.

Another unusual feature of the lecture is the question and answer session at its end. Cage planned on there being questions after his lecture, and wrote six answers to give to the first six questions asked, no matter what they were. In addition to the obvious resulting *non sequiturs*, he made the answers themselves rather irrational and cryptic: "My head wants to ache," for example, or "According to the Farmers' Almanac this is False Spring." The questioning would be cut off by the sixth answer: "I have no more answers." The nonsense of these answers was perhaps inspired by the style of the Zen *koan* or *mondo*, which Cage would have been familiar with through his reading of Huxley and Alan Watts, and Cage himself called this "a reflection of my engagement in Zen."[18]

The body of the lecture itself represents the full statement and elaboration of the ideas about the emptiness and discipline of rhythmic structure that were so obliquely presented in "Forerunners of Modern Music." Cage uses various analogies and images to convey the voidness of rhythmic structure with regard to content, beginning with "an empty glass into which at any moment anything may be poured." Here, the glass represents structure and that which is poured into it represents the content. A further analogy is made to the State of Kansas, which he asserts is "like an empty glass, nothing but wheat, or is it corn? Does it matter which?" At one point, the text of the lecture refers to the units of its own rhythmic structure as they pass by, and in this context the independence of content from structure is clearly stated: "As you see, I can say anything. It makes very little difference what I say or even how I say it." He also reiterates here the portrayal of rhythmic structure as a necessary discipline: "It [structure] is a discipline which, accepted, in return accepts whatever, even those rare moments of ecstasy, which, as sugar loaves train horses, train us to make what we make."

These "moments of ecstasy" are the focus of Cage's discussion of form in the first section of the lecture. The sort of form or continuity that he presents could be characterized as "instantaneous" form, a continuity in which "each moment is absolute, alive and significant." In music demonstrating such instantaneous form (which is made possible by the emptiness of rhythmic structure), events can happen suddenly, at any time, and then disappear just as suddenly. The text of the lecture repeatedly refers to its own manifestation of this quality, as in the following passage:

> As we go along, (who knows?) an idea may occur in this talk. I have no idea whether one will or not. If one does, let it. Regard it as something seen momentarily, as though from a window while travelling.

In such an instantaneous form, the composer is in the position of no longer attempting to hold onto ideas or events. This sense of detachment is certainly related to the statement in "Forerunners of Modern Music" that a work of art should be "attractively disinteresting," but the sense of non-possession is more vivid in "Lecture on Nothing," and its positive results are made clearer, as in the following:

> Our poetry now is the realization that we possess nothing. Anything therefore is a delight (since we do not possess it) and thus need not fear its loss.

> Continuity today, when it is necessary, is a demonstration of disinterestedness. That is, it is a proof that our delight lies in not possessing anything.

The third and largest section of the lecture is devoted to the subject of musical materials. Prior to this lecture, Cage had said very little in his writings about either the nature of materials or their handling, and the large space devoted to this subject here shows how his work within the gamut technique in the *String Quartet* had focused his thinking. The section on materials is largely autobiographical: an account of how he became attracted or repulsed by various sorts of intervals and pitch combinations and how he took up noises as a means of getting away from pitches. The important new idea presented here is one learned from the *String Quartet* – the necessity of discipline and structure in one's way of handling materials: "The technique of handling materials is, on the sense level, what structure as a discipline is on the rational level: a means of experiencing nothing." A structured way of dealing with materials (such as the strict use of the gamut in the *String Quartet*) produces a sense of emptiness akin to that of rhythmic structure, allowing the sounds to exist as themselves rather than as tokens manipulated by the composer's mind. Cage makes his realization of this clear in his account of his renewed interest in pitched materials:

> I begin to hear the old sounds – the ones I had thought worn out, worn out by intellectualization – I begin to hear the old sounds as though they are not worn out. Obviously, they are not worn out. They are just as audible as the new sounds. Thinking had worn them out. And if one stops thinking about them, suddenly they are fresh and new.

The notion that sounds should be themselves, that they should be free from the intellect, is the new idea that will take Cage through the 1950s and beyond. It appears here – for the first time – only briefly, but soon will become the central point around which his compositional activity revolves.

These ideas – the independence of structure and content, the notion of instantaneous form arising from disinterest and detachment, the need to avoid letting thought about sounds cloud their identities – these relay the essential content of the "Lecture on Nothing," but communicate little or nothing of the beauty of the lecture. While rigidly structured around the four-fold division of composition, the lecture goes far beyond simply describing these divisions, crossing over into poetry. We see this in the gentle aimlessness of the text, in which ideas and images appear briefly from nowhere and then are dropped. The lecture is full of personal touches, such as the autobiographical treatment of materials or the self-references to the act of giving the lecture. There is poetry in the stories and personal anecdotes, sometimes clarifying, sometimes cryptic, such as the story of the man on the hill who is there for no reason, but "just stands." In sum, the "Lecture on Nothing" is a lecture that serves professional, personal, and musical ends; it is at once technical, religious, and entertaining. This is a mixture that fuses perfectly here, and results in as memorable a piece of writing as Cage had yet produced.

Of all the many memorable features of the lecture, perhaps the most prominent is the overriding tone of negation. From the title onwards, Cage persistently repeats various phrases that connote the negative: "we possess nothing," "we are going nowhere," "there is no point or the point is nothing." Perhaps the most frequently quoted line from the lecture is of this sort: "I have nothing to say and I am saying it and that is poetry as I need it." But this atmosphere of negation is not to be confused with a perverse negativism or nihilism; rather, this is a negation that has its roots in the "divine unconsciousness" of Meister Eckhart. This is a negation only of fixed ideas, the sort of self-denial that leads ultimately to an acceptance of all. Note that Cage does not state only the negative – that he has nothing to say – but goes on to state the positive – that he is saying it. Cage's "nothing" is analogous to what D. T. Suzuki says about the Void of Buddhism: "it is a zero full of infinite possibilities, it is a void of inexhaustible contents."[19]

The negative phrases and the aimlessness of the text together lend a rather bleak and flat quality to "Lecture on Nothing," an effect similar to that of the *String Quartet*, and best exemplified by the fourth section of the lecture. This section is lengthy (as long as the section on materials), but consists only of seven repetitions of the following lines (with changes made to reflect the passing of the structural units):

> Here we are now at the beginning of the fourth large part of this talk. More and
> more I have the feeling that we are getting nowhere. Slowly, as the talk goes
> on, we are getting nowhere and that is a pleasure. It is not irritating to be where

one is. It is only irritating to think one would like to be somewhere else. Here
we are now, a little bit after the beginning of the fourth large part of this talk.
More and more we have the feeling that I am getting nowhere. Slowly, as the
talk goes on, slowly, we have the feeling we are getting nowhere. That is a
pleasure which will continue. If we are irritated, it is not a pleasure. Nothing is
not a pleasure if one is irritated, but suddenly, it is a pleasure, and then more and
more it is not irritating (and then more and more and slowly). Originally we
were nowhere; and now, again, we are having the pleasure of being slowly
nowhere. If anybody is sleepy, let him go to sleep.[20]

This section forms a great pause in the flow of the talk, a kind of mantra for
settling the mind, a concrete demonstration of "saying nothing." The regularity
and static character of this passage suggests the canon movement of the *String
Quartet in Four Parts*, and perhaps was inspired by that work.

These images of "nothing" and "saying nothing" call to mind *4' 33"* (1952),
Cage's "silent piece," in which no sounds are made by the performer at all. This
piece is perhaps his most famous creation, and has been written about extensively:
practically no discussion of the composer or his work fails to mention it. The
work has most often been presented either as the ultimate chance composition,
or as the perfect example of indeterminacy of performance – both chance and
indeterminacy entering into Cage's music at about the time *4' 33"* was composed.
What has been rarely noted is that he had the idea for the piece much earlier. In
"A Composer's Confessions" there appears the following:

> I have, for instance, several new desires (two may seem absurd, but I am serious
> about them): first, to compose a piece of uninterrupted silence and sell it to the
> Muzak Co. It will be 4½ minutes long – these being the standard lengths of
> "canned" music, and its title will be "Silent Prayer". It will open with a single
> idea which I will attempt to make as seductive as the color and shape or
> fragrance of a flower. The ending will approach imperceptibility.[21]

"Silent Prayer," as it was thus described in 1948, is clearly the first glimmer of an
idea that, four years later, would become *4' 33"*; while "Silent Prayer" is not
4' 33" itself, it is its ancestor. Thus the silent piece's origins lie not in Cage's
works of the 1950s and 60s, but rather in the aesthetic milieu we are considering
here: the late 1940s, the *String Quartet in Four Parts*, and the "Lecture on
Nothing." We are justified, then, in considering the significance of *4' 33"* in this
context and in attempting to understand what it would mean to Cage before the
invention of chance composition.

Because *4' 33"* is known far more by reputation than through direct experience,
it is worthwhile here to provide a precise description of the piece as it was
composed in 1952.[22] The piece is in three parts of fixed lengths: 30", 2' 23", and
1' 40" for a total duration (as given by the title) of 4' 33". These durations were
arrived at by chance means, via the addition of many shorter durations.[23]

Although chance was used in the compositional act in 1952, it surely was not considered in 1948 when he first thought of the work: he almost certainly would have used a consciously-chosen structure instead. What would remain the same about the piece from 1948 to 1952 is the idea of a structured silence.[24] Thus considered, *4' 33"* represents an instance of a truly empty rhythmic structure. If all sounds occur within the order of rhythmic structure (as Cage had asserted in "Forerunners of Modern Music"), then such a structure could not only encompass all possible sounds, but could function without any composed sounds at all: the ambient sounds of the environment – or even a dead silence – would themselves occur within the structural order. More to the point, a silent piece would serve a personal, spiritual purpose: by making and experiencing a piece of structure without content, Cage could follow Eckhart's injunction to empty himself entirely, and thus hear "the hidden word." As a disinterested action, a meditation on the discipline of rhythmic structure, an actual immersion in the emptiness of rhythmic structure – in these senses the silent piece may be seen as more a means than an end, a mental, spiritual, and compositional exercise. Its literal silence reflects the silence of the will necessary to open up a realm of infinite possibilities.

It is not hard to imagine Cage in 1948, before the *String Quartet*, realizing the need to keep still and quiet, to pursue such a discipline of self-control and denial. The situation here is reminiscent of that found in the "ox-herding pictures" of Zen Buddhism. In these pictures, the path of self-discipline that leads to enlightened knowledge is compared to the gradual taming of an ox. The ox becomes completely docile, and ultimately disappears entirely. In one version of the pictures, the last picture is only a blank circle and its accompanying text can be read as a commentary on *4' 33"*:

> Both the man and the animal have disappeared, no traces are left,
> The bright moonlight is empty and shadowless with all the ten thousand objects
>   in it;
> If anyone should ask the meaning of this,
> Behold the lilies of the field and its fresh sweet-scented verdure.[25]

From choice to chance

Chart technique: *Concerto for Prepared Piano*

The clarity and self-assurance of the *String Quartet in Four Parts* and "Lecture on Nothing" indicate the extent to which Cage felt he had solved at least one of the problems that had plagued him in the late 1940s: how to use harmony in a static or non-progressive way. The *String Quartet in Four Parts* brought together his ideas about empty rhythmic structure and a harmonic gamut technique; this combination excited him tremendously, as he indicated in a letter to his parents in 1949, written just as he was starting the quartet:

> This piece is like the opening of another door; the possibilities implied are unlimited and without the rhythmic structure I found by working with percussion and the newness, freshness of sound I found in the prepared piano, it would be impossible.

Although Cage saw unlimited possibilities in his new style of composition, and was undeniably ecstatic about its manifestation in the *String Quartet*, he did not continue in this style – the only other composition to share the style and technique of the *String Quartet in Four Parts* was *Six Melodies* for Violin and Keyboard, composed immediately after the quartet in 1950.[26] Rather than suggesting a relatively stable style within which he could work, the quartet, together with "Lecture on Nothing", instead suggested avenues for further stylistic development – directions that might have been unforeseen by Cage at the time he composed the quartet, but were made increasingly clear to him in retrospect. Specifically, the *String Quartet* (and in particular its third movement) pointed to a significant rearrangement of his four-fold division of music (structure, form, material, and method) with regard to the duality of law and freedom.

In his writings prior to 1950, Cage had insisted that musical structure should be the realm of discipline – a "law element." But as strongly as he felt that structure must be the self-negating discipline of music, equally as strong was his belief that musical form (i.e., musical content) should be the realm of expressivity in music – a "freedom element." As late as 1949, in "Forerunners of Modern Music," Cage said of form that "the law it observes, if indeed it submits to any, has never been and never will be written."

Cage's rigid stance on this opposition of structure and form was weakened by the very four-fold division of music this duality had engendered. For by subdividing musical form into the twin components of material and method, and by allowing both of these to be either law or freedom elements, he had left open the possibility that, if both were disciplined, then the resulting form would be a law element, too. This possibility only became apparent to Cage after the *String Quartet*, in which materials are controlled by the discipline of the gamut technique, and in which, in its third movement, the method is controlled by the rules of the canon. Here, through the disciplined handling of both materials and method, Cage had discovered a way of making music in which not only the structure was empty, but in which the content was empty as well. In short, he had discovered the "law of form" whose existence he had denied just one year earlier. This new approach to musical form had far-reaching implications. Cage's disciplined handling of materials via the gamut technique had been prompted by his need to negate the self-indulgence of Western harmony. The disciplined handling of form, however, went much further, extending to the negation of any musical self-indulgence whatsoever.

However, Cage did not immediately and fully embrace this notion of *musical* self-negation (as opposed to merely *harmonic* self-negation): while intuitively sensing the necessity of a completely disciplined approach to composition, he was reluctant to abandon completely his belief that expressive freedom had a necessary role in music. This inner conflict led him to take up, in his next work, a medium that has long been associated with the musical conflict of two opposing forces: the concerto.[27] In the *Concerto for Prepared Piano and Chamber Orchestra*, begun during the summer of 1950 and completed early in 1951, the orchestra and the piano would play the roles of law and freedom. As Cage describes it:

> I made it [the concerto] into a drama between the piano, which remains romantic, expressive, and the orchestra, which itself follows the principles of oriental philosophy. And the third movement signifies the coming together of things which were opposed to one another in the first movement.[28]

This drama of the opposition and reconciliation of piano and orchestra was to be portrayed through the handling of form in their respective parts. The prepared piano solo, while still subject to the discipline of the rhythmic structure, would have a continuity of events that came "from the heart," composed in that quasi-improvisational way that Cage had used throughout the 1940s. The sequence of events in the orchestral music, on the other hand, would be completely mind-controlled; through a self-imposed discipline in all aspects of the composition, even the note-to-note continuity of the orchestra would be a demonstration of emptiness.

In order to create a fully self-negating musical form, Cage needed to combine a highly structured way of defining his materials with an equally rigorous method for ordering them. He accomplished both of these through the use of a chart of sounds – a two-dimensional representation of the gamut. He described both the principle and its realization in the concerto in a letter to Boulez:

> A new idea entered which is this: to arrange the agregates [*sic*] not in a gamut (linearly) but rather in a chart formation. In this case the size of the chart was 14 by 16. That is to say: 14 different sounds produced by any number of instruments (sometimes only one) (and often including percussion integrally) constitute the top row of the chart and favor (quantitatively speaking) the flute. The second row in the chart favors the oboe and so on. Four rows favor the percussion divided: metal, wood, friction, and miscellaneous (characterized by mechanical means, e.g., the radio). The last four favor the strings. Each sound is minutely described in the chart: e.g., a particular tone, sul pont. on the 2nd string of the first violin with a particular flute tone and, for example, a woodblock. I then made moves on this chart of a "thematic nature" but, as you may easily see, with an athematic result.
>
> [May 1951]

The sounds themselves, as Cage described them to Boulez, are mostly single sonorities, much like those of the *String Quartet*'s gamut (although some of the sounds extend this idea by including short flourishes and grace notes). What made the chart different from the gamut is that, beyond acting as a means of organizing the sonic materials, it suggested a disciplined method of moving from sound to sound: by tracing simple patterns on the charts (Cage's "thematic" moves).

The structural proportions of the concerto are {3, 2, 4; 4, 2, 3; 5}, the larger divisions grouped into three movements of equal tempo. In the first movement, Cage set up his polarity of law and freedom. Here, the prepared piano solo was composed in a completely free manner, similar to that of his earlier prepared piano pieces, such as the *Sonatas and Interludes*. But while the piano solo is expressive and improvisational, the orchestral music is completely subservient to the chart technique (see Example 2–8). The sounds follow one another with no apparent musical logic – not even the melodic line that held the *String Quartet* together. In this case, Cage simply took a few simple moves (such as going down two cells and then over three) and used various permutations and orientations of these to generate sequences of sounds, one for each phrase unit of the rhythmic structure. This method did not address the matter of rhythm, however. Cage had no systematic way of assigning rhythms to the sounds; instead, given a particular number and series of sounds to be placed within a phrase of a particular length, he arranged the sounds rhythmically according to his own musical judgement. If, for example, as a result of his chart moves, the flute played in three or four successive sounds, he would usually take advantage of this continuity and make the rhythmic sequence such that the flute notes could be slurred together and suggest a brief, "accidental" melodic line.

In the second movement of the concerto, the conflict between piano and orchestra was to be resolved somewhat. For this movement, Cage maintained the same orchestral sound chart, but drew up a new sound chart for the piano as well, structured in the same way as the orchestral chart, thus bringing the solo part under the control of the chart technique, as well. While the orchestra and prepared piano have their own distinct charts, they share the same method for producing the continuity of sounds, which this time involved concentric circles and squares drawn on the charts. Once again, Cage used his compositional judgement to place these sounds rhythmically within the framework of his phrase structure.

The specifics of the chart technique – the precise arrangements of sounds within the charts and the specific patterns drawn upon them – are never audible as such to the listener. However, the use of charts does make a great deal of difference in the effect of the piece. In the first movement, it is immediately apparent that the piano solo and the orchestral music are composed in significantly different ways. The piano speaks clearly to us, with gestures and a sense of drama that is effortlessly understood. The orchestra in this movement, on the other hand, is elusive and cryptic; it does not speak, it simply exists. This perceptible difference (heightened by Cage's decision to have the pianist and orchestra play one at a time and never together) is the direct result of the difference in compositional means. Similarly, we are aware in the second movement that the piano solo has taken on the style of the orchestra; where the piano and orchestra traveled in different worlds in the first movement, they are clearly moving in

Example 2–8 *Concerto for Prepared Piano*: I, bars 1–9

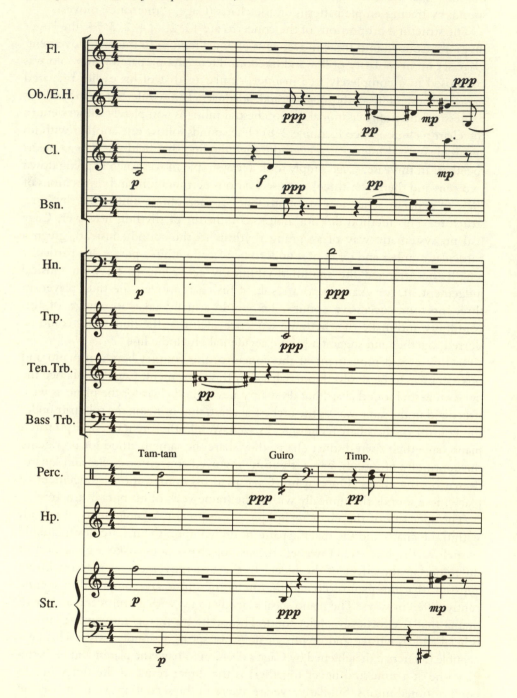

the same world in the second. But while they share a compositional method (and hence a musical style), the piano and orchestra in the second movement still speak only in alternation, never in unison. Cage has compared the technique of the second movement to the way "a disciple follows his master, in a sort of antiphony, then comes to join the latter in his impersonality."[29] He would completely integrate the piano and orchestra in the final movement of the concerto (as I will describe presently), but only after making some striking discoveries.

"Lecture on Something"

The chart music of the *Concerto for Prepared Piano* represents Cage's first deliberate attempt to create a completely disciplined musical continuity – a new, empty, self-negating form. This new form, which Cage dubbed "no-continuity," was unlike anything he had composed before, and became the subject of his next lecture: "Lecture on Something," first delivered in early 1951 at The Artists' Club. The title of the new lecture suggests a duality with the earlier "Lecture on Nothing": while "Lecture on Nothing" deals mostly with matters of structure, "Lecture on Something" is almost entirely about form or content, about the freedom of action that is made possible by the acceptance of an empty rhythmic structure. As with the earlier lecture, "Lecture on Something" is organized by means of a rhythmic structure, although here the arrangement of the content of the lecture within the structure is less strict, and as a result the ideas flow more freely and informally.

Cage's notion of no-continuity has its roots in the instantaneous form encountered in "Lecture on Nothing" and in his use of charts in the concerto. In "Lecture on Nothing" he stated that "each moment presents what happens": musically, this is exemplified by the use of the gamut in the *String Quartet*, where musical events happen with an aimless or static quality, but still reflect the personal intervention of the composer. This approach to instantaneous form was changed by the chart technique of the concerto. Here, the ordering of events had nothing to do with any perceived or composed relations between them, but rather was dependent only on the coincidence of their positions in the chart with the pattern of moves, both of which were arbitrary. The occurrence of a given sound was no longer the result of an imposed melodic or harmonic idea, but was now the result of nothing at all but geometry: the sounds simply "happened."

This sense of sounds emerging of themselves is the essence of no-continuity as described in "Lecture on Something." Cage defines no-continuity as "accepting that continuity that happens," as opposed to "making that continuity that excludes all others." For him, a continuity is the product of an artist's mind – it is an abstraction, something that the artist feels he may "securely possess." With no-continuity, on the other hand, each sound is just itself, and any relations among the sounds happen of themselves, not because the composer imposes them. In "Lecture on Something" Cage extends this concept of no-continuity from the musical to the personal. Large portions of the lecture are devoted to describing how an acceptance of the no-continuity of everyday life leads to a better way of living:

> [No-continuity] will let us allow our lives with all of the things that happen in them to be simply what they are and not separate from one another. . . . Anything may happen and it all does go together. There is no rest of life. Life is one.

While most of the lecture is about no-continuity and its implications, the "Lecture on Something" was ostensibly to be about Morton Feldman. In a sense, the lecture is about both, since Feldman's work played an important role in focusing Cage's thought on the subject of no-continuity. Cage met Feldman in 1950 after a performance of Webern's Symphony Op. 21 by the New York Philharmonic (both composers were leaving the concert hall early because they could not imagine listening to any other music after the Webern). The two immediately struck up a strong friendship, and soon they were sharing ideas. They spent hours in the Cedar Bar in Greenwich Village, talking about painting and music: "I can say without exaggeration," Feldman recounts, "that we did this every day for five years of our lives."[30]

The works of Feldman that prompted the "Lecture on Something" were the first of his "graph" pieces, *Projections* and *Intersections*, composed in late 1950 and early 1951. Example 2–9 is from the first such piece, *Projection 1* for solo cello (1950), and is a representative sample of the graph notation that Feldman used in the other *Projection* and *Intersection* pieces. The three large systems represent three timbres: reading from bottom to top, they are *arco*, *pizzicato*, and harmonics. The dotted lines are barlines, encompassing four beats in each bar. The smaller solid squares and rectangles each represent a single tone of the appropriate timbre. The vertical placement of the squares within a system gives the general pitch range of the notes: high, medium, or low. Any pitches can be played (so long as they are in the correct range), and their duration is given by the length of the rectangle or square. Part of the idea of using this graph notation was to compose using different weights of sound and not specific pitch combinations; to Feldman, the graphic notation seemed an appropriate and direct way of expressing them.

As shown by their treatment in "Lecture on Something," Feldman's graph pieces resonated strongly with Cage's emerging ideas about no-continuity and the importance of self-negating discipline. In the lecture, Cage portrays Feldman's graphs as the acceptance of all sounds in any combinations: "Feldman speaks of no sounds, and takes within broad limits the first ones that come along." Thus, the space of Feldman's graph cells was akin to the empty spaces of Cage's rhythmic structures, accepting all sounds equally at all times. As a result, Cage saw Feldman as one who "has changed the responsibility of the composer from making to accepting," hence a "heroic" figure. Feldman served as a model for Cage, an example of one who had accepted all musical possibilities – to an even greater degree than Cage himself had.

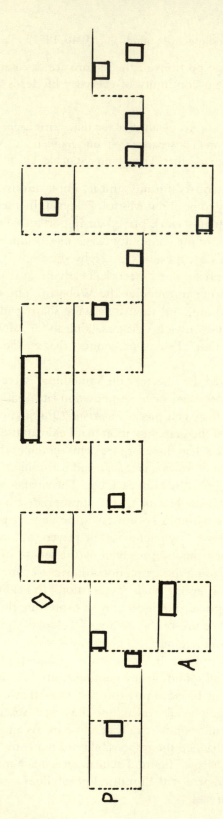

Example 2–9 Morton Feldman, *Projection 1* for solo cello (excerpt)

It is this emphasis on the acceptance of all that makes "Lecture on Something" so different from "Lecture on Nothing" in its overall tone and demeanor. Even though they cover similar material, "Lecture on Nothing" is all-negating, while "Lecture on Something" is all-affirming. Certainly, images of "nothing" persist in the new lecture: for example, Cage still insists on the emptiness of rhythmic structure, and on the necessity of possessing nothing, of being "submerged in silence." But the overriding image here is of gaining everything through this self-denial, of the relationship of "something" (content) to "nothing" (structure), as in the following passage:

> When nothing is securely possessed one is free to accept any of the somethings. How many are there? They roll up at your feet . . . There is no end to the number of somethings and all of them (without exception) are acceptable. If one gets suddenly proud and says for one reason or another: I cannot accept this; then the whole freedom to accept any of the others vanishes. But if one maintains secure possession of nothing (what has been called poverty of spirit), then there is no limit to what one may freely enjoy.

By its emphasis on what is to be gained by possessing nothing, "Lecture on Something" can be seen as not just the complement of "Lecture on Nothing," but as its completion. Cage could be accused in "Lecture on Nothing" and *4' 33"* of endorsing a kind of musical quietism, of sitting quietly and doing nothing. But "Lecture on Something," in affirming action and creation, balances the emptiness of "Lecture on Nothing," making it clear that "saying nothing" does not mean mere idleness. This relationship between emptiness and abundance can be related to the Zen ox-herding pictures mentioned earlier. In a later version of these pictures, the empty circle is followed by a picture of a "return to the origin" (portrayed as a stream), and ends with a picture of a fat man bearing gifts. In this version of the pictures, it is made clear that the emptiness of the circle was needed to get back to the source of all things, so that ultimately, "There is no need for the miraculous power of the gods, for he touches and lo! the dead trees are in full bloom."[31] Just as the ox-herding pictures relate a gradual path to enlightenment through self-discipline, so the "Lecture on Nothing" and "Lecture on Something," taken as a pair, show Cage's gradual attainment of a release from the musical problems that had plagued him in the mid-1940s. The emptiness of rhythmic structure, the silence of *4' 33"* (thought of, if not yet experienced), and the discipline of the chart technique were necessary to reach the source of "all the somethings." "Lecture on Something" reads like one great sigh of relief at the easing of these burdens.

> If you let it, it supports itself. You don't have to. Each something is a celebration of the nothing that supports it. When we remove the world from our shoulders we notice it doesn't drop. Where is the responsibility?

Chance

That Cage had reached a resolution of some of his compositional and musical problems is also reflected in the last movement of the concerto. This movement was to represent the resolution of the opposition of orchestra and piano, law and freedom. For it, Cage needed a means of suggesting this coming together of opposites. One device he used was to create a single new chart that would contain sounds for both piano and orchestra. Some of the sounds in this unified chart would be for piano alone or orchestra alone, these drawn from the separate charts used in the second movement. Others would be new sounds that combined piano and orchestra, thus providing the first moments in which the two would play together.

The other tool used to suggest the integration of law and freedom was the *I Ching*, or Chinese *Book of Changes*. The *I Ching* is based on the interpretation of figures made of six solid or broken lines, which represent the basic principles of weak and strong, *yin* and *yang*. There are sixty-four such hexagrams, which are numbered one to sixty-four, and which are said to represent various situations in life. To consult the *I Ching*, one throws three coins to determine each individual line of a hexagram. These lines, whether strong (solid) or weak (broken), may be either stable or moving; moving lines are considered to be in the process of changing into their opposites. If the hexagram obtained in consulting the book contains any moving lines, a second hexagram is formed in addition to the first by changing all the moving lines into their opposites.[32] Cage had recently been given a copy of the book by his student Christian Wolff and was struck by the similarity of its chart of hexagrams to his own sound charts. He no doubt also saw in its philosophy of mutually-embracing opposites a parallel to his concerto in progress, and so, for the last movement, he adapted his chart technique to include the use of the *I Ching*.

Cage applied the *I Ching* concept – of strong and weak forces either remaining constant or changing into one another – to create the new sound chart for the third movement. For each cell in the chart, three coins were tossed to obtain a single *I Ching* hexagram line. If a stable strong or weak line was obtained by the coin toss, that cell of the new chart would be filled by the corresponding cell from the orchestra or piano chart, respectively. If a moving line was thrown, a new sound combining piano and orchestra would be composed and placed in the chart.

The *I Ching* was also used to determine the continuity of sounds and silences in the third movement. Cage first chose a collection of thirty-two simple moves that could be made on the sound chart. Then he consulted the *I Ching* once for each measure, noting the hexagram numbers obtained; because of the possibility of moving lines, each measure could be assigned either one or two numbers in the range of one to sixty-four. Each number represented a single sound or silence: thirty-two possible numbers were assigned to the thirty-two moves (thus resulting in sounds), while the remaining thirty-two hexagrams caused silences to occur. Durations were kept simple: if only one number had been obtained for a measure, then the sound or silence filled the measure. If two numbers were used in a measure, the two sounds or silences were each assigned a half-bar's duration. In this manner, Cage adapted his technique of patterned moves made on the chart to the mechanism of the *I Ching*: where in the first two movements the series of moves was determined by regular geometrical means, in this final movement the *I Ching* chose which moves to make, thus resulting in a random series of sounds from the chart. Beyond this, the method of the third movement takes the theme of integrating opposites and extends it to the integration of sound and silence.

Considering the development of Cage's ideas about the emptiness of rhythmic structure and the acceptance of no-continuity, that the concerto should include his first use of chance is no surprise. Cage himself realized as he wrote the first movements of the concerto that his use of arbitrary moves on the charts "brings me closer to a 'chance' or if you like an un-aesthetic choice."[33] While the time was ripe for him to take on chance as a compositional tool, his introduction to the *I Ching* by Christian Wolff may have been the impetus for its actual use in the concerto. The third movement represented the resolution of the dualisms of piano and orchestra, sound and silence. Cage's use of the *I Ching* as a model and method for the composition of this movement makes perfect poetic sense: the book's philosophy of strong and weak forces in constant flux directly parallels the changing roles of piano and orchestra in the concerto. In later works, the *I Ching* would become more or less a faceless device in the compositional process, but Cage's attraction to the book may be traced to its singular appropriateness to the message of the concerto.

The use of a combined piano and orchestra chart, the extensive use of silences, and the simple rhythms combine to give the third movement of the concerto a substantially different sound from the rest of the work (see Example 2–10). It is not just the use of chance that produces this effect; the sound orders produced in the last movement are free of pitch relations to no greater degree than those of the first two movements. What makes the third movement sound so different from the others is Cage's arrival at the single most important new discovery of the concerto: the interchangeability of sound and silence. In the first two movements of the concerto, he had used silences much as he had in his earlier works: musically, to articulate groupings of sounds. In the final movement of the concerto, however, the continuity proceeds one sound or silence at a time, these two opposing possibilities being considered as events of equal standing. In doing this, Cage created a music that "speaks *Nothingness*."[34] The experience of this music can best be characterized by a passage from "Lecture on Something":

> Listening to this music one takes as a springboard the first sound that comes along; the first something springs us into nothing and out of that nothing arises the next something; etc. like an alternating current. Not one sound fears the silence that extinguishes it. And no silence exists that is not pregnant with sound.

The sounds of the concerto's final movement come of themselves, as a Tibetan poem says, "as from the surface of a clear lake there leaps suddenly a fish."[35]

Example 2–10   *Concerto for Prepared Piano*: III, bars 1–10

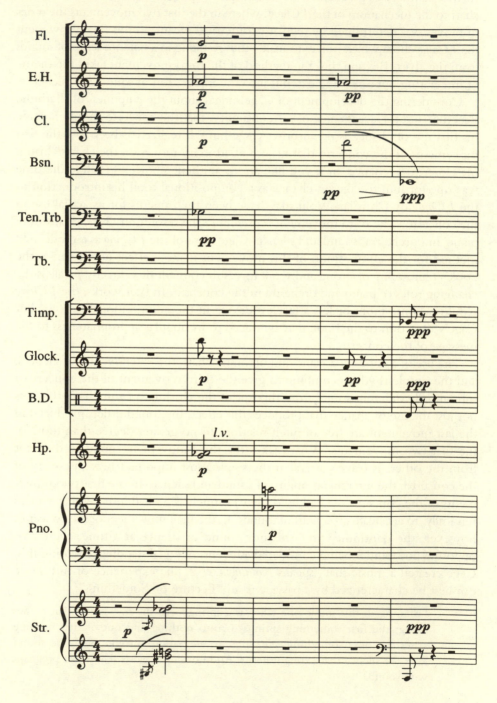

3

"Throwing sound into silence" (1951–1956)

Changes in aesthetic

The period of the late 1940s can be seen as a journey for Cage, a period of experimentation in which he attempted to find a way of composing that he could feel comfortable with. With the last movement of the *Concerto for Prepared Piano*, he had arrived at the end of this journey, and he found himself in a musical world quite different from any he had inhabited before: one in which each sound emerges of itself from the empty space of the rhythmic structure. The use of the gamut technique as subsequently transformed into the charts of the concerto had led Cage to a compositional approach in which materials were no longer a supporting element to structure and form, but were now central, an approach in which the selection of materials almost completely defined the resulting composition. In the concerto, the charts of sounds *are* the piece, or viewed conversely, the concerto is an articulation of the charts: a "sounding" of the charts in time. In a 1950 letter to Boulez, Cage aptly describes this sort of composition as "throwing sound into silence": not making an expressive continuity, but simply composing individual sounds and letting them find their own expressiveness within a blank canvas of empty time.

This approach to composition was enhanced and extended by experiences that Cage had shortly after finishing the concerto, experiences that would help him to build an aesthetic around the primacy of materials. The first of these was his exposure to Zen Buddhism, particularly through Daisetz Teitaro Suzuki, the Japanese philosopher and scholar who was instrumental in presenting Zen Buddhism to the West. The relationship of Cage's composition to his study of Zen Buddhism was not one in which Zen "influenced" him to act and think in certain ways: Cage's understanding of Zen was shaped as much by his compositional concerns as his composition was shaped by his interest in Zen.

In particular, Cage connected his musical world of sounds in silence to the Zen concepts of "unimpededness and interpenetration." He explains his understanding of these concepts in a lecture given in 1951 or 1952:

> This unimpededness is seeing that in all of space each thing and each human being is at the center and furthermore that each one being at the center is the

74

most honored one of all. Interpenetration means that each one of these most honored ones of all is moving out in all directions penetrating and being penetrated by every other one no matter what the time or what the space. . . . In fact each and every thing in all of time and space is related to each and every other thing in all of time and space.[1]

In this view, a perfect balance exists between the individuality of things on the one hand (their unimpededness) and their common and simultaneous reflection of the universal on the other (their interpenetration). A consequence of such a conception is that reality must be completely non-dualistic, since the complete interrelation of all things cannot allow for any divisions or distinctions.

Cage quickly saw how this doctrine of unimpededness and interpenetration related to his newfound musical world. For him, the things that interpenetrate are *sounds*; compositionally, he found that silence produced the proper effect, noting in his "Juilliard Lecture" of 1952 that "silence surrounds many of the sounds so that they exist in space unimpeded by one another and yet interpenetrating one another." The chart technique of the *Concerto for Prepared Piano* itself could be seen as a musical translation of the doctrine of interpenetration. For example, when one hears a sound in the last movement of the concerto (say a combination of harp and percussion), one is hearing a unique, individual sound, isolated from all others in the piece by silence and the lack of a conscious continuity. At the same time, this sound is, with all the other sounds in the movement, a member of the same chart – the chart is thus a single entity that permeates the entire composition. The sounds of the concerto are both independent (in the way they occur in time) and simultaneous (in the way they exist in the chart).

The chart technique could thus be interpreted in terms of these aspects of Zen philosophy, but the relationship was less than perfect. While the spaciousness of the chart music displayed an affinity with the image of unimpededness, Cage's conception of music as the alternation of sound and silence was incompatible with the Zen view of a totally interpenetrating and non-dualistic reality – Cage was still thinking of sounds as existing in opposition to the silence that contained them. The full acceptance of the non-dual nature of musical reality was made possible only by his experience in an anechoic chamber at Harvard in 1951. According to Cage, while in this supposedly "silent" room, he heard two sounds: one the sound of his blood circulating, the other the sound of his nervous system.[2] This experience was a revelation for him. It demonstrated that there was no such thing as silence, but rather that there were only sounds: what he had referred to as silence was simply the sounds he had not intended. Thus the opposition of sound and silence became the opposition of intention and non-intention, which was a duality he found easy to transcend.

The realization that the musical world was completely filled with sound served to further accentuate the role of musical materials in Cage's composition. Where the chart technique had affirmed the primacy of materials, the epiphany of the anechoic chamber incident, placed in the context of Zen philosophy, allowed for materials to so grow in importance that they completely dominated all other aspects of composition. Rhythmic structure, no longer a true physical silence, became strictly an agent of compositional discipline, no longer perceptible or all-controlling. Instead of working with a compartmentalized space of silent rhythmic structure, Cage now saw his field of action as an infinite space of sounds that are completely interconnected, yet unique. Among the clearest presentations of this new view is that in the article "Experimental Music: Doctrine" (1955), in which he refers to this space as "a totality of possibilities" that are "impermanently involved in an infinite play of interpenetrations." In this context, form ceases to be an issue at all: since all sounds are interrelated, there can be no matter of making a continuity. Instead, form simply becomes any arbitrary path traced within the total space of possibilities. In his 1954 lecture "45' for a Speaker" Cage gives various such definitions of form: "It is right here right now"; "It is yourself in the form you have that instant taken"; "It is wherever you are and there is no place where it isn't." This new role of form is an extension of his earlier ideas about *accepting* rather than *making*. There he was speaking of accepting a disinterestedly-made continuity of sounds; here he realizes that there was no need to make anything in the first place.

It is in this context of the dominance of materials that Cage's use of chance is to be understood. As the first two movements of the *Concerto for Prepared Piano* show, he could have summoned up the image of unimpeded and interpenetrating sounds existing in a field of silence without the use of chance. However, to go beyond this and to explore freely the infinite space of musical possibilities, chance was essential. Cage gives the reason for the necessity of chance in "Experimental Music: Doctrine": "In view, then, of a totality of possibilities, no knowing action is commensurate, since the character of the knowledge acted upon prohibits all but some eventualities." The assertion here that musical knowledge limits the scope of compositional action has its parallels in passages from Cage's earlier writings: in "Lecture on Nothing," where he describes how materials can be "worn out" by thought about them; in the part of "Lecture on Something" that deals with the way in which thought (as expressed in traditional musical continuity) tends to exclude "non-profound" events; and in the "Juilliard Lecture," where he adapts a Zen metaphor to point out that "sounds are sounds and men are men," and that "the wisest thing to do is to open one's ears immediately and hear a sound suddenly before one's thinking has a chance to turn it into something logical, abstract, or symbolical."

In Cage's view, then, any useful compositional method or technique should serve as a means of emptying the mind of thoughts that would exclude possibilities. Chance operations are particularly effective here, since chance effectively blocks the exercise of one's accumulated knowledge and prejudices. Chance techniques are an example of what Cage, in "Experimental Music: Doctrine," came to call "experimental actions" – actions "the outcome of which [is] unknown." He contrasts such experimental actions to the thoughts or "knowing actions" that get in the way of our understanding of the nature of sound, and makes it clear that such actions, free from abstract thoughts, are the only reasonable way to apprehend the totality of possibilities.

In supporting and elaborating on his method of experimental action, Cage drew upon another Zen doctrine: the doctrine of "no-mindedness," as expressed in the Zen master Huang Po's "Doctrine of Universal Mind." The overriding theme of Huang Po's teaching – virtually identical to Cage's thinking about music – is the need to rid oneself of conceptual thought in order to apprehend ultimate Reality. The following is a typical formulation:

> A student of the Way, by allowing himself a single . . . thought, falls among devils. If he permits himself a single thought leading to differential perception, he falls into heresy. . . . Nothing is born, nothing is destroyed. Away with your dualism, your likes and dislikes. Every single thing is just the One Mind. When you have perceived this, you will have mounted the Chariot of the Buddhas.[3]

The no-mindedness that Huang Po espouses is not a matter of non-action or even non-thought, but rather is a state of non-attachment to thoughts:

> Every day, whether walking, standing, sitting or lying down, and in all your speech, remain detached from everything within the sphere of phenomena. Whether you speak or merely blink an eye, let it be done with complete dispassion. . . . Why do they [most students of Zen] not copy me by letting each thought go as though it were nothing, or as though it were a piece of rotten wood, a stone, or the cold ashes of a dead fire? Or else, by just making whatever slight response is suited to each occasion?[4]

For Cage, no-mindedness meant that the mind should be alert to sounds, but empty of musical ideas; as Huang Po puts it: "The ignorant eschew phenomena but not thought; the wise eschew thought but not phenomena."[5]

To summarize Cage's model of composition: there exists an infinite, completely non-dual space of unique but interconnected sounds; by means of chance techniques, the composer can empty his mind of thoughts about sounds, and thus identify with this infinite space. Such "purposeless," "unknowing," or "experimental" actions trace the path that constitutes the continuity or form of the piece. A story from Irish folklore that Cage refers to in his lectures and writings is a useful analogy to this model. The story deals with a hero who goes on a quest with the aid of a magical horse – a "shaggy nag" – that gives him advice along the way. The horse gives the hero a metal ball and instructs him to cast it in front of them and to follow it wherever it leads. The hero does this, and thus, by abandoning himself to chance, passes safely through his various trials.[6] For Cage, the composer is like the hero of the legend, chance composition is like the rolling of the metal ball, and the resulting musical form is the passage from one situation to another. He found this model of music and the approach to composition it implied attractive; it served as a point of departure for his works through most of the 1950s. Cage's aesthetic point of view does not change significantly during this period (as compared to the upheaval seen in the late 1940s); instead, what changes during this period is his compositional technique. The last movement of the *Concerto for Prepared Piano* had opened up the vision of infinite musical possibilities. Cage then spent the next decade finding compositional methods which, like the metal ball of the Irish legend, would make more and more of that infinite space available to him.

Chart systems

Music of Changes

The *Concerto for Prepared Piano* had been the point of entry to Cage's new musical world of sounds in silence. It is therefore understandable that the first new compositional systems he devised following the concerto should be variants of its chart technique. The use of chance within the chart technique of the concerto was something of an afterthought; Cage realized that the technique of materials organized into charts and ordered by chance was capable of a much greater flexibility and range than the concerto had demonstrated. After completing the concerto, he immediately began work on a more extensive and consistent chart system, first used in the monumental *Music of Changes* for piano (1951), and then subsequently applied to a number of different media in works dating from 1951 and 1952.

That Cage's next work was to be for piano solo was largely the result of his new association with the pianist David Tudor, whom he had met in 1950 through Morton Feldman. Cage was tremendously impressed with Tudor's virtuosity and meticulous approach to the challenges his music offered. It was Tudor's unique abilities that made *Music of Changes* possible for Cage; without them, such a work would have been a mere compositional exercise. *Music of Changes* became a sort of collaboration between Cage and Tudor, who would learn each part of the score as soon as it was completed. "At that time," says Cage, "he *was* the *Music of Changes*."[7]

In his new chart system, the first modification Cage made was to the structure of the charts themselves. In the concerto, he had used the *I Ching* in an indirect way, largely because the 14 × 16 structure of its sound charts did not allow them to be easily related to the 64 hexagrams. In *Music of Changes*, he simplified the system: all of the charts contain 64 cells (arranged into eight rows of eight columns each), so that the cells could be related one-to-one with the 64 hexagrams of the *I Ching*. To select an element from a chart, Cage would simply need to obtain a hexagram by tossing coins, find its number in the *I Ching*, and then look up the corresponding cell in the chart. This new approach, therefore, did away with the patterned moves on the charts used in the concerto; as a result, each element in each chart was equally possible at every moment.

The next extension of the chart technique – and perhaps the most significant – was the application of the chart idea to all aspects of sound. Every event in *Music of Changes* was the combination of one element from each of three charts individually referring to sonority, duration, and dynamics. Thus in these new chart pieces, the individuality of each event would not be compromised by the conscious choice of dynamics or of rhythm. The use of multiple charts – even though their contents might be arrived at deliberately – would insure combinations that Cage would never have considered himself, thus widening the scope of the piece.

The charts of sounds for *Music of Changes* – as with all the related chart works – contain sounds only in the odd-numbered cells, with the even-numbered cells representing silences. Example 3–1 shows the contents of one of the sound charts (omitting the silences).[8] The equal division of the sixty-four cells between sounds and silences is clearly derived from the similar arrangement used for the third movement of the *Concerto for Prepared Piano*. The result here is the same as well: the equivalence and interchangeability of sound and silence, thus producing a spaciousness and isolation of individual events in time. The sounds used are sonorities of various complexity and not just simple single pitches. Cage categorized these sounds as single notes, intervals (two-note sounds), aggregates (chords), and "constellations" (more complex arrangements of notes, flourishes, chords, and trills). Although the piano is not prepared, a number of unusual timbral effects are used. Tones are produced by plucking the strings of the piano, by muting the strings with the finger, and by using various sticks or beaters on the strings. In some sounds, keys are depressed silently (notated as diamond-shaped notes) while others are struck sharply, creating resonances by sympathetic vibration. The sound charts also include noises produced on or in the piano, such as by slamming the keyboard lid. In some sounds, the use of the sustaining pedal is indicated as an integral part of the sound.

The duration charts (a portion of one is shown in Example 3–2) differed from the sound charts in that they were completely filled with sixty-four different durations, since duration applied to both sounds and silences. The durations themselves are described by Cage as being "segmented." Rather than being only simple metrical values (such as quarter or eighth notes), the durations used in *Music of Changes* and similar chart works are the result of adding several different simple durations. The individual components of these durations consist of values ranging from one thirty-second note to a whole note, and include sevenths and fifths of beats as well as the common binary and ternary divisions. Although the durations are measured using traditional rhythmic notations, they are not used within any metrical framework. No attempt was made to fill out whole units of duration (e.g., a sixteenth note can exist by itself), or to relate all the segments of a duration to a simple common denominator. In order to facilitate both the composition and performance of the odd fractional durations, Cage applied a simple procedure: he standardized the horizontal distance between notes with the same rhythmic value. In the score of *Music of Changes*, one quarter note is equal to two and a half centimeters of length. All other rhythmic values are related

Example 3–1   *Music of Changes*, sound chart 2

Example 3–2   *Music of Changes*, durations chart 8 (excerpt)

to this scale, so that an eighth note takes up one and a quarter centimeters, while a half note takes up five centimeters. Using this system, Cage was able to display easily the ametrical durations within the framework of the metrical structure.

The charts of dynamics (see Example 3–3) operate in a slightly different manner from those for either sounds or durations. In these, only every fourth cell contains an entry. If, in the course of composing, Cage selected one of the sixteen filled cells, the dynamic marking contained therein would be used. If, on the other

Example 3–3   *Music of Changes*, dynamics chart 8

ffff>f	*fff>ff*
f>pppp	*ff*
p>ppp	*f>ppp*
ffff	*f>pp*
ffff>f	*ffff>ff*
mf>pp	*fff>mf*
p>pppp	*p>pp*
ffff>ff	*mf>mp*

hand, he selected one of the forty-eight blank cells, the dynamic used for the previous sound would continue to apply. The dynamics used are notated traditionally and range from *pppp* to *ffff*. In addition to simple (single) dynamics, Cage also used combinations of two, such as *f* > *pp*, which could be used as accents, crescendos, or diminuendos. The dotted lines beneath some of the dynamics in the charts indicate that the *una corda* pedal was to be used.

Each event in *Music of Changes* was thus a product of consulting not one, but three charts. First, an *I Ching* hexagram number was used to select one of the sixty-four rhythmic patterns of a duration chart. A second hexagram number was then applied to the chart of sounds: if it was an even number, a silence was indicated, and the duration chosen was filled with rests. If an odd number turned up, then the sound from that cell of the chart was coordinated with the duration chosen.[9] Finally, if the event was a sound and not a silence, a dynamic marking was chosen from a chart using a third hexagram number; in most cases this number indicated a maintenance of the previous dynamic, as noted above. An example of the coordination of sound and duration is shown in Example 3–4.

Example 3–4 *Music of Changes*, an event from bar 75

(a) sounds

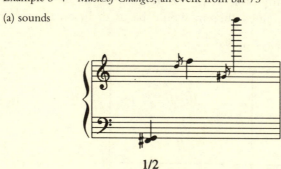

(b) durations

(c) result

This figure shows the sound and duration chosen for an event in bar 75 of the piece, together with the event produced by the coordination of these two elements.

In this example we see the strength of the multi-chart approach: the production of unforeseen possibilities. In the sound as it exists in the chart, the pairing of the grace-note figures and their registral contrast with the initial bass notes suggest that the initial component of this sound should be given a rhythmic emphasis – it should be longer – in order to balance the gesture. The use of pedal on the first attack indicates that Cage probably had this "natural" reading in mind when he composed the sound for the chart. Nevertheless, by selecting the rhythmic pattern randomly, the unexpected happens: the initial notes are the shortest by far, and the rhythmic emphasis is on the first of the grace-note figures. The application of a random duration transformed Cage's musical idea into something quite different than he had originally imagined. This is the usefulness that Cage found in chance operations: to take his own musical ideas and alter them, producing a fresh and spontaneous world of sound.

Both the greater diversity of sounds, durations, and dynamics and the unusual combinations of these generated by chance operations contributed to a sense of the *Music of Changes* taking place in a wider musical space than that of the concerto. But even this space would seem cramped if the charts had remained fixed in their content, and if the same elements had thus appeared and reappeared over and over during the forty-five minutes of the piece. For this reason, Cage devised a replacement technique which operated continuously throughout the work. Each chart alternated between states of mobility and immobility, this alternation controlled by the *I Ching*. As long as a chart was immobile, its contents did not change. While a chart was mobile, however, any sound, duration, or dynamic in it was replaced as soon as it was used. This system assured that the available pool of sounds, durations, and dynamics would continually be refreshed with new elements as the composition progressed.

This constitutes the basis of the new chart technique. The remaining changes in Cage's compositional methods were more structural in nature. He continued to use rhythmic structures created as in the past. In the case of *Music of Changes*, proportions are large: {3; 5, 6¾; 6¾; 5, 3⅛}. The overall structure of 29⅝ × 29⅝ is divided into four large parts of one, two, one, and two sections respectively, and the whole work lasts well over half an hour. In order to make the structure more flexible, Cage decided to have the tempo vary during the course of the piece, with these tempo changes determined randomly by means of a chart and the *I Ching*.

While the structure in time remained relatively unchanged, the vertical structure of *Music of Changes* was quite different. Cage's previous works, such as the *String Quartet* or the concerto, were conceived of as essentially monophonic in texture. In them, he had composed a single series of sounds that followed one after the other. Beginning with *Music of Changes*, he created a polyphony by simply adding several of these layers – what he called "superimposed parts" – to one another. In *Music of Changes*, for example, he decided that at any given point in the piece there would be anywhere from one to eight of these layers. The number of layers changed with each phrase unit of the rhythmic structure, the precise numbers being determined by the *I Ching* and a density chart. Each layer of a given phrase would be composed independently, event by event, in the manner outlined above; each layer had its own unique set of sound, duration, and dynamic charts.

Example 3–5 *Music of Changes*, bars 1–3

(a) sounds selected

(b) score and constituent layers

A large portion of the compositional effort involved here was the arrangement of rhythms in the denser sections so that all the sounds of all the layers could be played and heard. In Example 3–5, the first phrase (measures 1–3) of *Music of Changes* is broken down by layers. Example 3–5a shows the sounds obtained for each of the six layers of this phrase. Example 3–5b shows how these sounds were arranged rhythmically within the phrase. At the top of the figure is the music as it appears in the score; beneath this are the individual layers that make up this final product. The extent of the strategy and patience necessary to fit the various layers together becomes clear when such a disentangling of the polyphonic texture is studied.

Changes in density are among the most prominent musical features of *Music of Changes*. When density is low, silences in the layers overlap, producing gaping holes in the texture; the sounds that do occur take up their entire assigned durations, since there are few other sounds to interfere with their rhythmic expression. The result is a spacious sound akin to the last movement of the *Concerto for Prepared Piano*. When the density is high, on the other hand, even though each layer individually is half silences, the silences are rarely aligned, so that there is more continuous sound. In sections of very high density, the texture becomes saturated: so many sounds must be expressed within a relatively short time that Cage tends to abbreviate durations to mere attacks. These changes affect the perception of the music. During phrases of low density, the listener attends to the contours of individual events; during periods of high density, the ears are overloaded, the events become unfocused, and the impression is predominantly textural.

It is the composition of the materials – the charts of sounds, durations, and dynamics – that most strongly determines the effect of *Music of Changes* and that gives it its unique and unmistakable voice. In this work, perhaps more clearly than in any other, chance appears as a means and not an end in itself. It was necessary for Cage to use the chart technique in order to have his musical materials – which are completely products of his compositional choice and judgement – speak by themselves, without being forced into a particular sort of continuity. Chance here is the mechanism by which materials can assert their dominance of the composition: Cage's primary role as composer is to create the collection of materials that will, through the offices of the chance system, then become the sole identity of the work. Virgil Thomson, in reviewing the premiere of *Music of Changes*, compared it to a kaleidoscope,[10] and this seems a perfect analogy: the world of *Music of Changes* is one of abrupt juxtapositions of a variety of transparent, brightly-colored, and incisive materials.

Other chart pieces

With the development of the chart system used in *Music of Changes*, Cage's work entered a brief period of stability. The system he built around rhythmic structure and charts of musical materials was flexible enough to encompass a variety of media and to produce a wide range of interesting results.[11] Therefore, we find that most of the works written in the period 1951–52 use the chart system in one form or another. In the case of *Seven Haiku* (1951–52) and *For MC and DT* (1952), both for solo piano, not only the method, but the actual charts of *Music of Changes* were used. These pieces can be seen simply as miniature "spin-offs" of the *Music of Changes*, perhaps meant as gifts for the people to whom they are variously dedicated.

With the *Two Pastorales* (1951–52), Cage returned to the prepared piano. The major difference between these pieces and the *Music of Changes* is that the *Pastorales* employ only two layers, thus generating a significantly thinner texture. As a result, there is less fragmentation of the individual sound events, and in several places long empty spaces appear between the sounds. At times, Cage chose to fill these gaps by holding down the pedal for the duration (pedalling being outside the system and wholly at his discretion both here and in *Music of Changes*). The prominence of these lengthy pedals focuses one's attention on the decay of the sounds as they slowly dwindle into silence. *Music of Changes*, on the other hand, with a higher density of sounds, is notably lacking these long, drawn-out sounds. Thus one simple change in the system – from eight layers to two – makes for a piece of a pronouncedly different character.

Two other piano pieces from this time employ slight variants of the chart method. In *Water Music* (1952), "for a pianist, using also a radio, whistles, water containers, a deck of cards, a wooden stick, and objects for preparing a piano," Cage incorporated deliberately theatrical actions into the charts: at one point the pianist deals playing cards into the strings of the piano, for example. More importantly, *Water Music* is the first piece in which Cage used clock time rather than metrical time in his durations. These were calculated by taking *I Ching* hexagram numbers and multiplying them by a factor of one quarter, one half, or one second. The resulting score is rather strikingly notated on a single large page, which is to be mounted as a poster and displayed for the audience to see during the performance. *Waiting* (1952), another dance commission, is a brief and simple piece that uses ostinato patterns instead of individual sounds as its raw materials. Durations were then calculated as numbers of repetitions of these ostinati.

Imaginary Landscape No. 4 (1951), composed concurrently with *Music of Changes*, is scored for twelve radios. The score requires two performers for each radio: one to manipulate the tuning, and the other to manipulate the volume and tone controls. The score uses traditional music paper to very precisely notate the changing radio tunings, and numbers ranging from 3 to 15 are used to show the changing volumes. The method of composition used in *Imaginary Landscape No. 4* is essentially the same as that for *Music of Changes*; the only real difference is in the materials, specifically the sounds. In the case of *Imaginary Landscape No. 4*, the charts of sounds contain combinations of radio tunings, arranged into patterns of varying complexity.

One might suppose that twelve radios playing at once would produce an extremely raucous effect – a blaring futurist gesture. But Cage was no Luigi Russolo in his intent, and *Imaginary Landscape No. 4* has exactly the opposite effect. The use of silences, the clarity of distinction among the various sound events, the predominantly thin texture – all hallmarks of the new chart music – together with the relatively low dynamic level make this a sparsely-populated and hushed landscape. This was considered a flaw by the audience at its premiere, and the thinness of sound was blamed on the late hour at which it was performed (when many local radio stations were no longer broadcasting), and on Cage's miscalculation of the dynamic range of the instruments.[12] However, the example of *Music of Changes* should make it clear that bombast was not Cage's goal. As he describes *Imaginary Landscape No. 4*, "it certainly was not . . . a rabble-rouser."[13]

The other major work from this period is *Williams Mix* for magnetic tape (1952). The title refers to Paul Williams, an architect who funded the composition of *Williams Mix* (along with other works by Morton Feldman, Earle Brown, and Christian Wolff) as part of a project known as "Project: Sound" or "Project for Music for Magnetic Tape." *Williams Mix* is a piece of *musique concrète*, made up of recorded "real" sounds. For the purposes of organizing the materials, Cage divided the sounds into six categories:

A) city sounds
B) country sounds
C) electronic sounds
D) manually-produced sounds (including music)
E) wind-produced sounds (including songs)
F) "small" sounds requiring amplification

The sounds were further categorized by the predictability or unpredictability of their frequency, timbre, and amplitude. Each of these aspects of a sound could be "controlled" and predictable or "variable" and unpredictable. Thus the designation of a sound consisted of a capital letter representing the sound type, followed by three lower-case letters ("c" or "v", for controlled or variable) representing the predictability or unpredictability of the three aspects of the sound (e.g., Dvvv). Sounds could be mixed electronically to produce "double sources," or looped to create regular rhythmic patterns. A rather complex system was used to fill the sound charts with such generic descriptions, and Cage, together with Louis and Bebe Barron and David Tudor, collected sounds to fit these descriptions.

Since amplitude was already given in these sound descriptions, Cage dispensed with charts of dynamics in *Williams Mix*, and instead used charts for attacks and decays. He described them to Boulez as follows:

> The attacks and decays are specific cuts of the tape . . . [and] also "cross-grain" use of the tape (which affects the overtone structure as well). I have organized single and double cuts . . . and then use a "+" to indicate more complicated cuts or curves which are invented at the moment of cutting.

Cage goes on to explain that the system of determining the splicing patterns could have some odd results: "It often happens . . . [that] a sound 'ends' before it 'begins' or even that the sound that 'follows' it happens first."

The process of composing *Williams Mix* produced a full-size drawing of the tape fragments, which served as a "score" for the splicing. The excerpt of this score shown in Example 3–6 gives a sense of the variety of splicing patterns found in the piece, and includes a specific example of a sound whose "end" precedes its "beginning" (the sound AcccBccc in track 3, middle of system 1). The arrows crossing some of the sounds represent the direction of cross-grain tape splicing. Examples of Cage's notation for "more complicated" splicing are found in tracks 4, 6, and 7 (the last sounds on the first system). Once the score was finished, the tape was cut from this, just like "a dress-maker's pattern."[14]

Example 3–6 · *Williams Mix*, excerpt from score

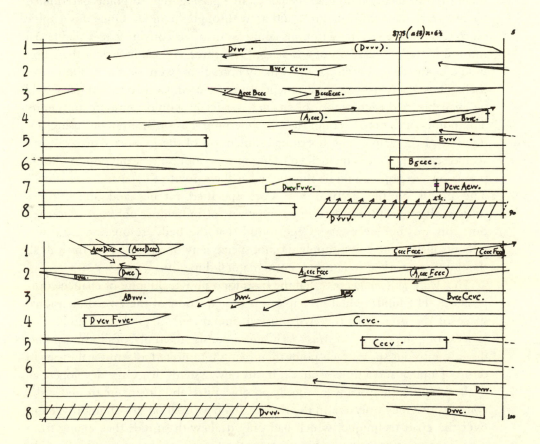

Point-drawing systems

The process of composing using charts involved an excessive amount of rather tedious work: for each of the thousands of sound events in *Music of Changes*, eighteen coin tosses were necessary just to determine the sound, duration, and dynamic components that would need to be coordinated with each other and with the sounds of other superimposed layers. In 1952, while still working with charts, Cage began experimenting with quicker and simpler ways of composing. The first of these experiments was *Music for Carillon No. 1* (1952). The work was drawn on quarter-inch quadrille graph paper (see Example 3–7). The method of composing the piece consisted of plotting points onto this graph by means of templates, made by arbitrarily folding pieces of paper and then making holes at the intersections of the folds. Once these stencils were made, Cage superimposed them on his graph-paper score – placing them at points determined by an overall duration structure – and drew through the holes. Once this graphic score was completed, transcriptions could be made to convert it to a traditional musical score for a carillon of any range. The three vertical inches of the graph would be divided according to how many notes there were on the carillon to be used. Thus, if a two-octave instrument was to be used, twenty-four notes would be available, and each eighth of an inch vertically would represent one note. The points of the score could then be interpreted as precise pitches using this division of the graph. The horizontal dimension of the graphic score, in turn, would represent time (one inch equalling one second), so that the position of the points on the graph could be interpreted as their point of occurrence in time.[15] The points on the graph-paper score specified pitches and attack times sufficiently, but did not determine durations of individual notes. As it turned out, this was not necessary: Cage found that the bells' resonating time was uncontrollable, and so he simply did not specify any durations at all. Instead, all the notes are marked to last their entire natural duration.

The *Music for Carillon* revealed the basis for a new technique of chance composition. The fundamental principle was the equation of the two-dimensional space of the page with the two musical dimensions of pitch and time. The process of composition in *Music for Carillon* consisted simply of plotting points directly into this space, each point then being interpreted as a musical event in terms of a pitch and a time of attack. In the new systems that Cage developed, all of the points in the space were equally possible; pitch and time were treated as the continua that they truly are. In this respect, the new method was an improvement over the chart technique, which had only dealt with sounds that sprang from Cage's imagination, and not directly from the totality of acoustic possibilities. In the *Music for Carillon*, Cage was working within a space bounded by sonic parameters of pitch and time; in the chart pieces, the space was one of prefabricated sonorities and rhythms.

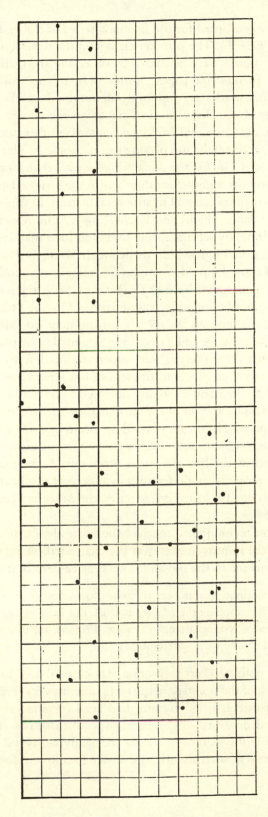

Example 3–7 *Music for Carillon No. 1* (excerpt)

This point-drawing system was adapted for use in a new series of eighty-four pieces called *Music for Piano* (1952–56). The primary change in the technique of these compositions was that the points were generated by observing and marking minute imperfections in the manuscript paper, rather than relying on the manipulation of templates. After marking a randomly-determined number of imperfections on a blank page, Cage drew musical staves on the sheet, thus turning the points into notes. Coin tosses and *I Ching* hexagram numbers would determine such matters as clefs, accidentals, and playing techniques (e.g., plucked or muted strings). As in the *Music for Carillon*, the durations of notes were left open.

Most of the differences among the eighty-four numbers in the series relate to how the number of points was determined and to structural matters. In *Music for Piano 1* (1952), written for the dance "Paths and Events" by JoAnne Melcher, Cage composed one staff at a time, by setting a time limit and then marking as many paper imperfections as he could find within that time. In *Music for Piano 2* (1953), composed for dancer Louise Lippold, a rhythmic structure was used to control the density of notes. Beginning with *Music for Piano 3* (1953), the pieces are one page long each, and the number of notes was determined by the *I Ching*. *Music for Piano 4–19* (1953), composed as an accompaniment to Merce Cunningham's dance "Solo Suite in Space and Time," was designed to be played by more than one pianist with the ordering and superposition left to the performers. Similarly, the last sixty-four pieces in the series (four separate sets of sixteen pieces each, composed in 1955 and 1956) are designed to be performed together.[16] They differ from *Music for Piano 4–19* in that they include noises produced inside or outside the piano. Noises are notated by means of a single line drawn between the staves of each system: notes drawn above the line are noises made inside the piano, those below the line are noises made outside the piano. Paper imperfections – or more properly, imperfections in a piece of cardboard – were used for the next entries in the *Music for Carillon* series, the *Music for Carillon Nos. 2 and 3*, composed in 1954.

With the paper-imperfection technique, Cage had the more direct, simple system he wanted. But despite the improvements over the chart method, he saw the new system only as an alternative to the old and not a replacement of it:

> Certainly I intended to continue working on *Williams Mix* and other pieces as I had started out doing, by consulting the *I Ching* as usual. But I also wanted to have a very rapid manner of writing a piece of music. Painters, for example, work slowly with oil and rapidly with watercolors.[17]

That Cage wished to continue with his chart technique may be attributed to his realization of the main drawback of the point-drawing technique: its very limited results. Speed and flexibility (particularly of rhythm) had been obtained at the expense of the complexity and diversity of the basic musical materials. The materials of a chart piece such as the *Music of Changes* are of myriad types; we could compare the beautiful chaos of such a work to that of a meadow or forest, in which different recognizable organic and inorganic forms are repeated, juxtaposed, and scaled in arrangements of varying densities and effects. In the *Music for Carillon* and *Music for Piano*, on the other hand, the forms are all identical and of the simplest type: the single point. Hence their beauty is not as complex and rich, but is akin to that of a starry night sky: not an unsatisfactory result, but a limited one. The superimposition of multiple pieces changes only the density of points, but not the overall effect. Cage realized this limitation and compared the works composed in this fashion to "the first attempts at speech of a child or the fumblings about of a blind man."[18]

"The Ten Thousand Things"

Development of a new system

While he would continue to use paper imperfections in the *Music for Piano* until 1956, Cage found by 1953 that the chart system had outlived its usefulness. At this point, then, he set out to develop a new system that could replace the charts, one that could give the depth that charts provided but without the limitations of the prefabricated collections of materials. The result of this new system was a series of pieces whose rather unwieldy titles are their durations (e.g., *26' 1.1499" for a String Player*), but which Cage privately called "The Ten Thousand Things."

The key to Cage's new design was again in the treatment of materials. In the chart systems, he had selected specific sonorities, rhythms, and dynamics, and then used the *I Ching* to arrange them within his rhythmic structure. Thus, while the random system operated in the ordering of materials, the materials themselves – often of great complexity and intricacy – were the product of Cage's imagination, of his mind. The musical results were as diverse as the collections of materials he composed. The new approach was to keep the sense of materials as complex events, but to remove the charts and replace them with point-drawing methods related to those of *Music for Piano*: in short, a synthesis of the chart and point-drawing systems.

Although the systems varied from piece to piece, the general outline and principles are the same for each work in the series. Cage first enumerated and categorized all the possible types of events that could occur in a piece (e.g., single pitches, aggregates, constellations) and used the *I Ching* to select randomly from this list of possibilities, much as he had used it to select materials from the charts in earlier pieces. To determine specific pitches and durations, however, he used the technique of measuring randomly drawn points within a pitch-time space. In "The Ten Thousand Things," he consciously defined the possible structures of events, and then used chance to provide the specific pitch and rhythmic content of these events. Thus the ability to work with the continua of pitch and time provided by the point-drawing method was used to fill the event profiles of varying complexity that had been the strongest point of the chart technique. In

1951 Cage wrote to Boulez that his concern as a composer was to understand "the quantities that act to produce multiplicity" in music. In "The Ten Thousand Things" he realized that those quantities were of two sorts – discrete and continuous – and that two different methods were necessary to manipulate them effectively to "produce multiplicity": one the method of enumeration and selection, the other the method of measurement and scaling. The result of this integration was as flexible and diverse a system as Cage had yet fashioned.

The compositions

After completing *Williams Mix* in 1953, Cage started on his new project. As he described it at the time in a letter to Boulez, his vision was grand:

> From time to time ideas come for my next work which as I see it will be a large work which will always be in progress and will never be finished; at the same time any part of it will be able to be performed once I have begun. It will include tape and any other time actions, not excluding violins and whatever else I put my attention to. I will of course write other music than this, but only if required by some outside situation.[19]

Cage's plan was to compose many independent pieces for various media, each of which could be played as a self-contained work in its own right, or performed together with any number of the others. Such an open work could be constantly enlarged – since the ensemble would not be fixed at any time, the total need never be finished, but would remain a work "in progress."

The actual structure for the ensemble piece was itself on a grand scale: 13 parts with the proportions {3, 7, 2, 5, 11, 14, 7, 6, 1, 15, 11, 3, 15}. The sum of these proportions is 100, so that the overall structure would consist of 100 units of 100 measures each, or a total of 10,000 measures. The number 10,000 had a special significance for Cage, as he revealed in his 1954 lecture "45' for a Speaker":[20] "That [the structure is based on 10,000] is pleasing, momentarily: The world, the 10,000 things." Cage refers here to the symbolism of the number 10,000 in Chinese philosophy and writing, where it represents the infinite. Hence, the phrase "The Ten Thousand Things," commonly found in Taoist and Buddhist writings, connotes the material diversity of the universe. While the individual pieces were given titles based on their durations, Cage never publicly gave a title to the ensemble project as a whole. However, in two places in his early manuscript notes for these works, he uses the phrase "The Ten Thousand Things"; I will take advantage of this poetic reference to the structure and refer to the general plan for the work as "The Ten Thousand Things."

The structure of these pieces has had a rather confused history, and I feel it worth the time to clarify it here. The proposed structure of 10,000 measures turned out to be too large to be manageable. Therefore Cage decided to reduce the size of the structure by making the units 100 *beats* in length, rather than 100 *measures*, so that the overall structure would be 100 units of 100 beats each, or 2500 bars of $\frac{4}{4}$ meter. If he had followed the principles of rhythmic structure, this smaller unit size would have resulted in phrases that were too short to be useful: phrases would be as short as a single beat. His solution to this problem was to form five larger groupings of the thirteen structural proportions as shown below.

$$\{3, 7, 2 \; ; \; 5, 11 \; ; \; 14, 7, 6, 1 \; ; \; 15, 11 \; ; \; 3, 15 \; \} \; = \; 100 \; \text{(sections)}$$
$$\{ \quad 12 \quad ; \quad 16 \quad ; \quad 28 \quad ; \quad 26 \; ; \; 18 \; \}$$
$$\{ \quad 3 \quad ; \quad 4 \quad ; \quad 7 \quad ; \quad 6\tfrac{1}{2} \; ; \; 4\tfrac{1}{2} \; \} \; \times \; 4/4 \; \text{(phrases)}$$

This resulted in five phrases with lengths of 12, 16, 28, 26, and 18 beats, respectively, or, 3, 4, 7, 6½, and 4½ measures of 4/4. In short, there were two separate proportion series in this work: a five-part structure which functioned only at the small scale, and a thirteen-part structure functioning only at the large scale. This structure was the basis for all of the pieces produced during this time, although variations were to occur from piece to piece. In fact, the large-scale plan – works of 100 units each – was never fully realized, with the four largest works each consisting of only twenty-eight units.[21] In addition to the two-level rhythmic structure, Cage altered his original rhythmic structure by allowing it to be open-ended. In performance, any number of the 100-beat units could be performed in any order.

The first works to be composed in this large "never-ending" project were six short pieces for a string player. Composed between May and July of 1953, each of these pieces is only one unit long (this reflects Cage's emphasis on the 100-beat unit as the fundamental building block of his open structure). The first five of these pieces were ultimately to become part of the larger string piece *26' 1.1499" for a String Player*, while the last, *59½" for a String Player*, remained independent.

The notation of these pieces is illustrated in Example 3–8. In the notation, time is measured in a manner similar to that of *Music of Changes*; here two centimeters equal one beat. The tempo varies with every phrase; at the beginning of each, Cage puts a two-centimeter "ruler" with the new tempo marking. Vertically, the four large areas or bands (marked B through E in the figure) represent the four strings of the instrument being played, from highest to lowest. The vertical placement of points within these bands indicates the location at which the strings are to be stopped. Points connected by vertical lines represent multiple stops, with the arrows giving the direction of breaking triple or quadruple stops. This notation allowed the pieces to be performed on any four-stringed bowed instrument (violin, viola, cello, or contrabass). The smaller band below the four string bands (marked F in the figure) represents noises of any type. The vertical placement of points and lines within this band gives the relative pitch of the noise. The smaller band above the string bands (marked A in the figure) represents the bowing pressure, or amplitude of the sounds. This is

Example 3–8   *1′ 18″ for a String Player* (excerpt)

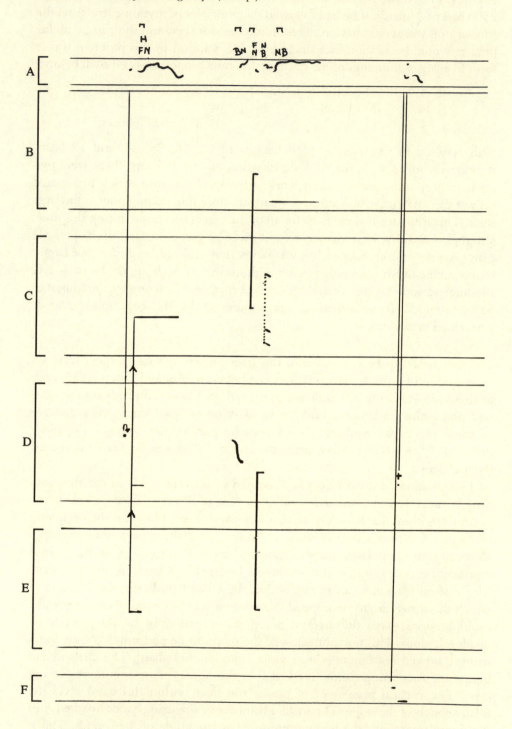

notated graphically so that the top of the band is the least pressure (softest) and the bottom the most pressure (loudest). The notations here correspond one-to-one with the sound notations below them (Cage occasionally draws vertical lines to make these correspondences clearer). In the case of sounds that extend in time, a pressure curve is notated, showing the changing amplitude of the sound. The notations at the top of the page also relate to bowing. The traditional up- and downbow symbols are used. The letters H and W ("Hair" and "Wood") denote *ordinario* and *col legno* bowing. The letters F ("Fingerboard"), N ("Normal"), and B ("Bridge") give the location of the bowing. Compound notations (e.g., "FN") denote intermediate positions.

At the outset of composing the string pieces, Cage defined the seven types of events that could occur: points (i.e., *pizzicato*), lines (sustained tones), aggregates (multiple stops), angles (linear slides), curves (non-linear slides), noise points (noises of no duration), and noise lines (noises of some duration). A randomly distributed *I Ching* table was established for these seven types at the start of each phrase, and the sequences of sounds and silences determined by the use of the *I Ching*: odd numbers were interpreted as sounds, even numbers as silences. After this was done, Cage determined the other characteristics of each sound event. The types of determinations made depended on the particular type of event involved. There were to be four different ways to play point events, for example: *ordinario*, stopped against the fingerboard, stopped against the fingernail, and played with a slide following the pluck. This last category of points had four further subcategories: downward slides, upward slides, down-up slides, and up-down slides. In the case of line events, there were two further decisions to be made. Line events could be constant or intermittent in time, and could be played either *ordinario* or as harmonics. For aggregate events, there were six categories: double, triple, or quadruple stops played either constantly or intermittently in time. If a triple or quadruple stop was obtained, the direction of its arpeggiation was also randomly chosen. Angle and curve events could be either constant or intermittent in time.

At this point, only the structure of events had been determined: the piece existed as a series of generic descriptions in Cage's working notes. For example, a notation might consist of the indication that a sound was to be a triple-stop aggregate, intermittent in time, or a continuous pitch curve, or a fingernail-stopped *pizzicato*. In order to fill these empty forms with pitch and rhythmic content, Cage used the point-drawing technique. First he calculated (by means of adding *I Ching* hexagram numbers) a number of points to be inscribed in each phrase. Then he would mark the phrase lengths on paper and inscribe the points, the locations of points determined by observing imperfections in the paper. This done, he began drawing the sound events, coordinating the abstract descriptions of his notes with the precise pitch and time information given by the points. Durations of all events and silences were measured by counting the points from left to right. Presumably the first point of each event would determine its starting pitch. For point and line events, this was the only pitch involved, but in aggregate, angle, or curve events, other intermediate points of the event's duration must have been used to determine the other pitches of aggregates and the pitch contours of the angles and curves. Finally, to complete the score, he added the bowing indications: pressure, up- and downbows, bowing material (hair or wood), and location.

The other pieces in the series follow similar procedures, and I will limit myself here to a brief summary of their major features. In 1953 Cage worked briefly on a piece for magnetic tape using the same structure and basic system of the short string pieces. This piece was to use the same sort of sound materials as had been used in *Williams Mix*. The work was abandoned early on, however. From the same time, there exists a sketch for a similar work for voice, which was also never completed.

In the fall of 1954 Cage was commissioned by the *Donaueschinger Musiktage* to compose a new work for two pianos, and he used this opportunity to compose two more parts for his ongoing "Ten Thousand Things" project. The resulting work was not just a piece for two pianos, but rather consisted of two pieces that could be performed either separately or together, or with the short string pieces he had already composed. *34' 46.776" for a Pianist*, written for David Tudor, was the more difficult work, while *31' 57.9864" for a Pianist*, written for Cage himself to perform, was "relatively easy to play."

The new pieces were for prepared pianos, the last large works Cage would compose for that instrument. Unlike the instructions in his previous works for prepared piano, the preparation tables found in these two scores list only the notes to be prepared and the types of objects to be used (e.g., wood, cloth, metal). The exact choice of objects and their placement on the strings was left to the performer, so that the sounds of the instruments would vary from performance to performance. In addition, Cage introduced the device of having the preparations change during the course of the work. At points throughout the score he indicates that preparations should be moved along their strings, or that objects should be added or removed.

The method of composition used in the piano pieces is essentially the same as that used in the earlier string pieces. Cage even attempted to find a pianistic equivalent of the string player's bowing pressure notation. The score (see Example 3–9) contains no traditional dynamic notations, but rather includes three narrow bands with markings corresponding to the notes below them. These bands denote force of attack, distance of attack from the keyboard, and speed of attack, the three physical factors that Cage thought determined dynamics.

There were three major differences between the composition of the piano pieces and of the earlier string pieces. First, in the piano pieces, Cage used clock time (minutes and seconds) rather than "musical time" (beats). The metrical structure with changing tempos was still used but was converted to clock time early on in the compositional process, so that no traces of it appear in the finished

Example 3–9 31' 57.9864" for a Pianist (excerpt)

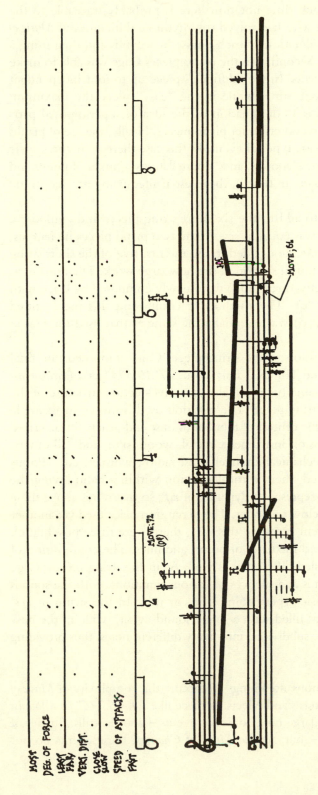

score. That Cage used clock-time notation here is probably traceable to the influence of David Tudor, who had solved the rhythmic difficulties of *Music of Changes* by calculating the duration of each phrase in seconds and then using a stopwatch in performance. Secondly, in the piano pieces Cage was able to make use of multiple layers of events. In the "difficult" piece up to four independent layers are present at any one time, while in the "easy" piece the maximum density is two layers. This is a continuation of the idea of superimposed parts found in *Music of Changes* and other earlier piano pieces. Finally, the use of pianos required a different set of basic types of event. In this case there were three basic types: point events, aggregates (chords), and "constellations" (mixes of points and aggregates forming "aggregates in time"), these last-named being notated in the score by the use of beams.

In 1955 Cage decided to add to the six short string pieces and compose a piece for string player that was equal in size to the two piano pieces he had just finished. Perhaps to save time, he decided to use the first five of the short string pieces of 1953 to form the fourth section of the new large work. The remaining four sections, totalling twenty-three units, were newly composed by Cage with assistance from David Tudor. The method of composing this piece (titled *26' 1.1499" for a String Player*) was essentially the same as that used for the six shorter string pieces.

After finishing the extension of the string piece, Cage composed one final score in "The Ten Thousand Things." This work, *27' 10.554" for a Percussionist* (1956), was to follow the same twenty-eight-unit, five-section structure of the two piano pieces and the string piece. The notation used is shown in Example 3–10. The four lines mark the centers of four bands of sounds, each characterized by a general type of percussion instrument: metal, wood, skin, and "all others, e.g., electronic devices, mechanical arrangements, radios, whistles, etc." Points represent notes to be played, their vertical position within a band giving the amplitude: the center lines represent a dynamic of *mf*, so that notes above these lines are louder and those below are softer. The percussion piece used yet another categorization of sound event types. In this case, there were three possibilities: point events, line events, and mixtures of points and lines. The composition of individual events was handled differently as well. As in the string pieces, Cage determined a series of sounds and silences of various durations, with the sounds being one of the three basic types: point, line, or mix. In the string pieces, however, each duration was filled with a single sound event, while in the new percussion piece, it could be subdivided into many different notes, thus providing a more active texture.

The pieces of "The Ten Thousand Things" recapture the complexity of *Music of Changes*, its diversity of patterns and effects. A piece like *34' 46.776" for a Pianist* presents the listener with a large range of sonic events – chords, trills, flurries of quick notes, single points – but, unlike *Music of Changes*, these events do not

Example 3–10 *27' 10.554" for a Percussionist* (excerpt)

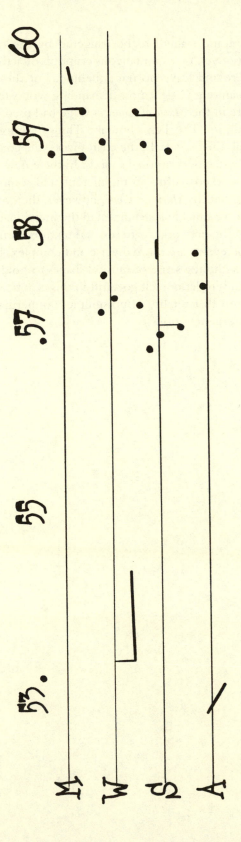

appear to be carefully rehearsed and staged, to be triggered by the random process. Instead the impression is given of a spontaneous eruption of activity, of figures that appear from nowhere and leave no traces behind. For this reason "The Ten Thousand Things" is among Cage's most demanding works for both audiences and performers. Where in the *Music of Changes* Cage had used chance only to order his musical materials, in "The Ten Thousand Things" he used it to erase his control over the materials themselves. In the chart pieces, the continuity occurs within a *musical* space – a space of composed sounds. In these new pieces, as in the *Music for Piano*, Cage worked within an undifferentiated sonic space, thus making for a less "musical" result. In *Music for Piano*, however, the events are so simple, pure, and uniform that we quickly lose interest in the individual points and instead attend to the whole – the networks, patterns, and textures formed. In "The Ten Thousand Things" the events are more diverse and complex, leaving the listener without landmarks, without a sense of musical shapes to hold on to. Instead, perhaps the best approach is to let oneself go adrift in this chaotic swarm; to be drawn – like it or not – into that totality of possibilities "impermanently involved in an infinite play of interpenetrations."

4

Indeterminacy
(1957–1961)

Sources of indeterminacy

The New York School

4' 33" and the first chance compositions of the early 1950s ushered in a period of tremendous activity for Cage. Surveying the music he composed during the first years after his discovery of chance composition, one is struck not only by the large number of works written, but also by the size of those works. *Music of Changes* and *Williams Mix* are not minor efforts (they both took nine months to complete), and in "The Ten Thousand Things" Cage had created four half-hour compositions of great complexity. His prolific creation during this period was inspired by his initial encounters with chance composition, by the musical vistas he saw opened before him as a result of the new approach. At the same time, his composing during these years was necessary in order to develop and explore his intuitions and ideas. Chance had opened doors for him; simultaneously, it demanded that he explore the possibilities it afforded in order to reveal their full extent.

Cage was not the only intrepid explorer of a new musical world during these years: the younger composers surrounding him – Morton Feldman, Christian Wolff, and Earle Brown – were inspired by Cage's ideas and by visions of their own. The circumstances surrounding Cage's first meeting with Feldman in 1950, and his subsequent introduction to David Tudor, were recounted in previous chapters. Shortly thereafter, Christian Wolff, a music student still in high school, joined Cage, Feldman, and Tudor. Earle Brown, an engineer-turned-composer steeped in the Schillinger method of composition, met Cage in Denver in 1951, was impressed with his music and ideas, and came to New York in 1952 to join the group. Cage, Feldman, Tudor, Wolff, and Brown have been sometimes referred to as The New York School, thus drawing a parallel with the similarly-named group of Abstract Expressionist painters active at the same time. All five collaborated in "Project: Sound," working together to produce Cage's *Williams Mix*, Feldman's *Intersection*, Wolff's *For Magnetic Tape*, and Brown's *Octet*. Cage assisted the others in their work in other ways, introducing them to Merce Cunningham (who used scores by all four composers for his dances), and by performing their works both in America and in Europe. The members of the group were in close contact with each other from 1950 to 1954, but became less closely knit after 1954, when Cage and Tudor moved from New York City to Stony Point in upstate New York.

Feldman, Wolff, and Brown are often considered to be students of Cage – or at least his "followers." This is a misapprehension: the members of the group conversed together and shared their works with one another, but there was no teacher-student relationship between them. The younger composers were not followers of Cage, either, since Cage was as likely to be inspired by their work as the other way around. The most prominent example of this was pointed out in chapter two: Cage's use of chance certainly owed something to Feldman's first graph pieces. Cage and his younger contemporaries were thus more a "group" than a "school" – they were united only in their mutual support for the widening of musical possibilities.

Not only were Feldman, Wolff, and Brown not "followers" of Cage in the sense of being his pupils, but their work in the early to mid-1950s actually went *beyond* his in the pursuit of the new. While Cage was concerned primarily with new ways of ordering sounds, Feldman, Wolff, and Brown were changing the fundamental nature of the musical work itself – exploring new notations, new forms, establishing new relationships between composer and performer. Feldman's graph pieces are an example of this. He continued with works in this vein with the *Intersection* series (1951–53), a ballet score entitled *Ixion* (1958), and later in . . . *Out of "Last Pieces"* for orchestra (1961) and *The King of Denmark* for percussion (1964). Another of Feldman's experimental styles of composition involved the use of "free durations" beginning with *Piece for Four Pianos* (1957) and continuing in works such as *Last Pieces* for piano (1959) and the *Durations* series of ensemble pieces (1960–61). Interspersed among these experimental styles are traditionally-notated pieces, as well. In all his works, conventional or otherwise, Feldman's focus was on sonority and the individual sound. With the characteristic hushed dynamics and minimum of attack, his music avoids development and climax, instead presenting a flat surface of great beauty.

Christian Wolff's music also focused on individual sound events in a sparse texture. Through Cage, Wolff came to embrace rhythmic structure as being fundamental to composition, and he began to compose in ways that produced arbitrary (if not strictly random) results. One such method, used in *For Prepared Piano* (1952), was to compose a score vertically on the page (i.e., up and down in columns of measures), but have the score read traditionally, left-to-right. After this, Wolff began using a notation which, like Feldman's graph pieces, gave general descriptions of musical events (the number of notes to be played, a collection of pitches to choose from, and so on) and the time frames within which these were to occur. In later works, such as the *Duo for Pianists II* (1958), Wolff broke up the time bracket structure into several independent blocks of such material. The order of these blocks was not given, thus producing what could be called an "open structure" or "open form." In the *Duo for Pianists II*, cues are given for each block of material. As each pianist finishes a passage, he listens to the next sound made by the other player: this becomes the cue for the next block to be played. A performance of *Duo for Pianists II* is thus open-ended: it lasts as long as the performers are willing to continue.

While Wolff and Feldman were creating compositions based on the division of time into discrete brackets within which isolated events occurred, Earle Brown was exploring the notation of musical continua, particularly the continuum of time. "Time is the actual dimension in which music exists when performed and is by nature an infinitely divisible continuum," he noted in 1955. "No metric system or notation based on metrics is able to indicate all of the possible points in the continuum, yet sound may begin or end anywhere along this dimension."[1] In a series of short experimental works written in 1952 and 1953 (later published under the title *Folio*), Brown explored various spatial notations that could exploit the full continuous nature of time and pitch. Perhaps the most famous of these is his *December 1952* for any number and combination of instruments. The score consists of a number of rectangles drawn on a single page. These rectangles represent notes: their placement horizontally on the page gives their location in time, while their vertical placement gives their pitch. In other works, Brown used similar spatial notations within an open-form context. In *25 Pages* for piano(s) (1953), for example, the pages of the score can be played in any order by one to twenty-five pianists. In addition, the pages are so notated that they can be read with either end upright, thus providing two different readings for each page. In pursuing such physical mobility of the pages of a score, Brown was inspired by the mobiles of Alexander Calder.

Definition of indeterminacy

A common feature of the early experimental works of Feldman, Wolff, and Brown (as well as some of Cage's music from this time), is that they are designed so that they could be performed in a number of substantially different ways. With works such as Feldman's *Piece for Four Pianos*, Brown's *December 1952*, or Wolff's *Duo for Pianists II*, the differences between performances are more than just subtle changes in interpretation of an idealized score, but rather are radical differences that extend even to the nature and order of events. Any discussion of the sorts of compositional and performance techniques involved in such works soon faces the problem of terminology. In the literature on this subject, the terms "chance," "indeterminacy," and "aleatory" have all been used to describe the use of random procedures in composition, the variability of performance, or both. In addition, other terms arise regularly that refer to specific techniques or situations: "stochastic music," "open form," or "graphic notation," to name but three. Before proceeding further, then, we should settle on definitions of chance and indeterminacy; in this case I will draw upon Cage's own definitions, which I believe to be the most sound and useful.

In Cage's terminology, "chance" refers to the use of some sort of random procedure in the act of composition. *Music of Changes* is a perfect example of this, with the *I Ching* being used to order and coordinate elements from the charts in the score. "Indeterminacy," on the other hand, refers to the ability of a piece to be performed in substantially different ways – that is, the work exists in such a form that the performer is given a variety of unique ways to play it. Brown's *25 Pages* is a good example: it exists as twenty-five independent pages of music, the order or superimposition of those pages being left to the players to choose, thus varying from one performance to another.

Cage addressed this issue of terminology in a lecture entitled "Indeterminacy" (1958). In this lecture, he discusses seven works, five of which he calls indeterminate: Bach's *Art of Fugue*, Karlheinz Stockhausen's *Klavierstück XI*, Morton Feldman's *Intersection 3*, Earle Brown's *Four Systems*, and Christian Wolff's *Duo for Pianists II*. The remaining two works are determinate, but chance-composed: Cage's own *Music of Changes* and Earle Brown's *Indices*. The five indeterminate works represent several different types of openness. In the Bach, Cage notes, the instrumentation and dynamics are not given, so that "the function of the performer . . . is comparable to that of someone filling in color where outlines are given." Similarly, Feldman gives broad pitch indications, within which the performer can choose any notes, and Brown's *Four Systems* (which is similar to *December 1952*) indicates relative pitch and duration, but not specific notes. In the Stockhausen *Klavierstück XI*, the music is presented in short fragments which are played in any order by the performer, thus making for a rudimentary kind of open form. Wolff's *Duo for Pianists II* exhibits open form in a more subtle fashion; here, the content of the musical events is indeterminate as well (the performers choose specific pitches from the collections given, for example).

Cage makes it clear in the lecture that chance and indeterminacy are not identical. In discussing *Music of Changes* and *Indices* he shows that chance procedures can be used to create a work that is completely fixed from one performance to another – in other words, that chance can and has been used to produce essentially "traditional" scores. At the same time, that a score is indeterminate does not mean that chance is involved in its composition or performance. Stockhausen's and Feldman's works were composed without recourse to chance at all, and even in the other compositions, Cage points out that the performer may not necessarily make his decisions randomly or even arbitrarily.

Nevertheless, chance and indeterminacy are related in Cage's work. His use of indeterminacy can be seen as emerging from his chance music. Cage's twin compositional goals in his early chance works were flexibility and inclusiveness; the development of chance techniques in his works from *Music of Changes* to "The Ten Thousand Things" can be summarized as his pursuit of these qualities in his compositional systems. But the problem of creating musical works in a way consistent with the "totality of possibilities" that Cage saw in the world went beyond just designing more complex systems, as he was soon to discover.

By 1958, he found flaws in the conception of *Music of Changes*, as he revealed in "Indeterminacy":

> That the *Music of Changes* was composed by means of chance operations identifies the composer with no matter what eventuality. But that its notation is in all respects determinate does not permit the performer any such identification: his work is specifically laid out before him. He is therefore not able to perform from his own center but must identify himself insofar as possible with the center of the work as written. The *Music of Changes* is an object more inhuman than human, since chance operations brought it into being.

Cage realized that no matter how inclusive his system of composition, so long as it produced a specific, fixed score, the result would be closed and unchanging from performance to performance.

The introduction of indeterminacy into some of Cage's chance pieces early in the 1950s can be seen as an attempt to remedy this situation, mainly by embracing open form. In both the *Music for Piano* series and "The Ten Thousand Things" the various individual structural units can be rearranged into any vertical or horizontal combinations in performance. There are various other "open" aspects to these works as well: the choice of dynamics and tempo in the *Music for Piano*, the selection of preparation objects in *31' 57.9864" for a Pianist* and *34' 46.776" for a Pianist*, and the selection of instruments in *27' 10.554" for a Percussionist*. The indeterminacies of these pieces are still not central to their conception, however. Note, for example, that while the units of "The Ten Thousand Things" can be performed in an open arrangement, the pieces were composed following a strictly closed model: the indeterminacy was imposed after the fact of composition. It was only after 1957, perhaps inspired by the experiments of his younger colleagues, that Cage fully explored the possibilities of indeterminacy in his work.

New notations

Experiments in notation: *Winter Music*

In his attempt to make compositions that were less fixed, Cage developed new, indeterminate notations to change the nature of the scores his systems produced. His work in new notations derived from his approach to composition, which had become a combination of graphic and musical actions. This change in approach can be seen as having its origins in the composition of *Williams Mix*: here he had not dealt with *sounds*, but rather had drawn a *picture* of the spliced tape. The elements manipulated were graphic and spatial (splicing patterns or lengths of tape), rather than musical (pitch configurations or dynamics). With *Music for Carillon* and *Music for Piano* this substitution of graphic for musical elements was complete. Composing one of the *Music for Piano* pieces was simply a matter of drawing points on the page. These points took on musical meaning only after the addition of staff lines and clefs.

The system used in *Music for Piano*, then, suggests a two-stage model for Cage's graphic compositional systems. The first step was to make a drawing by means of some system involving chance (e.g., the paper imperfections). The second step was then to translate this drawing into music by providing some frame of reference, some means of measurement, by which musical instructions could be gleaned from the picture he had drawn (e.g., the musical staves). One line of development that Cage pursued in his indeterminate works centered upon this latter step: indeterminacy could be produced by using ambiguous frames of musical reference for the graphic tokens. In other words, one way to new notations was not through the use of new graphics, nor through new means of producing these graphics, but rather through the use of new and indeterminate ways to translate these into musical directions.

An early example of this sort of indeterminate notation is found in *Winter Music* for pianos (1957). The piece consists of twenty pages of music to be played in whole or part by one to twenty pianists. There are anywhere from one to sixty-one chords scattered over each page. Example 4–1 is taken from the score, and shows the different sorts of chords encountered in the work. Each chord either consists of one to ten pitches or is a cluster, these latter notated as two pitches with a rectangle above. There are two clef signs for each chord. If the two clefs are identical (treble or bass), then all the notes of the chord are read in that clef. If the clefs differ, then some of the notes are read in one clef and some in the other. For chords with two notes (or clusters), one note is read in each clef. For chords with more than two notes, a pair of numbers above the chord gives the proportion of notes to be read in the different clefs. The assignment of clefs to notes is not given by Cage, but is decided upon by the performer. Example 4–2 shows the eight different ways of reading one chord from the work – a chord of four notes, divided so that three are read in one clef and one in the other. In a performance, any one of these eight versions might be used. In performing *Winter Music*, each chord is to be played with a single attack, that is, with no arpeggiation. In cases where this is impossible (such as the last two readings in Example 4–2), then some of the notes are to be depressed silently ahead of time and held by the pedal while the remaining notes are struck, thus producing the "silent" notes by sympathetic vibration.

The compositional systems of *Winter Music* and *Music for Piano* are quite similar. In both, paper imperfections were used to generate points on a page, and the subsequent application of staff lines and clefs turned these points into notes. As a consequence, the resulting pieces are similar, as well: *Winter Music* presents the same sparse texture of individual attacks as the *Music for Piano*, although here the grouping of points into chords makes for a more varied array of events. But while the compositional systems – and hence the uses of chance – are similar, the use of indeterminacy in the two works is quite different. In the *Music for Piano*, the point-drawing system produced a configuration of notes that was fixed; the main indeterminacy of the work results from the myriad possible

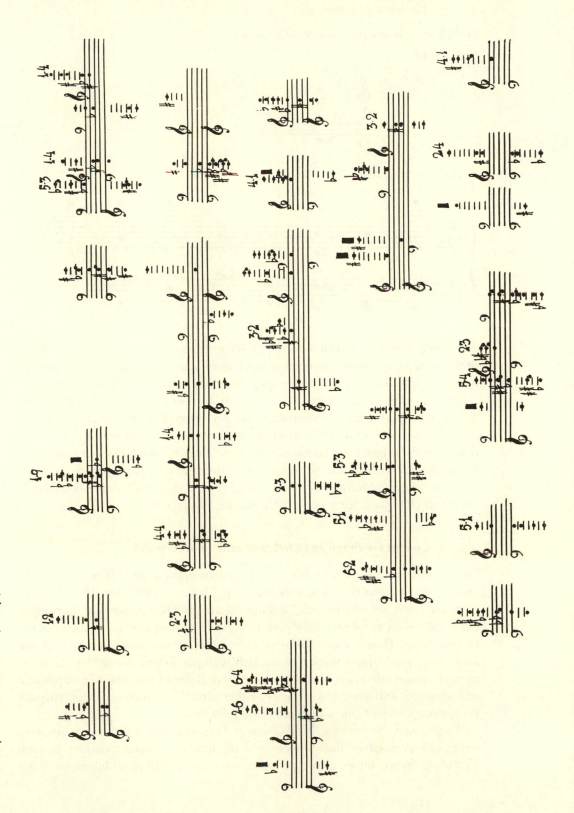

Example 4–1 *Winter Music* (excerpt)

Example 4–2 *Winter Music*, example of notation

(a) as notated

(b) possible interpretations

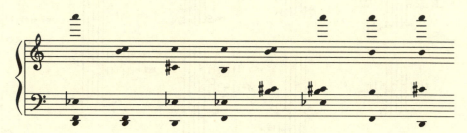

combinations of the individual pieces. In *Winter Music*, not only can different pages of the score be combined in different ways, but within a page no order is imposed on the chords. But an even more important indeterminacy results from the use of ambiguous clefs: these produce a configuration of notes in each chord that can change from performance to performance. Any given performance of any chord is but a "snapshot" of it in one of its possible states. The result of this change was that Cage no longer made music out of simple "atoms" or blocks, but now made his works out of little mechanisms or mobile structures that were to be fixed only for a single performance. In the case of *Winter Music*, this simple alteration in his use of clefs made for a vastly more flexible product.

Concert for Piano and Orchestra and related works

Of the indeterminate works that Cage began composing after *Winter Music*, the most important was the *Concert for Piano and Orchestra* (1957–58). He called it a "concert," and not a "concerto," because all the players – pianist and instrumentalists alike – act as soloists, their parts being totally independent of one another. In this piece, Cage's exploration of indeterminate notations accelerated and intensified, producing a work that was rich with possibilities for further development. Its piano solo is a collection of eighty-four different methods of composition and notation, and served as a source, either directly or indirectly, for virtually every composition Cage composed from 1958 to 1961.

The *Concert* consists of a *Solo for Piano* and separate solos for three violins, two violas, cello, contrabass, flute (doubling on alto flute and piccolo), clarinet, bassoon (doubling on saxophone), trumpet, trombone, and tuba.[2] In addition, there is a completely independent part for the conductor, who acts as a sort of human stopwatch, the movement of his arms imitating a sweep-second hand. His part consists of a table of timings by which he translates the true clock time into an "effective" time for the performers. Thus, for example, he may be told by the score to signal to the performers with his arms that they should play fifteen seconds' worth of their parts (the effective time), but over an actual period of one minute.

The instrumental parts were composed using a point-drawing system similar to that of the *Music for Piano*. The major difference is that in these orchestral parts, the notes are of three different sizes; differences in size represent either differences in dynamics (smaller meaning softer) or duration (smaller meaning shorter), or both, the decision being left to the performer. Each note is to be separated from the others by silence. Before composing each part, Cage consulted with the performer in order to ascertain what sorts of different playing styles, timbres, and unusual effects could be obtained from the instrument. Tables of these were made and the *I Ching* used to apply specific timbres and so forth to specific notes. Example 4–3 is taken from the *Solo for Flute*, and demonstrates the astonishing variety of playing techniques used, even within a short time span. In this brief excerpt one finds: non-vibrato playing, double- and triple-tonguing, microtonal variations (indicated by arrows), slapping the keys of the flute, fluttertongue, various dynamic changes, multiphonics ("intervals"), whistling, singing, and a change of instrument from piccolo to alto flute (all the notations are carefully explained in the score).

Most of Cage's compositional attention was paid to the *Concert*'s *Solo for Piano*. The solo is sixty-three pages long, with fragments of music scattered throughout and frequently crossing page boundaries. The location of the notations on the pages was randomly determined, as was the rectangular space allowed for each. The process of composing the piano solo was based on the premise of continuously inventing new notations and new methods of composition. For each musical fragment in the score, the first decision made (via the *I Ching*) was whether it would use a wholly new method of composition, a repeat of a method already used, or a variation on a method already used. As a result of this procedure, Cage was forced to invent new methods of composition as he went along, and through the course of the sixty-three pages, some eighty-four different types appear. These are identified in the score by letters: the first twenty-six are lettered A to Z, the next twenty-six AA to AZ, then BA to BZ, and finally CA to CF. This continuous invention of new notations results in a score that is striking in its diversity of graphics, even within just a single page, as illustrated in Example 4–4. Detailed instructions on the interpretation of these notations are given in the performance notes for the score.

The notations of the piano solo are diverse, yet most are subsumed under the same model of composition we found in discussing *Winter Music*: the compositional methods have produced drawings that have then been translated into musical terms. The piano solo is, in effect, sixty-three pages of changes rung on this

Example 4–3   *Concert for Piano and Orchestra: Solo for Flute* (excerpt)

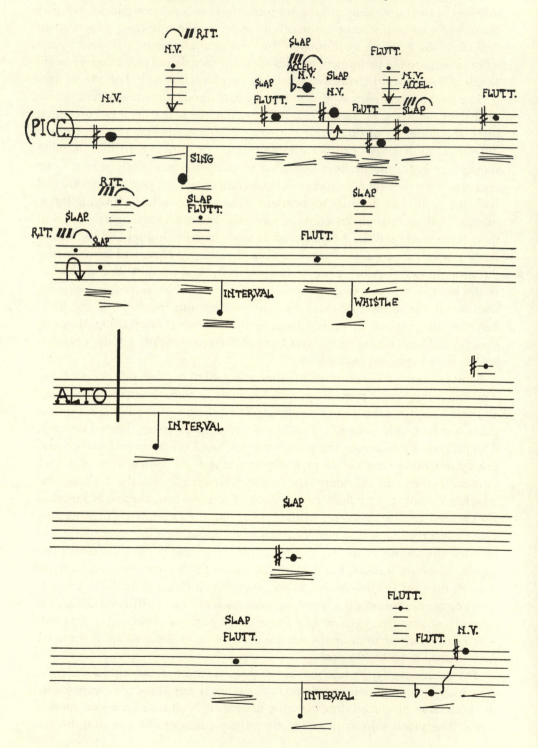

Example 4–4 *Concert for Piano and Orchestra: Solo for Piano* (excerpt)

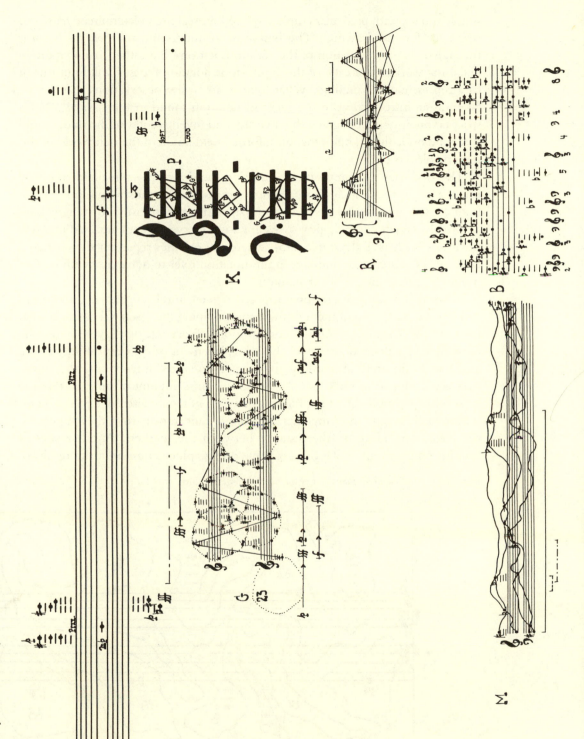

simple model, with particular emphasis placed on making indeterminate frames of reference for the drawings. The best way to understand the *Solo for Piano* is through a close examination of the various notations, but rather than explore in detail the workings of each of the eighty-four notation types, I will limit myself to a representative sampling. What follows are a few observations that can be taken as an introduction to the types of notation found in the *Concert* – not a strict taxonomy (which, given the diversity and inventiveness of the solo, would surely be inadequate), but rather an informal field guide to the rich world of this remarkable score.

The first stage of composition – making the drawing – remained relatively unchanged in the *Solo for Piano*. Simple points are the most common graphic tokens used (presumably derived from paper imperfections), and straight lines and freely-drawn curves appear as well. Closed curved shapes are used in a few notations, such as T (Example 4–5), where the outlines represent the changing contours of clusters (the numbers in this notation refer to dynamics, with smaller numbers representing softer dynamics).

In some notations, Cage superimposed several unrelated drawing actions in order to keep any one of them from strongly shaping the result. In notation AM, for example (Example 4–6), the compositional process is two-layered: first the drawing of the notes on the staff, then the placement of the vertical lines above and below the staff. According to the performance instructions, the music between each pair of lines should take up the same amount of time, so that the time relations implied by the distances between notes are altered: a pair of notes may actually occur closer together or more distant in time than they appear on the page, depending on the distance between the markers. Another way of transforming a simple notation is to have one graphic action limit the results of

Example 4–5   *Concert for Piano and Orchestra: Solo for Piano*, notation T

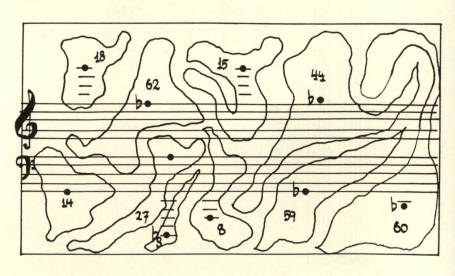

Example 4–6   Concert for Piano and Orchestra: Solo for Piano, notation AM

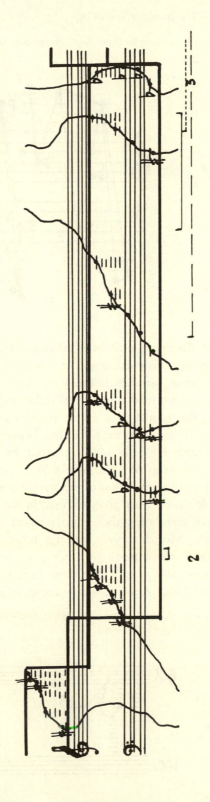

Example 4–7   Concert for Piano and Orchestra: Solo for Piano, notation O

Example 4–8   *Concert for Piano and Orchestra*: *Solo for Piano*, notation W

another. An example of this is in notation O (Example 4–7), where there are two drawings superimposed: one of curves and one of straight lines. Notes are inscribed on the curves, but only in the spaces between the straight lines (in performance, these notes are read from left to right, and the curves themselves are ignored). Finally, the results of a simple point-drawing process are modified in some notations by grouping the points into larger gestures, as in notations W and AH. In W (Example 4–8), the notes connected by lines are to be played *legato*, while the rest are *staccato*; in AH (Example 4–9), the pianist is to follow the lines connecting the notes in the direction of the arrows (clefs are ambiguous here).

While the drawing processes used in the *Solo for Piano* are relatively simple, the means of translating these into musical notations are diverse and frequently complex. Musical staves are the most common and the simplest sort of translation, these frequently being made indeterminate through the use of ambiguous clefs, as in *Winter Music*. In fact, notation B is identical to the notation of *Winter Music*. Another simple means of turning points into musical notes is to

Example 4–9   *Concert for Piano and Orchestra*: *Solo for Piano*, notation AH

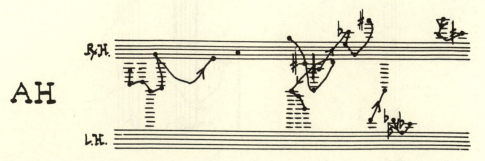

draw a rectangle around them, using their positions in vertical and horizontal space to determine the values of any two musical variables. In notation BY, for example (Example 4–10), the points represent noises of any sorts, with their relative pitch (high or low) given by their placement vertically within the space; the horizontal dimension here, as in most such notations, represents time.

For notations involving a fixed number of discrete possibilities, Cage uses a sort of "grid" to convert points into specific choices. In AC (Example 4–11), the points represent noises of three types: those made on the inside of the piano, those made on the outside, and "auxiliary" noises made off the piano. A three-space grid is used to sort the points among the three types. Similarly, grids are used in notation BD (Example 4–12) to represent the discrete choices of dynamics (the points represent notes of any sort), and in notation BE (Example 4–13) to represent the fingers, hands, or arms with which to play (the nature of the events played is not given). Notation Y (Example 4–14) is a more complex use of this same device. Here the eight bands are used to articulate eight pitch ranges, all adjacent to one another (the choice of pitch ranges is made by the performer). The size of these ranges changes: the numbers beneath the grid give the number of pitches in each range at various points in time, these times given in seconds by the numbers above the grid. This is another example of multiple compositional actions altering a basically simple process (the drawing of points within the grid): the changes in range size, the random placement of these horizontally, and the randomly-assigned time values all work together to alter drastically the musical meaning of the configuration of points originally produced.

All the notations examined so far have used two-dimensional spaces. Other notations use several different reference lines or axes to interpret points in terms of more than two parameters. In BJ (Example 4–15), the distances of the point from each of the four sides of the rectangle represent the pitch, duration, dynamic, and timbre (from simple to complex) of the note. This notation is indeterminate in that which side represents which parameter is decided by the performer. Other, more involved examples of this sort of multi-dimensional notation will be discussed later in conjunction with *Variations I* and *Variations II*, the two works that extend this principle to its most refined, pure state. One last projection used in the *Solo for Piano* merits our attention, if only for its novelty: in notation BT (Example 4–16), outlines of a grand piano are used to convert points into sound events. The location of a point gives the location on the piano where the sound is to be made.

The ambiguous projection of points, lines, and curves into musical space is the primary means by which indeterminacy is arrived at in the notations of the *Solo for Piano*, but it is certainly not the only one. In some notations, directions external to the basic musical signs modify their interpretation. In notations AC and BE, for example, a number indicates how many of the given notes are actually to be played. Indeterminacy is produced here in that the choice of notes is made by the performer. Notation D (Example 4–17) gives another example of

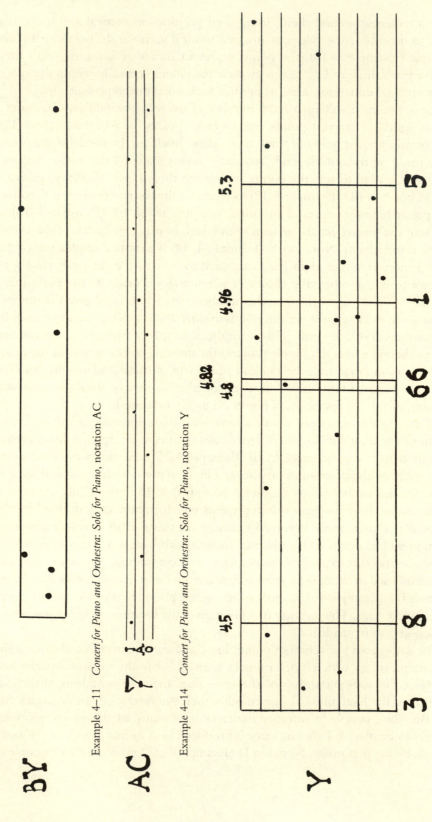

Example 4–10   *Concert for Piano and Orchestra: Solo for Piano, notation BY*

Example 4–11   *Concert for Piano and Orchestra: Solo for Piano, notation AC*

Example 4–14   *Concert for Piano and Orchestra: Solo for Piano, notation Y*

Example 4–12   *Concert for Piano and Orchestra: Solo for Piano*, notation BD

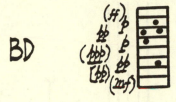

Example 4–13   *Concert for Piano and Orchestra: Solo for Piano*, notation BE

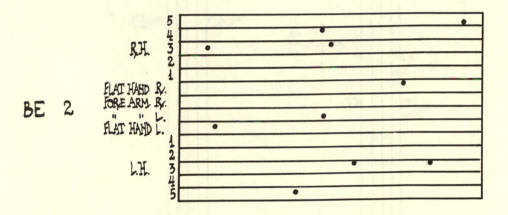

Example 4–15   *Concert for Piano and Orchestra: Solo for Piano*, notation BJ

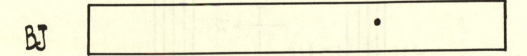

Example 4–16   *Concert for Piano and Orchestra: Solo for Piano*, notation BT

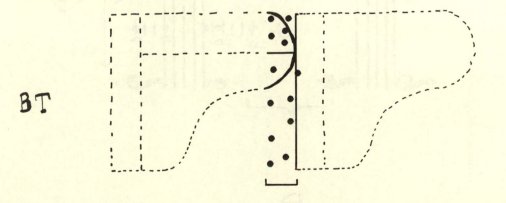

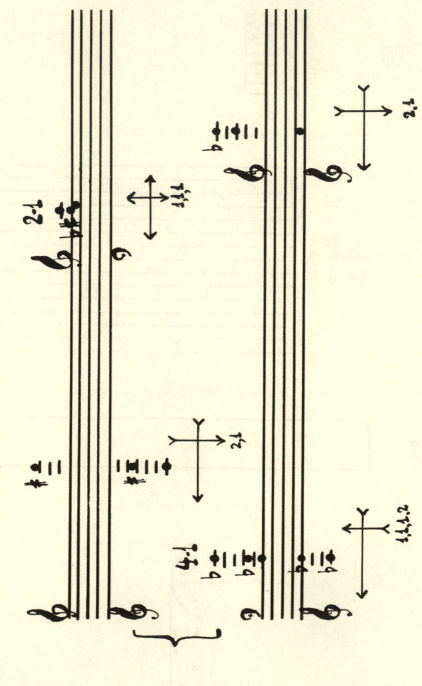

Example 4–17   Concert for Piano and Orchestra: Solo for Piano, notation D

such modification of the primary notation. The notation of the chords is to be read exactly as in *Winter Music*. The arrows and numbers below each chord modify its performance in time. Here, rather than being struck all at once, the notes of each chord are to be arpeggiated, with the numbers beneath the chords giving the numbers of tones to be played at a time (e.g., "1, 1, 1, 2" means to play three single notes followed by two notes together). The vertical arrows give the direction of arpeggiation (up, down, or both in alternation), while the horizontal arrows "refer to time and the tendency of the tones to sound sooner, later, or at the point of notation." The performer must choose the notes to conform to the arrow-and-number notations, which in many cases can be realized in several ways. Notation D is also a clear example of a notation that is a variation on an earlier one – in this case B, the *Winter Music* notation.

Some notations achieve indeterminacy by simply omitting information about one or more aspects of the sound to be produced. In notation BD, for example, only the dynamics of the sounds are given – any sounds of the required loudnesses would fulfill the notation (even sounds not made on a piano at all). Many such "partial" notations give information on *how* to play, but not *what* to play, as in notation BE (which specifies the fingers, hands, or arms to play with) or BT (which gives the location of the action). Notations such as AR (Example 4–18) – in which the performer is told to "play in any way that is suggested by the drawing" – can be seen as extreme forms of this style of indeterminate notation.

The extravagance of the *Solo for Piano* was made possible by David Tudor's meticulous way of working: Cage knew he could entrust such an idiosyncratic score only to an equally idiosyncratic performer. The importance of Tudor's abilities to Cage's work is immediately apparent if one compares the *Solo for Piano* to the instrumental solos of the *Concert*: the relative simplicity of the latter was necessary since they were to be performed by players Cage barely knew.[3] Listening to David Tudor's renditions of the *Solo for Piano*, one hears how the diversity and virtuosity of the score can be realized in performance. One hears the precision and inventiveness of Tudor's playing, while still being aware of the spaciousness of texture, the separation of sounds from each other that is the hallmark of Cage's style of the 1950s.

Several works can be seen as "descendants" of the *Concert for Piano and Orchestra*. In *Solo for Voice 1* (1958), for example, the method used to produce the orchestral

Example 4–18   *Concert for Piano and Orchestra: Solo for Piano*, notation AR

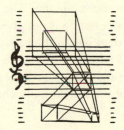

parts of the *Concert* was used to make a vocal piece. *Fontana Mix* (1958), *Variations I* (1958), and *Variations II* (1961) are all based on notations found in the *Solo for Piano* (since these works extend these notations dramatically, they will be discussed later). Because all these works have a loose family relationship, Cage allowed for their simultaneous performance. Thus, for example, in May of 1958, simultaneous performances of *Solo for Voice 1* and the piano solo, clarinet, trumpet, trombone, and tuba parts of the *Concert for Piano and Orchestra* were programmed as *Concert for Voice, Piano, and Four Instruments*.

Another major work that belongs – at least in spirit – to this period of notational experiments is *Atlas Eclipticalis* for orchestra (1961), commissioned by the Montreal Festival Society. In his early compositional notes for the piece, Cage indicated that he was trying to compose a version of *Winter Music* for instruments, and there are similarities between the pieces. In both, events contain from one to ten notes, divided randomly into two groups. Whereas in *Winter Music* this division is between the two clefs, in *Atlas Eclipticalis* it is between short and long durations. Example 4–19 is an excerpt from one of the cello parts, and shows the notation used. Pitches are given unambiguously, although the notation is somewhat unusual – rather than use accidentals, Cage altered the spacing of the staff lines to reflect the number of semitones between them. The relative size of notes gives their amplitudes. The numbers above the events divide the notes with regard to durations: the notation 6-3, for example, means to play either six short notes and three long ones, or three short notes and six long ones.

The compositional process used in *Atlas Eclipticalis* was very similar to others Cage used at this time: the random inscription of points followed by the super-imposing of the staves to create musical notes. In this case, however, the points were to come from the large star charts of the *Atlas eclipticalis 1950.0*.[4] By placing tracing paper over any of the thirty-two star maps in any of several different orientations, Cage was able to trace the star locations, thus producing random points. The brightness of stars is shown in the maps by their size, which translated into the size of notes in Cage's score. The maps also show the spectral class of the stars by their color: by tracing only stars of one color at a time, Cage was able to reuse the same part of a map without duplicating the pattern of points.

The structure of each of the eighty-six orchestra parts is identical: four pages with five staves each. The location of events on each page of a part, and then the individual notes within each event, were both determined using the star charts. In performance, the score can be played in whole or in part by any number of players up to a full eighty-six-member orchestra. The systems are to be read left to right proportionally in time, but the tempo is not given: the conductor determines the duration of each system and then signals the passage of time to the performers. *Atlas Eclipticalis* can be performed simultaneously with *Winter Music*, thus reflecting their compositional similarities. In addition, Cage indicates that contact microphones can be attached to some or all of the instruments, thus amplifying their sound.

Example 4-19 *Atlas Eclipticalis*: cello 1 part (excerpt)

CELLO 1

Musical tools

From scores to tools: *Music Walk*

Cage's composition of the *Concert for Piano and Orchestra* was a great stimulus for his imagination in designing notations for his music. By the time he had finished the *Solo for Piano*, he had tremendously expanded and diversified his approaches to composition, to notation, to the ways in which a score could describe a musical action or event. After the *Concert for Piano and Orchestra*, Cage's work took a different, even more radical turn. In the pieces composed from 1958 to 1961, he ceased making musical *scores* in any sense of the term, and began making what I refer to as "tools": works which do not describe events in either a determinate or an indeterminate way, but which instead present a procedure by which to *create* any number of such descriptions or scores.

An early example of this change in direction is *Music Walk* for one or more pianists (1958). The performers share a single piano, and also may play radios. Cage presents the performers with ten pages containing various numbers of points, and an oblong transparency with five parallel lines on it, much like a musical staff. The transparency is to be placed on any one of the sheets of points, as shown in Example 4–20. The points represent sound events and the five lines represent five different categories of such events. Four of the categories can be interpreted as either piano or radio sounds, as summarized below:

	Piano	*Radio*
1)	plucked or muted strings	"kilocycle glissando"
2)	notes played on keyboard	radio speech
3)	external noises	radio static
4)	internal noises	radio music

The fifth category is "auxiliary sounds" (i.e., all other sounds). The placement of the points within the five-line grid thus determines what kinds of events will take place. Each performer can independently create a score by means of any number of such readings; the interpretation of the dual piano-radio categories (i.e., when a point in the second category will be a keyboard sound or radio speech) then depends upon the availability of the piano or of a radio – that is, upon the actions of the other performers.

The notation using points and a five-line grid is clearly related to certain notations found in the *Solo for Piano* of the *Concert*. In particular, it is reminiscent of the grid notations such as AC, BD, or BE, in which randomly inscribed points are positioned within some regular grid that places them in one of a discrete set of categories. What distinguishes *Music Walk* from such earlier grid notations is made clear if we compare it to a closely-related work composed the same month, *TV Köln* for piano. The notation of *TV Köln* is almost identical to that of *Music Walk* – points placed within a five-line grid representing here only piano sounds

Example 4–20 *Music Walk*: sample configuration of score

of different sorts – but without the use of a transparency, so that the points and lines are fixed on the printed page. *TV Köln* is thus quite similar to a work like *Winter Music* or part of the *Concert for Piano and Orchestra*: a point-drawing process used to create an indeterminate score for the performer to interpret. *Music Walk*, on the other hand, can hardly be called a score at all. The pages of points (which are akin to Cage's observation of paper imperfections) and the five-line transparency (which represents the musical frame of reference) have no fixed relationship to each other and hence can describe no musical events. Instead, the point pages and transparency are the means by which the *performers* can describe a series of events. *Music Walk* has no existence as a *score*, but rather exists as a means of *making* scores – a compositional process handed over to the performer to execute. If, in the indeterminate notations of the *Solo for Piano*, Cage had gained flexibility by creating scores that moved fluidly among their multiple meanings, with his musical tools of the late 1950s he gained even more flexibility by removing the need for scores of any sort. Throughout the 1950s Cage had become more and more aware of the act of composition as being a process; now he extended this principle so that the work itself exists solely as a process.

This turning over of the score-making process to the performer should not be confused with the abandonment of the role of composer altogether. In *Music Walk*, while the performer defines the events by overlaying the transparency on a page of points, it is Cage who has set up this process and who has fashioned the rules for its operation and interpretation. Cage has still decided upon the possible event structures and variables, but the process of determining specifics for any given realization of the work is left in the performer's hands. Thus, while the performer's role has changed greatly in these new works, that of the composer has not: he still is primarily a designer of compositional systems. In fact, the case can be made that by presenting the system itself rather than any specific score it might produce, Cage is in fact offering the work in its most fundamental form, since it is the system that is the source of the work's identity. What he has produced in his ten pages of points and the five-line transparency is truer to the real identity of *Music Walk* than any one score that could be derived from it, such as *TV Köln*.

Fontana Mix and its descendants

Music Walk and *TV Köln* had been composed during the first leg of Cage's European tour in the fall of 1958. His next major work, *Fontana Mix* (1958) was the product of the next part of this tour, a three-month stay in Italy. Cage had been invited to Milan by Luciano Berio in order to create a work for magnetic tape at the studio of the Milan radio. Arriving there in November, Cage immediately created a new work, a tool that would generate the score for the tape piece. Both the utility and the tape piece itself were originally to be called *Performance Mix*; however, during the creation of the tapes, Cage decided instead to name it after his Milanese landlady, Signora Fontana.[5]

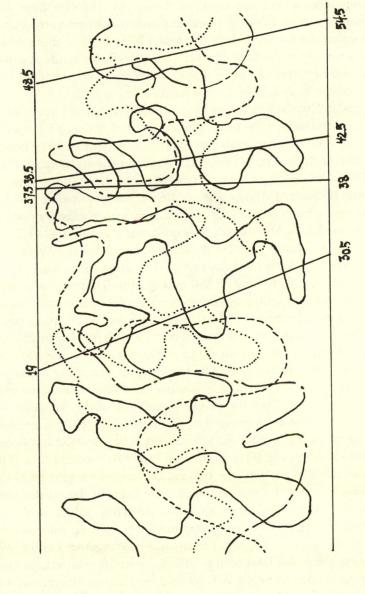

Example 4–21 Concert for Piano and Orchestra: Solo for Piano, notation CC

The work was derived from notation CC of the *Solo for Piano* (see Example 4–21). In this notation, the four curving lines represent the four acoustic variables of frequency, amplitude, timbre, and duration. To obtain values for these variables, measurements are made from the points at which they intersect the slanted straight lines to either the top or bottom horizontal lines. Each of these slanted lines represents a time-span or "time bracket" during which sounds described by these measured parameters take place (the numbers at either end of the lines give the starting and ending times of the brackets).

Fontana Mix makes few changes to this notation, the primary difference being the use of transparencies to turn this into a musical tool rather than a fixed score. In *Fontana Mix*, there are ten pages with curved lines of six types (solid or dotted, each in three different thicknesses). These lines represent the six variables Cage wished to manipulate in creating the tapes: type of sound (he used the same six classifications as in *Williams Mix*), means of modifying the amplitude of sounds, means of modifying the frequency of sounds (such as playing at a faster or slower speed), means of modifying the timbre of sounds (such as filtering), splicing patterns, and duration controls (specific durations, or tape loops). To use the utility, any sheet of lines is chosen, and any one of ten transparencies with various numbers of randomly-inscribed points is laid on top of it. There are two more transparencies: one inscribed with a rectangular grid of 100 squares horizontally by 20 vertically, the other bearing a single straight line. The grid is superimposed on the lines and points, and becomes the reference for all measurements: the horizontal dimension represents time (in the case of the tape piece, the 100 units represented thirty seconds) and the vertical dimension gives a means of measuring values for the six variables. The straight line acts like the slanted lines of notation CC, selecting a time bracket from the overall time frame of the rectangle. To determine the bracket, the line is arranged so that it connects one point falling within the rectangular grid to a point outside the grid. Example 4–22 shows one possible arrangement of curved lines, points, grid, and the straight line. The intersection of the straight line with the top and bottom of the grid gives the starting and ending times of the bracket, and intersections of the curved lines with the straight line within this bracket are measured. These values for the six variables determine the types of sounds, sound modifiers, splicing patterns, and durations to be used within the bracket. For any given arrangement of the grid on a sheet of points, there may be several possible positions for the straight line.

To create the tapes, Cage first collected and cataloged his sound materials. He then proceeded to use the utility to create descriptions of time brackets within the piece. Two stereo tapes were to be made, each seventeen minutes long. Since each grid represented thirty seconds, thirty-four arrangements of the grid on sheets of points and lines were made for each tape, and all the possible time brackets used for each. Cage filled notebooks with descriptions of bracket timings, the types of sounds to be used in each bracket, along with the other sound modifiers, splicing patterns, durations, and tape loops to be made. The collected

Example 4–22 *Fontana Mix*: sample configuration of score

sound materials were then mixed and modified according to these specifications, and then spliced together. Where two time brackets overlapped, their sounds were placed in different tracks of the tape; where more than two overlapped, the sounds interrupted one another, creating what Cage called "fragmentation" of the brackets.

Thus the *Fontana Mix* tool was used to create the two stereo tapes. While this was the project for which it was designed, Cage soon realized that it could be applied in a more general way to other compositional situations. Specifically, it could be used to determine random time brackets within any time frame, and then to choose from collections of materials, coordinating these materials within the time brackets chosen. In essence, then, the approach of *Fontana Mix* is the same as that of the earlier chart pieces – defined materials randomly ordered and coordinated within random time units. After making the tapes, Cage decided to make *Fontana Mix* more generalized by not restricting the types of materials it controlled, but rather having the definition of those materials become part of the process of using the tool – he indicates in the score that "the use of this material is not limited to tape music, but may be used freely for instrumental, vocal, and theatrical purposes." *Fontana Mix*, as a means of creating a tape piece, was a more flexible version of the original notation in *Solo for Piano*; by applying the tool to other musical situations, Cage made *Fontana Mix* even more flexible and open.

Cage used *Fontana Mix* to compose several other works, beginning with *Aria* for solo voice. This work was composed for Cathy Berberian immediately after the *Fontana Mix* tapes were completed in 1958, and was premiered together with those tapes on January 5, 1959. The twenty pages of score (to be sung at any tempo), contain scattered events notated as pitch curves in ten different colors, each color representing a different style of singing (the choice of styles is made by the singer). Vocal noises also occur in the piece, notated in the score by black squares. The text consists of vowels, consonants, words, and phrases in five different languages: Armenian, Russian, English, French, and Italian. Here, *Fontana Mix* was used to determine the placement and durations of the events, along with the colors and languages to be used. *Aria* can be performed together with the *Fontana Mix* tapes and any parts of the *Concert for Piano and Orchestra*, thus indicating the common ancestry of these three works.

Two other works composed with *Fontana Mix* were *Sounds of Venice* (1959) and *Water Walk* (1959). Both works were the product of Cage's appearance on a television quiz show in Milan. In the show, called *Lascia o raddoppia* ("Double or Nothing"), Cage was asked questions for five straight weeks on the subject of mushrooms; by correctly answering the questions one week, he was allowed to continue the next week, until the end of the five weeks, at which point he won the jackpot of five million lire.[6] Before each of the five programs, Cage was asked to perform some of his music for the television audience. *Sounds of Venice* and *Music Walk* were composed for performance on these programs. In both, Cage made a list of twenty props, instruments, and noise-makers, then

Example 4–23 *Theatre Piece* (excerpt)

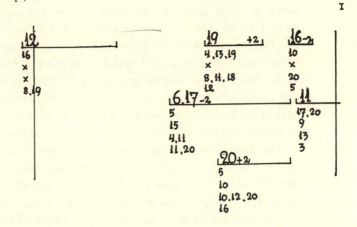

used *Fontana Mix* to make a three-minute score using this list as a collection of materials. The props and instruments of *Water Walk* all relate to water: a mechanical fish, a duck call, a bathtub, a soda siphon, steam released from a pressure cooker, and ice cubes crushed in a blender all make an appearance. *Sounds of Venice*, as its title implies, uses a collection of objects and sounds that reflect that city, including bells of various kinds, boat horns, and even a toy that meows like a cat.

The last of the *Fontana Mix* progeny was *Theatre Piece* (1960). This work is for one to eight performers of any sort ("musicians, dancers, singers, et al."). Each performer is to make a collection of nouns and verbs that could be used to describe actions to be made, or objects to be used as props. Twenty of these nouns and verbs are to be active at any given time in the piece, and are assigned numbers from 1 to 20. The score (see Example 4–23) consists of time brackets indicated graphically, each with numbers that represent which words from the collection of twenty are to be interpreted in that time bracket. Four sets of other numbers (also in the range of 1 to 20) are given for each bracket to answer any other questions that might arise about the type of action to be performed. Finally, two more numbers given for each bracket cause either new words to be added or old words to be restored to the collection, thus creating a constantly changing pool of materials.

The score was, in fact, a simple transcription of readings of the *Fontana Mix* utility. Eighteen arrangements of the grid on sheets of lines and points were made for each of the eight parts of *Theatre Piece*, and all possible time brackets used for each. The timings of the brackets were used to control the size and placement of the notated brackets in the score. One curved line was used to produce the numbers referring to the noun-verb collection, one was used to generate the numbers controlling the replacement of words in the collection, and the remaining four curved lines produced the four sets of numbers appended to each bracket. Thus the score for *Theatre Piece* consists of "prefabricated" *Fontana Mix* readings, to be applied to arbitrary collections of theatrical actions. *Theatre Piece* shows a kinship with *Sounds of Venice* and *Water Walk*, in which *Fontana Mix* was applied to specific collections of theatrical properties. As in the case of *Fontana Mix* itself, Cage generalized a score by simply removing any reference to specific materials, leaving only the process of selection, ordering, and coordination.

Other tools

After returning from Europe in 1959 Cage made a number of works using the same model of score-making tool that he had used in *Music Walk* and *Fontana Mix*. Some of these tools were relatively minor works, limited to a single medium or use, rather than generalized as *Fontana Mix* had been. Works that fall into this category include *Music for Amplified Toy Pianos* (1960), *Solo for Voice 2* (1960), and *Music for "The Marrying Maiden"* (1960), this last being a tool for making audio tapes that would accompany Jackson MacLow's play *The Marrying Maiden, a play of changes*.[7] All three works are similar to *Music Walk*, consisting of sheets of points or circles and a transparent rectangle or grid. The points and circles represent events, and the placement of the rectangle or grid over them thus selects events, places them in time, and further defines their musical characteristics. In *Solo for Voice 2*, the tool materials are also used to create the text to be sung, using a circle with letters written on its perimeter: the intersections of a curved line with the circle produce a vocalise of vowel and consonant sounds.

Cartridge Music (1960) is an example of a more generalized composition. Although it was originally designed as a means for producing performances using phonograph cartridges with various objects inserted into them, it was, like

Fontana Mix, later extended to various other media. In the phonograph cartridge version, sounds are produced by striking or rubbing the objects; these sounds are picked up by the cartridges and then amplified and played over loudspeakers. In order to create a score from *Cartridge Music*, the performer first decides on how many cartridges are to be used. The *Cartridge Music* materials include twenty sheets with from one to twenty irregular shapes drawn on them; the sheet with the same number of shapes as there are cartridges is used in realizing a performance. This sheet is overlaid with four transparencies marked with points, circles, a curved line, and a circle marked like a stopwatch. The points and circles represent events in the performance. Points are sounds made either on or off the cartridges (depending on whether they land inside or outside the shapes), while circles mark changes of amplitude and "tone" (again depending on their location inside or outside the shapes), or they can indicate that a new object is to be inserted into the cartridge (if the circle lies *on* a shape). The curved line is read from one end to the other and gives the sequence of events by its intersection with various points and circles. The intersections of the line with the "stopwatch" give the time brackets in which these events take place.

Cartridge Music can be extended to other media by the abstraction of this method: the materials can be used to control any medium in which there are one to twenty amplified instruments. Points inside or outside the shapes then represent sounds made on or off the instruments, and circles represent amplitude and tone alterations made at the amplifiers, or radical changes in the timbre of the instruments. In the instructions to *Cartridge Music*, Cage gives two examples of its use with other media: a *Duet for Cymbal*, in which there is one instrument (the cymbal), and a *Piano Duet* in which the piano is treated as two instruments, one for keyboard sounds and one for sounds made on the strings.[8] In addition, *Cartridge Music* was used by Cage to create several lectures and articles, such as "Where Are We Going? and What Are We Doing?" (1960), "Rhythm, etc." (1962), and "Jasper Johns: Stories and Ideas" (1963). Here, rather than sounds occurring on or off an instrument, the materials were used to indicate passages to be written "on" or "off" a list of various subjects.

The last of the generalized tools – and the ultimate end of their development – were the *Variations I* (1958) and *Variations II* (1961). As with *Fontana Mix*, these works have their origin in notations appearing in the *Solo for Piano* – *Variations I* was composed before the *Concert for Piano and Orchestra* was completed. The specific notations involved are BB and BV, shown in Example 4–24. In BB, the five lines represent the parameters of frequency (F), amplitude (A), duration (D), overtone structure (S), and point of occurrence within a time frame (O). In BV, the lines have the same meanings, although the assignment of lines to parameters is not fixed. The size of a point in BV determines the number of sounds in the event it represents: the largest points are events of four notes, the next smallest are events of three notes, and so on. In events of more than one note, different

Example 4–24   *Concert for Piano and Orchestra: Solo for Piano*

(a) notation BB

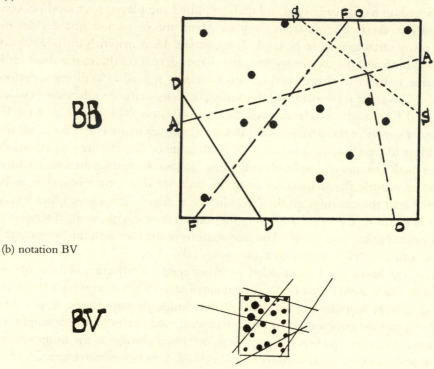

(b) notation BV

pitches, amplitudes, and so forth are generated by using a different assignment of parameters to lines for each note.

The *Variations I* is derived from notation BV. It consists of a transparent square with twenty-seven points of four sizes, interpreted as in notation BV. There are also five different transparent squares with randomly-arranged configurations of five lines. A sheet of lines is superimposed in any of four orientations on the points, and is interpreted as in BV; in events of more than one note, different sheets of lines, or different orientations of the same sheet are used to make measurements for each separate note of the event. The *Variations I* thus uses transparencies to make notation BV mobile and more flexible, but the use of a single sheet of points fixes the number and structure of events in the piece. This, combined with the very limited number of orientations in which the sheets of lines can be used, makes *Variations I* less flexible than some of the other tools. In essence, this is only an extension to other performance media of the BV notation of the *Solo for Piano*, with the transparencies used here to offer more possibilities in describing events of multiple notes.

The *Variations II*, on the other hand, represents the most flexible tool composition that Cage ever created. The materials are deceptively simple, consisting of five small transparencies, each with a single point, and six larger transparencies, each with a single line. These are to be arranged in any manner at all, thus creating a configuration of points and lines that can be measured in a way similar to *Variations I*. Five of the lines have the same meanings as in *Variations I* (frequency, amplitude, timbre, duration, and point of occurrence), while the sixth represents the structure of the event (i.e., number of notes), thus taking over the role that the different sizes of points played in the earlier work. Each arrangement of points and lines thus generates five events; the materials can be rearranged as many times as desired, generating any number of events.

By removing the fixed relationships among the points and lines, Cage turned the mechanism of *Variations I* into an open-ended tool, capable of producing an infinite number of scores. But *Variations II* goes far beyond this, as Cage makes the following direction in the score: "If questions arise regarding other matters or details . . . put the question in such a way that it can be answered by measurement." This means that not only can there be as many events as desired in the realization, but there can be as many variables as needed to describe those events. The basic unit of *Variations II* is the measurement of a point to a line. The interpretation of that measurement is completely open: it can represent anything at all, at any level, structural or particular. A point can represent any event or component of an event, and a line can represent any characteristic of such events. In his other tool compositions, Cage presented rules for the creation of a score and had the performer execute them. Here there are no rules: there is a single, simple model – the measurement of distances – to be used in making whatever rules the performer deems necessary. In this sense, *Variations II* is more than a tool, it is a meta-tool.

When boiled down to its essentials, this piece takes Cage's goal from the early 1950s – to understand the quantities that act to produce multiplicity – and approaches it in the most fundamental way possible: by having a performer enumerate all the variables and then measure them. By making the number of parameters open-ended, Cage created a piece in which any actions in any orders and combinations whatsoever can be described. Cage's pursuit of flexibility and inclusion in his compositions from 1951 onwards had led to his removal of his compositional actions at various points. He abandoned the composition of specific sound events when he gave up the chart technique for that of "The Ten Thousand Things," and he abandoned the construction of specific scores with the indeterminate notations and tools of the later 1950s. With the generalized tools such as *Fontana Mix* and *Cartridge Music*, Cage stopped specifying the materials to which his rules would be applied, but even these works shaped their possible results by using rules of specific sorts – the fragmentation of time into brackets, or the indication of sounds as being made either on or off an instrument. *Variations II*, by removing even these meager shaping influences, reduced Cage's compositional voice to a near silence. With this work as his compass, he had finally attained the freedom to explore any part of that space of interpenetrating sounds that had been his quest throughout the 1950s.

5

"Music (not composition)" (1962–1969)

Changes in Cage's life and work in the 1960s

Signs of change: 0' 00"

In May of 1965, concert-goers entering the Rose Art Museum at Brandeis University were treated to an unusual musical experience. They were attending a concert of contemporary music, organized by Alvin Lucier, which featured works by Lucier, John Cage, and Christian Wolff. As the audience entered the museum, they were greeted by loud noises – squeals, gulps, clacks – coming from speakers located at various locations in space. They soon discovered the source of the strange sounds: John Cage, sitting in a squeaky chair on a staircase landing between the two floors of the museum, was writing letters on a typewriter, and occasionally drinking from a glass of water. He was equipped with microphones connected to the museum sound system, so that every movement he made – every squeak of the chair he sat in, every tap of his typewriter, every gulp of water – was greatly amplified so that it filled the space of the museum. When Cage was finished writing letters, the sound equipment was shut off, and the next work on the program was prepared.

What the Brandeis audience witnessed that night was a performance of Cage's composition *0' 00" (4' 33" No. 2)*. Composed in 1962, the score for the work consists of a single sentence: "In a situation provided with maximum amplification (no feedback), perform a disciplined action." The first performance of the piece, given in Tokyo during Cage's first tour of Japan, consisted of Cage writing that very sentence. The day after the Tokyo performance, he added four qualifications to the basic score: the performer should allow any interruptions of the action; the action should fulfill an obligation to others; the same action should not be used in more than one performance, and should not be the performance of a musical composition; and finally, the performer should pay no attention to the situation he finds himself in, whether electronic, musical, or theatrical. These qualifications were perhaps suggested by that first performance, their inclusion in the score thus clarifying Cage's intention for the work.

138

Given the history of Cage's compositions of the 1950s, *0′ 00″* is a difficult piece to understand. It is astonishing to realize that this is the work that immediately follows *Variations II* and *Atlas Eclipticalis*: nothing in these earlier works prepares the ground for *0′ 00″*, which at first glance seems to be completely unlike the chance and indeterminate music Cage composed in the 1950s. Any similarities one might find lie entirely on the surface. The use of amplification suggests a connection with *Cartridge Music*, but in that work the amplified objects are treated as instruments to be played, and the amplification system is used as a source of other musical parameters to manipulate; there is no sense of either "instrument" or "parameter" in *0′ 00″*. Similarly, while the focus on action and theatre calls to mind the earlier *Theatre Piece*, in fact no comparison is possible. The one work consists of a fragmented series of actions distributed among random time frames, while the other is a single deliberate and directed action that recognizes no measurement of time at all.

Part of the problem of approaching *0′ 00″* is that it does not appear to be "music" in any sense that we might use the term – even in the somewhat expanded sense of Cage's music of the 1950s. Its character instead would seem to place it under the category of theatre, or more properly what has come to be known as "performance art." Cage, in fact, has a long-standing connection to the performance art movement. Some authors cite the event he organized at Black Mountain College in 1952 – a joint performance with Merce Cunningham, Robert Rauschenberg, David Tudor, M. C. Richards, and Charles Olsen – as the first example of a "happening." A simple structure of random time brackets was used to control the performance, which included film, slides, poetry, music, and dance. Later in the 1950s, Cage taught classes in composition at the New School for Social Research in New York City, classes that were attended by artists who would go on to develop the performance art genre: George Brecht, Allan Kaprow, Al Hansen, and Dick Higgins, among others. *0′ 00″*, with its simple prescription of concrete action, is similar to many of their performance art pieces, especially the "events" of George Brecht, where the focus is on a single action described in simple prose – Brecht's *Piano Piece 1962* consists of the phrase "a vase of flowers on(to) a piano."

But whatever affinities *0′ 00″* may have with early 1960s performance art, the fact remains that it stands apart from all that Cage composed before it. In it, we find a different relationship between Cage as a composer and the external world of sounds that was his medium. In general, we might say that his earlier chance and indeterminate works were indirect in their approach to music. In all of them – even such open-ended compositions as *Variations II* – a score (or a score-making tool) is used to act as a buffer between mind and sound. Uppermost in Cage's thoughts at that time was the image of a world of interpenetrating sounds, a world in which each sound was unique and centered on itself. The actions of the performer were methodically worked out via the score so that this external sound world could be apprehended unconditionally, without the obstruction of the mind. In *0' 00"*, this situation is reversed. There is no score to speak of here at all, and there is no sense of an objective sound world to be apprehended. Instead, there exists a totally subjective situation, in which the performer acts in a deliberate and personal fashion. The actions of a performer in *0' 00"* are not arranged according to any elaborate plan or process, but are arrived at simply and directly. In its clear presentation of a musical world quite different from that of the 1950s, *0' 00"* represents that rarity in music history – a clear line of stylistic demarcation.

Increasing notoriety

Substantial changes in a composer's work, such as those that occurred in Cage's work in the 1960s, do not just happen of themselves. Behind sudden stylistic change there usually stands a change in the composer's life, and this case is no exception. What happened to John Cage in the late 1950s and early 1960s, simply put, is that he became famous – not just well-known, but notorious. Many of the changes in his life and work in the 1960s can be connected in some way to his increasing notoriety, and it is worthwhile here to examine the course of his widening reputation.

Cage was already a noted composer by the late 1940s, at least in New York circles. His name appeared regularly in the New York press, and in such national publications as *Musical America* and even *Time* magazine. By the time of the *Sonatas and Interludes*, he was receiving consistently favorable notices in the press, being referred to with such honorifics as "one of this country's finest composers." At this time, Cage was usually considered an "experimental" composer, in the vein of Henry Cowell or Edgard Varèse, and his invention of the prepared piano was undoubtedly his most famous "experiment."

Even after his adoption of chance techniques in the early 1950s, little changed in the way Cage was received by the musical press – except that they found the new works less attractive than the old. Cage was still called an "experimentalist," but his innovations were known to extend only to such matters as unusual piano-playing techniques and the use of radios as instruments. The aesthetic and com-positional underpinnings of Cage's chance music were almost entirely unknown to critics (whether favorable or not), with the exceptions of Henry Cowell and Virgil Thomson. A review of the premiere of *Imaginary Landscape No. 4*, for example, treated the work as if the new ideas that it presented were no different in substance or manner from Cowell's new piano techniques; the review does not mention chance at all.[1] The failure of Cage's aims and compositional methods to become known among critics resulted in the works being completely misunder-stood and poorly received; Cage, Feldman, Wolff, and Brown were described as "being naughty in the manner of horrid children," and their music derided as "so aggressively unattractive, so utterly hideous, so insistently repellent."[2]

While New York *musicians* had no context in which to put Cage's chance works, New York *artists* did. Cage had always been prominent in the New York art world, as a contributor to art journals, a lecturer at the Artists' Club, and as a friend of various artists. As Cage would say later:

> I had early seen that musicians were the people who didn't like me. But the painters did. The people who came to the concerts which I organized were very rarely musicians – either performing or composing. The audience was made up of people interested in painting and sculpture.[3]

Cage was an important early friend and supporter of the painters Robert Rauschenberg and Jasper Johns; their subsequent rise to stardom in the art world indirectly helped to further Cage's work.

Rauschenberg and Johns joined forces in 1958 to put on a large concert of Cage's music in New York's Town Hall. Since Cage's earliest works dated from 1933, the concert was billed as a twenty-five-year retrospective of Cage's work, a tribute to the importance of that work over the years. Well-attended (one review estimated that there were 1,000 people in the audience), the concert marked the beginning of Cage's new rise to prominence in the avant-garde music world. The concert was followed by another trip to Europe, this time to appear at the Darmstadt summer festival, where Cage's music was well-received and influential. But while these concerts helped to put his music in perspective, it was the release of two recordings in 1959 that was pivotal to the understanding of Cage's work. The first of these was the recording of the lecture "Indeterminacy: New Aspect of Form in Instrumental and Electronic Music," a collection of ninety stories drawn from Cage's personal experience, from friends, and from Zen literature. Cage read the stories at the precise rate of one a minute (thus changing speeds depending on the length of the story), while David Tudor performed the piano solo from the *Concert for Piano and Orchestra*, using bits of *Fontana Mix* tape music as auxiliary noise sources when needed. The stories reveal a good deal of Cage's approach to music in a highly entertaining fashion. The other recording, privately produced by George Avakian, was of the twenty-five-year retrospective concert. Complete with copious program notes and fully-explained excerpts from the scores, the Avakian recording, together with the "Indeterminacy" record, finally put Cage's music in a clear aesthetic context – the context that New York music critics had lacked throughout the 1950s. As a result, the first informed appraisals of Cage's chance works date from 1960. It was the availability of resources like the twenty-five-year retrospective recording that, in 1960, permitted Leonard Meyer, in an essay on "Art by Accident," to treat Cage not as a "naughty child," but as one of many "serious and thoughtful people who are creating an art which expresses a consistent, clearly defined set of attitudes and beliefs about the nature of the universe and man's place in it."[4] To be sure, Meyer was less than sympathetic to the idea of chance composition, but his acknowledgement that Cage's work reflected a serious and consistent musical point of view contrasts sharply with the attitudes expressed by other music critics only a few years earlier.

Cage's work received an added measure of exposure in 1961 with the simultaneous publication of his writings and music. The release by Wesleyan University Press of *Silence*, a collection of virtually all his writings from 1937 to 1961, was perhaps the most important event in Cage's career as a composer. *Silence* generated even more interest in Cage than the recordings had: the audience for the book was wider than that for his recordings or concerts. At the same time, Cage's music was taken on by Henmar Press, his scores thus becoming available through the publisher C. F. Peters. Peters published a descriptive catalog of all the compositions (written by Cage in conjunction with Robert Dunn) in 1962, which included accounts of compositional techniques, a bibliography, and an interview with Cage. Thus the entirety of Cage's musical thought, in the form of both compositions and writings, was made public almost all at once. Where in 1958 only a thousand had heard the premiere of the *Concert for Piano and Orchestra*, in 1962 it was possible for anyone in America, Europe, or Japan to listen to that same performance on the Avakian recording (or hear Tudor's rendition on the "Indeterminacy" record), peruse a copy of the score, and read Cage's comments on the work in *Silence*.

With this new publicity came new opportunities for lectures, writings, and performances. *Atlas Eclipticalis*, it will be recalled, was a commission from the Montreal Festival Society in 1961, and by 1964, Cage was sufficiently renowned to merit a performance (albeit a catastrophically irresponsible one) of that same work by the New York Philharmonic.[5] Cage received several university appointments during the 1960s; he held positions at Wesleyan University (1960), the University of Cincinnati (1967), the University of Illinois (1967–69), and the University of California at Davis (1969). Cage lectured extensively, as well, speaking not only at the expected venues (universities or art conferences), but also at such unlikely events as the International Design Conference of 1966. In 1968, he was elected to the National Institute of Arts and Letters, a prestigious honor for an American composer.

Cage's music was also being made known world-wide as a result of the increased activities of the Merce Cunningham Dance Company. Cage and Cunningham gave their first joint recital in New York in 1944, and Cunningham went on to form his own dance troupe in the early 1950s. Cage acted as musical director for the company from the start, and many of the dances were accompanied by Cage scores. The dance company toured regularly in the 1950s, although performances were limited mainly to small colleges and so forth. Cunningham, like Cage, began receiving more and more attention in the 1960s, with the biggest boost coming from a world tour in 1964. Cage participated in all these tours, and the performances of his music at Cunningham dance concerts were instrumental in establishing Cage's reputation throughout the globe.

Life and music

The sudden increase in attention paid to Cage created changes in his work and working methods. Perhaps the clearest example of this is the decrease in compositional productivity that he experienced in the 1960s. In the eight-year period of 1952 to 1959, for example, he completed about forty compositions, including such substantial efforts as the *Music of Changes*, *Williams Mix*, all of "The Ten Thousand Things" pieces, the *Concert for Piano and Orchestra*, and *Fontana Mix*. In the eight-year period of 1962 to 1969, on the other hand, Cage completed only about fifteen pieces, some of which have no scores at all (such as *Musicircus*), many of which are unpublished, and only one of which is of any substantial size (*HPSCHD*, which was actually a collaboration with Lejaren Hiller).

The immediate reason for this sudden reduction in productivity was simple: Cage was too busy touring, lecturing, and performing to compose in the manner he was accustomed to. In the 1950s, he had had few commitments other than his compositional work, thus he was able to use the extravagantly detailed methods of his chance works, such as "The Ten Thousand Things." In the 1960s he no longer had that surplus of time, and this change in his daily life forced him to change the way in which he composed, a change that he had some difficulty in adjusting to. In 1966, he explained to Morton Feldman the conflict he felt between his new life and his old habits, especially the need to be "at home" in order to compose:

> The telephone ringing, the correspondence, and having to travel here, there and the other place – there seems to me to be no time because I still have the notion that I should be in one place and waiting, so to speak, for something to come to me which I would then do.[6]

As he then put it, the problem was "to get the notion that I'm at home wherever I am."

In reading the interviews Cage gave during this period, it also becomes clear that part of his compositional troubles stemmed from his discomfort with all the attention that was being paid to him. His resistance to fame comes through most clearly in a 1969 interview:

> What I do and say and so forth has become of interest to people. It would be much better had it not. But it did. And I think it's actually a result of my having lived a long time . . . Had I died at 44 I surely would be quite unknown. And yet I would have done much as I've done. The Chinese say the best thing to do is to leave no traces. To remain unknown.[7]

Cage's primary quarrel with all this attention was that it got in the way of his deeply-felt need to pursue the new and original:

> It seems to me that one of the dangers that exists, and may exist more and more, is that once you pass the point of interesting people in what you're doing, and

they become interested, then what they want is not anything new from you but rather what you have done before. So that you could be kept busy week after week, never having a chance to do anything but fulfill engagements, answer the telephone, and answer your correspondence.[8]

For this reason, Cage disliked commissions: "There is a resistance in me to have a new idea *for* an occasion. If I have a new idea I would like it to be somehow free of occasion."[9]

It was in part to reconcile himself to this situation that Cage pursued a new course in his work; where before he had attempted to make his musical works be more like life, he now turned to transforming his life into his work. *0' 00"* offers a perfect example of this – a piece that consists of a very personal action, one that is ephemeral, not to be repeated. It requires no rehearsal or elaborate preparation, and the action performed is one that he would have done in any event. *0' 00"*, in short, takes a moment from the everyday life of John Cage and through electronics and concert-hall setting transforms it into a musical work. If notoriety was going to mean spending all his time answering correspondence, then Cage would adjust his art so that answering correspondence became a musical performance.

This informal and ephemeral quality is reflected in the kinds of scores he produced during this period. *0' 00"* consists of but a single sentence, for example. In *Rozart Mix*, the score consists of the correspondence between Cage and Lucier about how the premiere of the piece was to be produced – another example of turning the mundane chore of answering letters into art. In *Variations V* Cage invented "*a posteriori*" scoring: the score is simply a description of the first performance, written after the fact. Finally, many of the events that he staged during the 1960s, which he considered to be musical works in their own right, have no scores at all (*Musicircus* and *Reunion* are two such examples). In works such as these, music became whatever it was that Cage was doing, and the lack of scores served to keep at bay the possibility of his fixing the experience and possibly repeating himself.

This new informality extended to Cage's writings as well as his music. Gone were the rhythmic structures of works such as "Lecture on Nothing" and the formal explanation of concepts found in "Experimental Music: Doctrine." Instead, the new writings were more personal, chatty, anecdotal, and aphoristic. The most extended prose works of this time were the yearly installments in his "Diary: How to Improve the World (You Will Only Make Matters Worse)," in which he used the *I Ching* to determine how many statements to write each day, as well as how many words each statement should have. The result is a mosaic text, in which there is no need to connect one statement to another, and where one gets the impression that many of the statements were written off the top of his head. Cage's adoption of the diary as his preferred literary form (as opposed to the essay or lecture) is another clear example of his tendency to make his daily life into his art.

This notion that simply *living* could be art created a new interpretation of *4' 33"*. Where before the piece had represented a demonstration of empty time structure or a showcase for unintentional sounds, Cage now considered it as a musical work that went on constantly, an intimation of the ultimate unity of music and life. In the 1960s, Cage felt that his work could show all listeners how to find that "daily beauty" that was not obtained through the offices of any composer, but "which fits us each moment (no matter where we live) to do our music ourselves. (I am speaking of nothing special, just an open ear and an open mind and the enjoyment of daily noises.)"[10]

While a lack of time and a distaste for fame are important factors in Cage's new attitude towards music during the 1960s, it should not be overlooked that during this time he was feeling less and less interested in composition itself. Cage stated this plainly in the Foreword to his second collection of writings, *A Year From Monday* (1967), and at that time he told Morton Feldman that, unless asked to, he would not be inclined to compose at all.[11] Cage's declining interest in composition parallels the case of the artist Marcel Duchamp, who supposedly stopped working as an artist in 1923 – when asked what it was that he did, Duchamp claimed to be a "*respirateur*." Cage became quite close to Duchamp in the 1960s, and felt that he was in a similar situation: in his 1963 essay "26 Statements Re Duchamp" Cage's description of Duchamp's activities in the 1960s – "Now that there's nothing to do, he does whatever anyone requires him to do" – could just as well be a description of himself.

That Cage should be less and less interested in composition should not come as a complete surprise, considering the extent of his work in the late 1950s. If *Variations II*, as I have suggested, stood as the ultimate exploration of the total sound space, then it is understandable that Cage would find that line of development no longer compelling. While his adoption of chance techniques in 1951 came to be viewed by many as his abandonment of music and composition, it had exactly the opposite effect – it sparked a period of intense compositional activity. It was only in the 1960s, after having so thoroughly explored the world of pure sound, that Cage lost interest in musical issues and began to pursue more social concerns. His "Diaries" of the 1960s deal less with art than with "world improvement," a reflection of his new interest in thinkers such as Buckminster Fuller and Marshall McLuhan. Music, he saw, was "child's play"; "Our proper work now, if we love mankind and the world we live in," he said in 1967, "is revolution."[12]

Despite such statements, however, Cage – like Duchamp – did not abandon his art completely. He gave many different answers throughout the 1960s to the question of why he still composed, perhaps the best being that art was a "celebration" of everyday life, a special occasion that was unnecessary, but nevertheless enjoyable and valid. In the 1968 installment of his "Diary: How to Improve the World," there appears the three-word statement "Music (not composition)."

This can be seen as a terse summary of the direction of Cage's life and work in the 1960s. Cage saw music as more than just making pieces by ordering sounds in some fashion or another (i.e., "composition"). Music, he felt, had a larger goal, a greater scope: it included action and new technologies, and could serve to change not just his own mind, not just other musicians' minds, but the "global mind" of society at large. Cage was aware that great changes were taking place in the world of the 1960s. As a result of this, he felt the need, in both society and his own work, to start over from scratch, to "begin again, assuming abundance, unemployment, a field situation, multiplicity, unpredictability, immediacy, the possibility of participation."[13] These new ideas were explored by him in a less than systematic fashion: his work of the 1960s lacks the focus and direction he maintained in the 1940s and 1950s. Much like the rest of Western society at this time, Cage threw caution aside and embraced change and uncertainty with optimism and a passion for the new and untried.

Process and action

Let me return now to the issue of *0' 00"* and how one is to understand such a composition in the context of Cage's prior work. The best course, I believe, in dealing with a difficult piece such as this is to try to see what is *there* in the work – in this case, to ask the question of just what is given in the score to *0' 00"*. All that Cage has supplied is a direction to act – to perform some disciplined action that will fulfill an obligation to others. Cage has also indicated some of the circumstances surrounding this action: it should be amplified and performed in an unselfconscious way. This is all that the score contains. What probably accounts for the difficulty in reconciling it to Cage's earlier work is what it does *not* contain: it lacks any reference to sound. The only acoustic information given at all is the instruction that the action be amplified, and this only *implies* that sound will be heard. Because there is no mention of sound, and no means for describing or measuring the sorts of sounds that the piece will entail, *0' 00"* does not exist as a compositional object – a series of sounds – but only as a process, an action by the performer.

This distinction between objects and processes is at the heart of the change in Cage's music from the 1950s to the 1960s. *0' 00"* is not an isolated case, but is in fact quite typical in its emphasis on action and process. A quick examination of the scores Cage produced during this period shows that few of them mention sounds directly. None at all (with the possible exception of *HPSCHD*, which was, in any event, a collaborative effort) is primarily involved with describing or ordering sounds. This attitude is made explicit in the instructions to *Variations VI*, where Cage indicates that "the notations refer to what is to be done, not to what is heard or to be heard." That statement fairly describes all Cage's music of the 1960s: he had moved from arranging *things* to facilitating *processes*.

This interest in action and processes – and hence theatre – can be seen in some of Cage's works of the 1950s. His theatrical "happening" at Black

Mountain College in 1952 has already been described; at the same time, he began including visual and theatrical elements (for Cage these are essentially the same) in his musical compositions. But even in such "theatrical" works as *Water Music* or *Sounds of Venice* sounds predominate, and the less strictly musical actions are marginal. Beyond this, the actions notated in these works are treated as if they *were* sounds – as if they were objects to be manipulated and ordered. This treatment of actions as objects is clearest in *Theatre Piece*, where the actions are reduced to a list of nouns and verbs written on index cards – the score simply serves as a means of selecting and coordinating the cards. In *0' 00"*, as in the rest of Cage's work of the 1960s, there is no such objectification of actions: these new works were invitations to what Cage called the "pure subjectivity" of process and action.

A concomitant to this replacement of objects by processes was Cage's avoidance of any sort of measurement in his musical scores. The title of *0' 00"* is a reference to this: it refers to the notion of "zero time" as derived from the work of Christian Wolff. In response to Wolff's notations of "zero time" in his *Duo for Pianists II* (an event so notated can have any duration at all), Cage changed his notion of time in music so that it became "less tangible than it was." As he explains:

> You see, if music is conceived as an *object*, then it has a beginning, middle, and end, and one can feel rather confident when he makes measurements of the time. But when it [music] is *process*, those measurements become less meaningful, and the process itself, involving if it happened to, the idea of Zero Time (that is to say no time at all), becomes mysterious and therefore eminently useful.[14]

Cage's pursuit of a music beyond measurement was also the result of his adoption of the complex natural world as an ideal model for his own art. He saw the world of nature, with its vast multiplicity of simultaneous activities, as surpassing all attempts to measure it. Indeed, he felt that the very act of measuring, by imposing a static arrangement on fluid experience, could produce a false, restricted view of experience. The solution to this dilemma was to make measurement irrelevant by dispensing with sounds-as-objects altogether, and simply to suggest actions, or to facilitate an environment for action. In his 1962 essay "Rhythm, Etc." he uses the image of being shut up in a house as a metaphor for his old habits of measurement and structure:

> The thing that was irrelevant to the structures we formerly made, and this was what kept us breathing, was what took place within them. Their emptiness we took for what it was – a place where anything could happen. That was one of the reasons we were able when circumstances became inviting (changes in consciousness, etc.) to go outside, where breathing is child's play: no walls . . .

Cage refers to *0' 00"* as *4' 33" No. 2*, thus implying that this is another silent piece. However, it is obvious that the piece is not at all silent, but in fact is quite noisy, given the extreme amplification involved. To understand this subtitle, it is necessary to consider what Cage meant by "silence" in the original *4' 33"*. There, he drew upon his experience in the anechoic chamber to point out that what we refer to as silence is in fact just the occurrence of sounds not intended; *4' 33"* embraces these unintentional sounds, and thus connects with Cage's chance works. *0' 00"* represents a similar realization, but this time in the field of actions, not sounds. In the early 1960s, Cage began to realize that his identification of silence as unintentional sound could be extended to inactivity, which he now saw as unintentional action. Where his music of the 1950s was an attempt to blur the distinctions between intentional and unintentional sounds, so with his music of the 1960s he became concerned with blurring the distinctions between intentional and unintentional actions.

In *0' 00"* this emphasis on unintentional action is manifested in various ways. The amplification system, for example, functions as a microscope, magnifying every tiny, uncontrollable detail of the performer's actions. Thus an action (such as writing letters) which is fully intentional on the part of the performer is transformed into a non-stop stream of minute, unintended acts. The encouragement of interruptions given in the score to *0' 00"* (and in other works) also represents the unintentional. When dealing with sound and silence, Cage had been fond of testing a musical work's validity by seeing if it could accommodate ambient noises (i.e., unintentional sounds); by 1966, the criterion had changed to whether it "can include action on the part of others."[15] Finally, the instruction that the action of *0' 00"* is to be performed in an unselfconscious fashion serves to de-emphasize the intentional side of the action – to make it appear as though the performer is doing what he would do anyway, without thinking of it as music or even as a performance.

The move from objects to processes, from sounds to actions, was swift, and is reflected in Cage's next work, *Variations III* (1962–63). Just as the first two *Variations* were abstractions of the chance systems he had employed in the 1950s, so *Variations III* represented a generalized approach to the action music that lay ahead in the 1960s. As in the earlier *Variations*, this work exists as a tool made of transparencies, rather than as a score. The performer is to take forty-two small pieces of transparent plastic with circles on them and let them fall upon a blank sheet of paper. From this mass of circles, a single interconnected group is isolated and will serve as the "score" for the performance. The performer starts with any circle in this group and makes an action that has as many variables as there are circles that overlap the chosen one. The performer then moves to any adjoining circle and makes another action, and so on. Nowhere in the instructions to *Variations III* is sound mentioned: even the title page fails to mention sounds or musicians, instead indicating that the work is "for one or any number of people performing any actions."

The *Variations III* explores the same themes as *0' 00"*. Here there is no measurement at all, only the counting of variables. Cage gives no indication as to how the variables are to be measured, varied, or otherwise used. *Variations III* was also concerned with the notion of unintentional actions: in the instructions to the piece, Cage not only allows the performer to count such actions as part of the performance ("Some or all of one's obligation may be performed through ambient circumstances . . . by simply noticing or responding to them"), but insists on it ("Leave room for the use of unforeseen eventualities"). The final line of the instructions – "Any other activities are going on at the same time" – continues in this vein: note that it is not a granting of permission, but is instead a statement of fact.

Cage's intent at the time that he made *Variations III* was that it would enable free and direct action in performance – one would simply do things and count the actions and variables involved. A performance of *Variations III*, then, might be similar to one of *0' 00"*, only with more than one action involved. In this sense, *0' 00"* might be viewed as a specialized case of the general situation outlined by *Variations III*. The actions Cage made in a 1963 performance of *Variations III* are, in fact, similar to those of the Brandeis performance of *0' 00"*: these included untangling electrical cords, putting on his glasses, smoking a cigarette, writing a letter, and drinking a glass of water. All these actions were amplified greatly, with the last producing a sound described by one witness as being "almost unbearable in its intensity."[16]

Another interesting case of Cage's turning to processes and actions is *Rozart Mix* (1965). *Rozart Mix* was written for the concert, described at the outset of this chapter, that was organized by Lucier at the Rose Art Museum at Brandeis University in May of 1965. The score consists of Cage's ideas for the piece as communicated in letters to Lucier prior to the concert. The instructions are simple enough: before the concert, eighty-eight loops of magnetic tape are to be made by splicing many fragments together. These loops should be of varying lengths, from very short to very long. In the performance, as many tape players as can be obtained are to be set up, and the performers then mount and unmount loops on these machines in any order and timing they desire. If a loop breaks (and this is inevitable), then a performer should give first priority to repairing that loop, replacing it in the meantime with another. There is no predetermined way to end the piece – at the premiere, Cage waited until all but twelve audience members had left, then had a small party for those remaining twelve to conclude the piece.[17]

Just as *Williams Mix* represents Cage's adaptation of his chance techniques to the tape medium, and *Fontana Mix* represents his application of the indeterminate tool idea to magnetic tape, so *Rozart Mix* represents the hybridization of tape music and action music. Again, sounds are barely mentioned at all: Cage only notes in passing that the tape loops should consist "mostly" of speech, and in any event, the heavy fragmentation caused by splicing would render the sounds unrecognizable. Instead, his instructions focus on the actions of making, mounting, unmounting, and repairing the loops, creating the rather unlikely circumstance of a purely theatrical piece for magnetic tape.

That Cage made an action-oriented tape piece underlines the substantial change in his attitude towards music in the 1960s. For Cage, tape music had always been the ultimate medium for the understanding of sound. It physically demonstrated that "sounds are just sounds," and it allowed for the free manipulation of all sonic parameters. In essays such as "Experimental Music: Doctrine" he identified the advent of magnetic tape with the understanding of the true nature of sound. *Rozart Mix* turns his earlier image of tape music on its head: here, the physical nature of sound is completely ignored, and in its place is a fascination with the logistics of threading tape recorders. In the premiere performance, performers removed their shoes and socks in order to extend tape loops over a shallow pool of water on the museum's ground floor, and in a performance at Wesleyan University in 1988, enormous loops were run from the stage down the center of the audience to the rear of the concert hall, with audience members lifting their arms to help support the fragile ribbons of tape.

Electronics

Electronic technology in Cage's music

I have already noted a difference in the use of electronics in *0′ 00″* as opposed to works such as the *Imaginary Landscape* series or *Cartridge Music*. Cage's treatment of electronic technology in those earlier works is, in essence, instrumental: the various devices are used as sources of particular sorts of sounds, and the musical scores – whether traditional, chance-composed, or indeterminate – are concerned with describing the ways in which these devices are to be played. In *0′ 00″*, on the other hand, the technology is that of amplification, which does not suggest the instrumental, but rather acts as a transforming force, elevating the mundane action of the performer to the realm of art. Cage used amplification in performances of all kinds during the 1960s; the gulping of water in his performance of the *Variations III* is one such example among many. Virtually any action he made or any device he used was likely to be amplified: in *Variations VII*, some of the performers' bodies were wired for sound, and in *Musicircus*, the sounds of the light switches were amplified. Cage saw amplification as a means to examine areas of action where nothing is definite, a way of making it clear that what one thought was inactivity is really full of uncontrollable, unintentional actions that produce sounds. In this way, he used technology in a more thorough way in the 1960s than he had in the past; the *spirit* of the music is electronic, not just its material.

Cage's attitude towards technology was shaped in part by his reading of the work of Marshall McLuhan, the prominent critic of media and technology. Cage read McLuhan's two major studies, *The Gutenberg Galaxy* (1962) and *Understanding Media* (1964), but he cites McLuhan's article "The Agenbite of Outwit" (1963) as the work "that I rank above all his [McLuhan's] books."[18] Cage refers to

McLuhan repeatedly throughout his diaries and other writings, and McLuhan, in turn, quotes from Cage in his own book *The Medium is the Message* (1967).

McLuhan's work is wide-ranging and hence precludes any quick summation; I will limit myself here to outlining the points that are essential for understanding Cage's attraction to his ideas. First, McLuhan saw all technologies as extensions of the human body: a wheel, for example, is an extension of the feet. Electronic media, he felt, were extensions of our own senses and central nervous system, thus producing a good deal of uneasiness in society. McLuhan felt that such changes in media and technology, no matter what specific uses they are put to, in turn change people – that, regardless of the content communicated, the way one interacts with a medium is built into the technology. This is the meaning of his oft-quoted dictum "the medium is the message" – as he puts it in *Understanding Media*: "any technology gradually creates a totally new human environment. Environments are not passive wrappings but active processes."[19] In McLuhan's view, much of the change in society in the twentieth century resulted from the weakening of the old mechanical environment (created by the technology of printing), and the ascendancy of the new electronic environment (created by the new technologies of telegraph, radio, and television). Print culture emphasized "*lineality*, a one-thing-at-a-time awareness and mode of procedure" that included detached analysis, specialization, and fragmentation. The new electronic media, on the other hand, "deal in *auditory space*," with total involvement, unification, and simultaneity. In "Agenbite of Outwit" McLuhan uses the structure of the newspaper page as an example of this way of thinking: the news items and advertisements on the page "have no interconnection of logic or statement. . . . It is a kind of orchestral, resonating unity, not the unity of logical discourse."[20]

It was this description of the new electronic environment – the new "global village" created by instantaneous electronic communication – in which Cage found a compelling and informative parallel to his own work. In his essay "McLuhan's Influence" (1967) Cage makes the connection between what he saw as McLuhan's message and his own ideas:

> We are now, McLuhan tells us, no longer separate from this environment. New art and music do not communicate an individual's conceptions in ordered structures, but they implement processes which are, as are our daily lives, opportunities for perception (observation and listening). McLuhan emphasizes this shift from life done for us to life that we do for ourselves.

But McLuhan did more than provide an explanation of the changes in society: he affirmed the primacy of the artist in dealing with those changes. Because the artist deals with the senses, he is best equipped to understand the changes in perception caused by new technology. McLuhan saw experimental artists such as Cage as prophets of the new technology, and offered them a new purpose: the instruction of society on "how to rearrange one's psyche in order to anticipate the next blow from our own extended faculties."[21] This is the point at which

Cage and McLuhan converge: Cage had always seen music as a means of "changing one's mind," and McLuhan provided a good reason to change it. After encountering McLuhan, Cage saw himself as the creator of musical experiences that would allow people to adjust to the new electronic media environment.

The composition as sound system

Cage's primary way of using the new electronic technology in the 1960s was by treating composition as the design of electronic sound systems. In "Diary: Emma Lake Music Workshop 1965" he makes the equation of electronic systems and compositional styles: "Seeing composition as activity of a sound system, whether made up of electronic components or of comparable 'components' (scales, inter-vallic controls, etc.) in the mind of a man." This view of composition is in keeping with McLuhan's image of the artist as the prophet of the new media, the designer of environments that can enlighten the audience as to the effects of the new technologies. McLuhan, by declaring that the new media are not passive wrappings but active processes, reinforced Cage's position that a composer, by designing an electro-acoustic system, is also creating a compositional process.

Cage, again in agreement with McLuhan, felt that it was totally irrelevant what sounds were to pass through these technological systems. Any interaction with the system would be conditioned by the system itself, and it was the nature of the transaction between participant and system that was musically and socially of greatest importance. *Rozart Mix* is a good example of this approach and its effects on Cage's compositional style. The sound system here consists of the multiple tape recorders, amplifiers, speakers, and the tape loops to play on the machines. Cage says little more than this about the piece – all he indicates about how to make the loops, for example, is that they should be diverse in splicing technique and length. It is the system – the arrangement of components, of machines and loops – that constitutes the identity of *Rozart Mix*. There is no need to give any specific plans of action for the performers (nor even to provide a means for creating such plans), because any particular series of actions is acceptable. The other sound-system pieces from the 1960s follow this same model: Cage describes how to set up the components of the system, and perhaps gives broad outlines of how to interact with it, but never offers a specific score for performers to follow.

In understanding the sound-system compositions that Cage made at this time, it is necessary to focus on the systems themselves, on the kind of musical environments they suggest, the themes they embody. In *Variations V* (1965), the first of these works, the theme is, fittingly, drawn from McLuhan: the translation of one medium into another, or what McLuhan called the "brushing" of information against information. The work, made in conjunction with Merce Cunningham, was a commission from the French-American Festival. In addition to the dance and music, a film by Stan VanDerBeek and video images by Nam

June Paik were projected onto screens behind the performers. The sound system was designed so as to maximize the interaction between the various elements of the production. For example, in addition to using tape recorders, radios, and oscillators, sounds were picked up by contact microphones applied to props used by the dancers – a table and chairs, for example. Thus the dancer's actions (such as sitting in one of the chairs) became translated via amplification into a sound signal that could then enter into the musical system. While the musicians were constantly mixing and routing their sound sources to the loudspeakers in the hall, these sources were gated (switched on and off) by various devices controlled by the dancers. Twelve antennae and a number of photoelectric cells were set up on the stage. The dancers' proximity to the antennae and their interruption of light sources on the photoelectric cells would trigger sound events. By such design of the technological system, Cage was able to "brush information against information," to cross one art with another, and thus to generate a complex experience.

A similar "thematic" sound system was that created for *Variations VII* (1966), one of a series of works presented in New York as collaborations between artists and engineers. In this case Cage's inspiration was electronic technology's ability to make the inaudible audible. The sound system was designed with the limitation that only sounds that arose during the performance were to be used – in other words, the performers would not make any actions to generate sounds deliberately, but rather would use technological means to discover sounds in the air "as though with a net." *Variations VII* is thus similar to *0' 00"*, in that it uses electronics to demonstrate that there is a great deal of activity going on even in apparently inactive situations. In this case the sound sources included: contact mikes attached to the performance platform; four assistants whose activities of heart, brain, lung, and stomach were detected and amplified; geiger counters; and various devices for receiving electromagnetic communication transmissions, such as twenty radios, two televisions, and fifteen telephones. The performers moved among all this equipment, amplifying, mixing, and routing the results to seventeen different speakers.

A much simpler sound system was used for *Reunion* (1968), a piece with the more personal theme of friendship. Cage invited David Tudor, Gordon Mumma, David Behrman, and Lowell Cross – all composers of live electronic music – to perform their own musics simultaneously. The outputs of their individual sound systems (of which Cage had no knowledge at all) were routed to a gating system controlled by a chess board: sensors in the board switched different outputs on and off as the pieces were moved. The performance lasted five hours, during which time Cage, Marcel Duchamp, and Mme. Duchamp played games of chess on the wired board. The various participants in this performance were all good friends; *Reunion* was a means for them to make music together, even though they had all gone their own ways artistically. The chessboard gating system allowed Cage to participate in the performance without actually creating any sound, and at the same time served to transform the actions of the four performers from four separate musics into a single entity.

In *Variations V*, *Variations VII*, and *Reunion* we find the arrangement of a specific electro-acoustic system, within which performers were then allowed to act in a free and unscripted fashion. *Variations VI* (1966), on the other hand, is a generalization of this idea, rather than a specific implementation. The work is an indeterminate tool, consisting of an opaque page with a straight line on it, twelve transparencies with straight lines on them, and a large number of transparent tokens. These last are of three different shapes, representing loudspeakers, sound sources, and components for sound modification (e.g., amplifiers or filters). A performer is to use as many of each kind as there are devices of the appropriate type available, and to drop them, along with the transparent lines, on the page with the straight line. The transparent lines (or their extensions) are used to group the tokens into individual sound systems: the orientation of these straight lines with regard to the line on the opaque page is to suggest the distribution of the sound in space. *Variations VI* therefore simply provides a means of creating arrangements of the available audio components; it is a tool for creating sound systems, just as *Variations II* was a tool for creating musical scores.

Simultaneity, abundance, and anarchy

Simultaneity in Cage's music

In *Reunion*, as in many other works from the 1960s, Cage brought together several completely independent performers to make their unique musics simultaneously. This use of simultaneity is not at all the same as that found in his earlier works such as *Double Music*, "The Ten Thousand Things," or even indeterminate works such as the *Concert for Piano and Orchestra*. In all these pieces, the various parts, while independent of one another, have some common feature or origin: a compositional technique, a rhythmic structure, a notation. They are, in short, independent parts that still exhibit a family relationship. Cage's use of simultaneity after 1962, on the other hand, does not require any common characteristic among the various parts. In *Reunion*, there is no given relationship among the various musics of Behrman, Cross, Mumma, and Tudor (other than Cage's inviting all of them).

Instead, Cage asserts here that it is the simultaneity of the various performances that constitutes their relationship. Rather than have independent parts performed simultaneously because they are related to one another, Cage here relates independent parts to one another by performing them simultaneously. This concept of simultaneity-as-relationship can perhaps be traced to the manner in which Cage was accustomed to working with Merce Cunningham. Beginning in the 1950s, the only relationship between Cage's music and Cunningham's choreography was that they took place at the same time and in the same space.

As Cage put it in "Where Do We Go From Here?": "Neither music nor dance would be first: both would go along in the same boat. Circumstances – a time, a place – would bring them together." In these dance productions, the complete independence of elements extended to the lighting, sets, and costumes, as well. In *Reunion*, the same approach is taken to the four musicians who perform together: their "reunion" on stage is in fact the only connection necessary in the piece.

This use of simultaneity can also be related to the idea of interpenetration found in Cage's chance works. Behind those compositions, it will be recalled, there stood the image of an infinite space of sounds that were all unique and completely interconnected: all sounds, in other words, were thought of as existing simultaneously in this space and hence were all interrelated to each other. In *Reunion*, this image is now applied to *processes* instead of *sounds*, so that the activities of the four composers are at once individual and interpenetrating. This notion of interpenetrating processes is reflected in other ways in Cage's compositions after 1962. Several scores allow for other performances or actions to go on simultaneously. The example of *Variations III* (with its statement that "any other activities are going on at the same time") has already been described, and in 1965 Cage himself performed it simultaneously with David Tudor's own realization of *Variations II*. The acknowledgement of interruptions in works such as *0' 00"* also represents Cage's awareness of the interpenetration of all activities. An interruption is simply an intrusion of an unintended process on an intentional one, and Cage began to encourage these in his work after *0' 00"*.

This image of the world as a place full of simultaneous, interrelated processes was the source of *Variations IV* (1964). The work is an indeterminate tool that consists of seven points and two small circles inscribed on separate transparencies. These are to be dropped onto a map of the intended performance space. Lines are drawn from one circle through each of the points to the edge of the map. These lines are then used to determine the location of the sound sources to be used (here again, the nature of the sound sources themselves is not described). If a line touches the second circle, then the sound source is to be located anywhere on the part of the line *inside* the performance space; otherwise, the sound is located on the part of the line *outside* the space. The notions of "inside" and "outside" depend a good deal on the type of space used – a theater, a building with multiple floors, a suite of rooms, a cave, and an outdoor space are all named as possibilities in the instructions. Multiple readings of the material are allowed, which can be interpreted either as additional sources, or as the movement of sources previously located.

To understand *Variations IV*, it is important to recognize that it was one of three compositions that were meant to be taken as a group: the other two were *Atlas Eclipticalis* and *0' 00"*. The grouping of these works was based on an interpretation of Japanese *haiku* poetry that Cage obtained from Hidekazu Yoshida. The first line of a *haiku*, Yoshida suggested, represents *nirvana*, the second *samsara*, and the third represents "a specific individual action – which, however, is completed through non-action."[22] In this arrangement, *Atlas Eclipticalis*, being based on maps of the heavens, corresponded to the *nirvana* line, and *0' 00"* corresponded to the "individual action" line. Cage's choice of *Variations IV* to represent *samsara* can be understood if we keep in mind that the image of sounds and activities occurring all at once in different places in space was Cage's image of nature – of life itself. Cage makes this connection of sound sources differentiated spatially with everyday life in "Where Do We Go From Here?":

> We're no longer satisfied with flooding the air with sound from a public-address system. We insist upon something more luminous and transparent so that sounds will arise at any point in the space bringing about the surprises we encounter when we walk in the woods or down the city streets.

The *Variations IV* represents the world of everyday life – *samsara* – by suggesting just the sort of abundance and simultaneity of activity that exist in a forest or a city.[23]

Circuses and anarchy

Just as McLuhan had served as a guide and inspiration for Cage's use of electronic technology, so Buckminster Fuller served as a source for his new approach to simultaneity and multi-media performances. The essence of Fuller's thought is that, through increased efficiency and design improvements, the technology is possible that would meet 100 percent of the material needs of 100 percent of the world's population. The history of technological advancement, he held, was to produce more with less raw material, thus making it possible to support more and more people at a higher and higher standard of living. In the future, if his plans and ideals were implemented, since everyone's needs would be met, there would be no need for wars, or even nations: a global utopian anarchy would be established. Fuller emphasizes, however, that this utopia is to be accomplished not by the efforts of political leaders, but simply by the forward march of technology, by the work of "comprehensive designers" who will make the global networks that will deliver resources to the world's peoples. It is by changing the technological environment – rather than by trying to change *people* – that success will be achieved, as illustrated by one of Fuller's favorite sayings:

> Take away all the inventions from humanity and within six months half of humanity will die of starvation and disease. Take away all the politicians and all political ideologies and leave all the inventions in operation and more will eat and prosper than now while racing on to take care of 100% of humanity.[24]

Other writers had similar ideas in the 1960s – Cage was aware of the economist Robert Theobald's writing about the economy of abundance, and was particularly taken with Edgar Kaufmann's ideas on the importance of disposability in the realm of modern design.

Cage was enthusiastic about Fuller's vision from the very beginning. He saw a connection of Fuller's concept of global planning and McLuhan's global village: the externalization of the nervous system on a global scale meant that just as meditation or yoga could lead the individual mind to enlightenment, so the discipline of comprehensive design science could lead the global mind to its enlightenment. Cage's world improvement texts were inspired by Fuller, and are full of Fulleresque ideas and quotations from his writings. Inspired by Fuller's prediction of near-unlimited global wealth, Cage began to speak of a similar abundance in music – a preference for quantity over quality:

> I find that through our experience of [contemporary] painting and now music, that everything we experience has, so to speak, quality, so what we would like to do is to continue to have experience – in other words, quantity. To go on having more and more experience, since it all has quality.[25]

In this regard, Cage refers to the development of an aesthetic of wastefulness – that experience could become so abundant that one doesn't mind wasting it:

> If you look at nature, for instance, it often seems to be wasteful: the number of spores produced by a mushroom in relation to the number that actually reproduce . . . I hope that this shift from scarcity to abundance, from pinch-penny mental attitudes to courageous wastefulness, will continue to flourish.[26]

This goal of superabundant, disposable music was approached not only by the adding of musics to one another through simultaneous performances, but through the lengthening of the performances themselves. In 1963 Cage staged the first complete performance of Satie's *Vexations*, a piano piece consisting of a few measures of music to be repeated 840 times, and thus lasting over eighteen hours. Performances of many of Cage's works were lengthy, such as the first performance of *Reunion*, which lasted five hours. In works such as these, Cage said, "tempo no longer exists. Just quantity."[27]

A kind of simultaneous, multi-media performance that derived from this line of thought was what Cage called a "circus." The first example of this was *Musicircus* (1967), an event staged at the University of Illinois. The performance was held in the University Stock Pavilion, a large space used for showing cattle. Cage invited a number of musicians to perform simultaneously in the pavilion in any way they desired – other than the invitation, no instructions were given to any of the performers. Thus, David Tudor and Gordon Mumma performed some of their own works (much as they would do the following year in *Reunion*), Salvatore Martirano gathered a group of performers and gave a program of his own choosing, two jazz bands played, and so on. For his own part, Cage operated the lighting console, which he had wired with contact microphones, so that the sounds of the switches would be broadcast into the space. There were non-musical elements to the show as well: films and slides were shown, balloons floated, and popcorn and apple cider were sold as refreshments. Each of the performing groups had its own platform, and the audience was free to wander around the main floor of the pavilion. An estimated 5,000 people came (no admission was charged), and, as the advertisements promised, they didn't hear a thing – they heard everything.

Cage applied this circus approach to whatever activities he was involved in. A classic example is his appointment as a guest composer at the University of California at Davis in 1969. Cage's class was anarchic: 120 students, divided into fourteen smaller groups of flexible membership, read 120 different selections from books in the university library (these chosen by means of the *I Ching*) and then discussed and acted upon their readings in any way they chose (the results included recipes, poetry, compositions, a film, and a chain letter). A one-day musical exposition, with concerts scattered all over the university campus, was also a part of Cage's stay at Davis, and was given the title *Mewantemooseicday*.[28] One of the events was a performance of Satie's *Vexations*; all other events were scheduled to occur within the roughly eighteen-hour span of this piece. Other activities included lectures by Cage, a concert of Satie's music, performances by the university orchestra and band, and film presentations, to name but a few. Also included was a new composition by Cage, *33⅓* (1969), in which twelve phonographs and over 300 LPs were made available in a large open space to anyone who wished to use them. The situation so produced was a sort of miniature version of *Musicircus*, with the phonographs filling the function of the performance platforms. With the exception of one performance, no admission was charged, and people were free to wander in and out of the various performances, lectures, and other activities. Cage, inspired by Fuller, had defined education as "people together without restrictions in a situation abundantly implemented";[29] *Mewantemooseicday* was exactly such a situation spread out over a large canvas of space and time.

The application of Fuller's ideas to music is clear in works such as *Musicircus* and *Mewantemooseicday*, where Cage functioned as a musical comprehensive designer, delivering aesthetic abundance to his audience. Cage felt that, as predicted by Fuller, such a rich situation eradicated the privileged role of the composer, and allowed the individuals of the audience the freedom to direct their attention wherever they wanted. Thus, the audience could take on a more active role, as Cage explained in his "Diary: Audience 1966":

> An audience can sit quietly or make noises. People can whisper, talk, and even shout. An audience can sit still or it can get up and move around. People are people, not plants. "Do you love the audience?" Certainly we do. We show it by getting out of their way.

In sum, a musical anarchy was produced, wherein the performers and listeners were no longer told what to do, and Cage retreated to such a distance that his role as organizer and designer, while crucial, was practically invisible. The circus events represented yet another variation on the music-as-process idea, this time turning music into an activity for society at large. Cage declared in his 1967 world improvement diary that: "Art's socialized. It isn't someone saying something, but people doing things, giving everyone (including those involved) the opportunity to have experiences they would not otherwise have had."

HPSCHD

The work that closes this period in Cage's career – *HPSCHD* for up to seven harpsichords and up to fifty-one tapes (1967–69) – presents an unusual case, a mixture of old-fashioned composition, multimedia event, and free-form circus. Composed at the request of the Swiss harpsichordist Antoinette Vischer, the piece was actually a collaboration between Cage and Lejaren Hiller, and these two facts – commission and collaboration – account for many of its seeming inconsistencies. Cage initially resisted the commission, not knowing how he could make the harpsichord an interesting medium. He decided to fulfill the commission only after he found an idea – the notion of a multiplicity of scales – that would bring the harpsichord into his contemporary world of abundance. Because of the short duration of harpsichord sounds, Cage felt the need for "an enrichment of the notion of scales . . . Necklaces of notes, or even rows of notes, and scales of notes, and modes of notes, and so forth. I would like to make a great multiplicity of such things."[30] As he had in the 1945 *A Book of Music*, Cage identified this notion of the simultaneity of several different scales with the music of Mozart, in which diatonic and chromatic passages coexist with arpeggiations, and so forth.

At this point, Cage began his residency at the University of Illinois, where he was asked by Lejaren Hiller, a composer of computer music, to propose a project to be realized at their computer music studio. Cage responded to Hiller's request with his ideas for the harpsichord commission, feeling that the work involved in generating music with a plurality of tunings and scales was well-suited to the computer. Having no computer skills, Cage relied on Hiller to do the programming for his project; soon Hiller began to have his own ideas about the piece, and so Cage suggested that they make it a collaborative effort. The title was derived from the name of a computer subroutine used in the program: in those days, the length of a subroutine name was limited to six upper-case letters, so that "harpsichord" was abbreviated to "HPSCHD".

The use of different scales was to be realized within the domain of the tape parts. Each of the fifty-one tapes was composed using a different division of the octave, ranging from five to fifty-six tones (excluding the standard twelve-note division). These tones could, in turn, be microtonally inflected by any of 128 degrees (sixty-four sharp and sixty-four flat), so that there was an enormous number of available pitches. A single line of tones was generated by the computer for each of the fifty-one tapes using a system of chance-determined goal notes, deviations, and ornaments. Although Cage would have liked to have overlapping notes, this was not technically possible, and so the tape parts were strictly monophonic.

In addition to the tapes, there are seven independent harpsichord solos. One was generated by the same program used for the tapes, this time applied to the standard twelve-note division of the octave. The other six are all related in some way to the theme of Mozart's music, since this had served as an inspiration for the multi-scale idea. Hiller suggested using Mozart's *Musical Dice Game* (*Musicalisches Würfelspiel*, K. 294d), no doubt seeing a connection between this piece and Cage's work. Mozart's piece consists of sixteen measures of minuet-style music and tables of numbers referring to these measures. Dice are used to select measures from the table at random, thus creating a chance-composed minuet. This game was programmed into the computer, and one harpsichord solo consists of twenty minutes of such music. Four other solos also use the dice game, but the results are altered by gradually replacing elements from the original table of measures with measures of various other music. Two of these solos use replacements drawn from other Mozart compositions: one in which the replacements occur simultaneously in the parts for both the left and the right hand, and another in which the replacements occur independently in either hand. Similarly, two solos (one "hands-together" and the other "hands-separately") use replacements drawn from a broad range of musical history, starting with Mozart, proceeding through the nineteenth century (Beethoven, Schumann, Chopin), and into the twentieth, ending with works by Hiller and Cage. The final solo consists of the instruction to play any work by Mozart.

As it stands, *HPSCHD* does not seem to have much in common with the rest of Cage's work of the 1960s. Of all the compositions examined thus far in this chapter, none have mentioned any specific sounds, and some do not mention sound at all (e.g., *Variations III*), yet *HPSCHD* not only deals directly with sound, but with notes, scales, scores – even Mozart and Beethoven! But it must be kept in mind that the tapes and the harpsichord solos were just the resources to be used in a performance: there was never any intent simply to play them all at once in a concert in a traditional setting. Instead, these sonic resources were only a small part of a five-hour multimedia extravaganza, held in the University of Illinois Assembly Hall. The harpsichords were placed on platforms distributed around this enormous circular arena, and the loudspeakers were arranged around the perimeter of the dome. Although each tape and each harpsichord solo had a duration of twenty minutes, they could be repeated as many times as desired, with pauses of any duration between repetitions, thus allowing the performance to last for hours. Several thousand slides were displayed (by means of eighty projectors) on large transparent screens hung from the center of the arena; several films were also shown on these screens. Blacklights, spotlights, and a discothèque-style mirrored ball completed the visual side of the event. Some 7,000 people came to the show, milling about among the performers and taking in the sights and sounds.

The performance of *HPSCHD* – as opposed to its raw materials, considered by themselves – is completely in keeping with Cage's attitude of the 1960s. It was, in effect, another circus event, with the difference that its components were all designed to go together. Besides its themes of scales, Mozart, and music history, *HPSCHD* was another essay on the subject of abundance. Cage saw the computer as a means of making an enormous number of decisions, hence producing an abundance of music for delivery in a circus atmosphere.[31] In the cavernous space of the Illinois Assembly Hall, among the thousands of spectators, dozens of tapes, and seven soloists, much of the Mozartean material created for *HPSCHD* was, indeed, wasted, played in a situation in which it could not be heard clearly. But, as with so much of Cage's music from this period, the content of the music was actually quite irrelevant to the experience: it was the quantity and the anarchic arrangement of the whole that created the effect, as one observer put it, of an auto show, with various performers "selling their wares of sights and sounds."

6

"Joy and bewilderment"
(1969–1992)

Return to composition

Change and contradiction: *Cheap Imitation*

In the previous chapter, I portrayed *0' 00"* as the turning point in Cage's work of the 1960s: a piece like no other before it, forming a sharp break with his compositions of the 1950s. Similarly, the period of Cage's work beginning in late 1969 – and extending, I think, through the rest of his life – is marked by a piece that is difficult to assess for similar reasons: *Cheap Imitation* for piano (1969). The work has a somewhat long and involved history. It is based entirely on a composition by Erik Satie, his *Socrate* of 1918. This work is a symphonic drama in three parts for voices and orchestra, the text taken from the dialogues of Plato. *Socrate* is considered by many to be Satie's masterwork, and, as one might expect, it was a work beloved by Cage. In 1947 Cage made a two-piano arrangement of the first part of *Socrate*, which was used as the accompaniment for a solo dance by Merce Cunningham entitled *Idyllic Song*. In 1968 he went on to make an arrangement for two pianos of the remaining two parts of the drama, and encouraged Cunningham to go back and similarly extend his 1947 choreography.[1] Cunningham decided to go along with this, and the new dance, consisting of the original 1947 solo plus two new ensemble dances made in a similar style, was to be premiered in early 1970. In December of 1969, however, a problem arose. Editions Max Eschig, the holder of the copyright for *Socrate*, denied Cage the permission to use his two-piano arrangement. Rather than cancel the premiere of the dance, Cage set out to compose a new piece to take the place of *Socrate*. However, because Cunningham's choreography followed the phrase structure of the Satie, Cage was not able to compose a completely independent piece, as he was accustomed to doing for Cunningham's more recent dances. What he did was to make a piece with the rhythms and phrases of *Socrate*, but with the pitches so altered that he could stay clear of any copyright problems. He called his composition *Cheap Imitation*; in response, Cunningham called his new dance *Second Hand*.[2]

In *Cheap Imitation*, Satie's symphonic drama is reduced to a single melodic line played on the piano. This line was made mainly by altering the voice part of

Example 6–1 Erik Satie, *Socrate* and John Cage, *Cheap Imitation*: I, bars 11–20

Socrate, although in places Cage used orchestral music as the basis for his work. Satie's music was altered by transposing it at random, using two different procedures. In the first movement, for each phrase of the original Satie, Cage used the *I Ching* to choose one of the seven "white note" modes (ionian, dorian, phrygian, etc.) and one of the twelve chromatic notes to act as tonic for that mode. Then, for each note of the melody, he randomly selected which of the seven tones of that particular mode was to be substituted for the original Satie; repeated notes were to be retained as such. An example of the transformation effected by this system is shown in Example 6–1. Note that rests in the original have been removed and converted into extensions of the previous notes. In the second and third parts of the piece, a slightly different system was used. As before, a new mode and tonic were chosen at the start of each phrase, but instead of choosing each note of the melody at random, Cage used the *I Ching* to choose only the first note of each half measure, with the remaining tones maintaining the same intervals as the original relative to this starting-point.[3] Example 6–2, drawn from the second movement of *Socrate* and *Cheap Imitation*, demonstrates the effect of this system. In all three movements, pedalling is added in places to blur some of the phrases, the line is at times doubled at the octave or at two octaves (this occurs almost throughout the entire last movement), and dynamic markings are independent of Satie's. Thus Cage arrived at the desired result: the phrases of Satie's

163

Example 6–2   Erik Satie, *Socrate* and John Cage, *Cheap Imitation*: II, bars 7–12

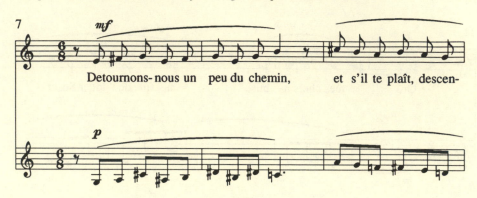

Detournons- nous un   peu du chemin,   et s'il te plaît, descen-

-dons   le long des bords   de l'I- lis-   sus.

music are intact rhythmically, but are, in almost every other way, completely unrecognizable. *Cheap Imitation*, however, has the spirit of Satie: the transparent simplicity of a single line, aimlessly and gently wandering from bar to bar.

As with *0' 00"*, *Cheap Imitation* seems completely unrelated to the works that immediately precede it. *HPSCHD* is the piece written just before it, but nothing could be further from that multimedia spectacle than this quiet, monophonic piano piece. *Cheap Imitation* lacks even that perennial component of Cage's work of that time, an electronic amplification system. But perhaps above all else, *Cheap Imitation* distances itself from the works of the 1960s in its being a *composition* – a composition in the old sense of the word, that which Cage had completely abandoned in 1962. In fact, with its severe limitations, modal melodies, traditional notation, and easily grasped contours, *Cheap Imitation* is even more of a recognizable composition than the chance works of the early 1950s.

The question arises, then: why did he make this piece? The answer that immediately comes to mind is that Cage wrote *Cheap Imitation* because he *had* to: it was no more than a response to the legal problems with his two-piano transcription of *Socrate*. But it should be recalled that the entire *Socrate/Cheap*

164

Imitation/Idyllic Song/Second Hand project was begun at Cage's instigation; one might just as well ask why he felt the need in 1968 to finish his two-piano transcription of *Socrate*. And whether or not *Cheap Imitation* started out as a purely expedient way of providing music for Cunningham's choreography, Cage didn't just let the matter drop there: he fell in love with the piece and the technique used to produce it. "I was so infatuated with my imitation of Satie," he said in 1970, "that I decided to convert it into a work for orchestra."[4] The orchestra version of *Cheap Imitation* was completed in 1972. For each phrase and each note of the single melody line, Cage used chance to determine how many and which instruments would play. Hence, he added nothing to the original piano version: it has just been colored, the orchestral combinations changing from note to note. And Cage wasn't finished there: a transcription of *Cheap Imitation* for solo violin appeared in 1977, made at the request of the violinist Paul Zukofsky. Beyond these transcriptions of the original piece, Cage employed the imitation technique in other compositions. It was used in parts of the *Song Books* (applied not only to the music of Satie, but to Schubert and Mozart as well) and in *Apartment House 1776*.

An alternative interpretation of *Cheap Imitation* is that it represents a giant step backwards in Cage's work: a rejection of the sort of unscripted, uncoordinated electronic spectacles that he had pursued in the 1960s. Certainly many of its features (traditional notation, rhythm, Satie) are things that had faded into the background in his work since the later 1950s, and his reassumption of the role of composer-as-craftsman is a sharp departure from his stated goals of only a few years earlier. But there is no reason to believe that Cage saw this as a conscious move away from what he had done in the past, and considering the reappearance of a 1960s-style use of electronics and theatre in *Song Books* and other works of the 1970s, *Cheap Imitation* cannot be explained as a turning away from the path his work had followed in the previous decade. While it may be tempting to see *Cheap Imitation* as a rejection, it is perhaps best considered as simply something different in Cage's work, a product of his devotion to Satie's music. When asked about the work in 1970, Cage made no apologies for his love of Satie: "Perhaps I could be blamed for my devotion to Satie. But I would never renounce it. . . . If my ideas sink into confusion, I owe that confusion to love."[5]

At the time he composed *Cheap Imitation*, Cage was quite aware of its apparent contradiction of his earlier work. In speaking about the piece with Daniel Charles in late 1970, he seemed troubled – or at least puzzled – by this: "Obviously, *Cheap Imitation* lies outside of what may seem necessary in my work in general, and that's disturbing. I'm the first to be disturbed by it."[6] He went on to make excuses for the piece and his subsequent orchestration of it: that he was only fulfilling commissions, and so on. But if *Cheap Imitation* bothered Cage, it was probably not just because of the piece itself (which he could explain away as an aberration made out of necessity): what took him aback was his unforeseen pleasure in composing and orchestrating it. In justifying it to Charles, the best face he could put on it was that it constituted a "detour" in his work. But later, he came to accept and even enjoy the whole idea of being contradictory. Taking a cue from Zen, he used this as an opportunity to transcend the notion of opposites. References to the acceptability of contradiction – and even its necessity – begin to appear in the 1970–71 installment of his world improvement diary: "Sometimes we blur the distinction between art and life; sometimes we try to clarify it. We don't stand on one leg. We stand on both"; "Do nothing for one reason only. Think it with respect to a large number of other reasons, preferably reasons that're seemingly contradictory." In 1972, in his Foreword to his third volume of essays, *M*, Cage cited Duchamp as an example of self-contradiction:

> A paper bag, a cigar, my membership card in Czechoslovakia's mushroom society, anything became a work of art simply because Duchamp was willing to sign it. At the same time he spent the last twenty years of his life making the most rigorously controlled work of art that anyone has ever made [Duchamp's *Etant donnés*]. . . . The extraordinary contradiction between this work and the world around us . . . is the contradiction in which we have the room to live.

It would be too neat, too facile to take the position that Cage deliberately pursued self-contradiction as a new aesthetic goal. From his comments to Daniel Charles in 1970, it is clear that he did not really understand or even fully accept the more traditional aspects of *Cheap Imitation* until later. Instead, it seems as if he composed *Cheap Imitation* without really thinking about the consequences, and it was only his strong positive reaction to it – a piece that by all rights he should have rejected – that led him to pay attention to the notion of contradiction. *Cheap Imitation* reminded Cage that there was more than one way to be a composer; that the things that drew him to Satie and *Socrate* in 1945 were still of value in 1970. *Cheap Imitation* has the air of being an unexpected encounter with an old friend one hadn't heard from in years; it reminded Cage that he certainly had changed, but that there was a good deal of his past work that was still alive within him.

Stylistic diversity: *Song Books*

Cheap Imitation was something of a jolt for Cage; the work that followed it, the massive *Song Books* of 1970, was the next step. A diverse work, it proceeds from the premise that contradictory styles and motives are to be embraced. Its subtitle – *Solos for Voice 3–92* – indicates that its ninety solos represent the continuation of the *Solo for Voice* series begun in 1958 as part of the *Concert for Piano and Orchestra*. Under the pressure of a deadline, Cage planned and composed this enormous amount of music (the score is 317 pages long) in only three months, completing the work in October of 1970. At the outset, he decided on a theme for the *Song Books*, a line taken from his 1969 world-improvement diary: "We connect Satie with Thoreau." Its meaning was unclear to him in 1969, and he took the opportunity of the *Song Books* commission to elaborate and explore the connections between Satie and Thoreau.

For each of the ninety solos of the *Song Books*, Cage used the *I Ching* to determine whether the solo would be relevant or irrelevant to his theme. Relevant solos contained references to Satie or Thoreau in some way, while irrelevant solos could be related to other people of interest to Cage (such as Marcel Duchamp or James Joyce), or they could lack any outside references at all. The *I Ching* was also used to determine into which of the following four categories each solo would fall: song (that is, a primarily sung piece), song using electronics, theatre (that is, *not* involving singing, but instead consisting of actions), and theatre using electronics. Cage then repeated the procedure he had used in the *Concert for Piano and Orchestra* to determine the compositional methods to be used in each solo. The *I Ching* determined whether each piece was to be composed using a method already employed in the *Song Books*, whether it was to use a variant of a previous method, or whether a wholly new method was to be invented for it. The effect of this system was the same as it had been in the *Concert for Piano and Orchestra*: to force Cage to invent new ways of working and thus to push himself beyond what he already knew into what he had never tried.

The result of this approach was that the solos of the *Song Books* encompass over fifty different methods of composition. Some are duplications of styles that Cage had used in the past. Solo 49, for example, revives the simple vocal line and closed piano accompaniment of *The Wonderful Widow of Eighteen Springs*. The 1950s are represented by new pieces following the models of the *Solo for Voice 1* (Solos 12, 13, 59, 66), *Aria* (Solos 52 and 53), and *Winter Music* (Solos 45 and 48). Cage's more recent works of the 1960s appear in the *Song Books* as well, with some five instances of *0′ 00″* scattered throughout the work. Parts of *Cheap Imitation* appear (with texts taken from Thoreau) in Solos 18 and 30, and the same method of composition is used elsewhere, applied to works by Schubert and Mozart.[7]

Besides repeating compositional methods he had employed in the past, Cage used similar techniques in new and different ways in the *Song Books*. The instructions of Solo 41 ("Produce feedback three times") recalls the use of electronics and the acceptance of feedback in some of Cage's performances of the 1960s. Star charts are used in several of the solos. They replace the use of *Fontana Mix* materials in composing the *Aria*-like solos, for example. In Solo 11 (Example 6–3), star maps were used to generate pitches, although only in a high tessitura, leading Cage to call this solo and others like it "coloratura songs." In Solo 40 (Example 6–4), the star-points were connected to form arabesques.

In addition to these repetitions and variations of past compositional methods, there are solos in the *Song Books* that do not resemble anything that Cage had done before. There is a whole family of theatrical solos that involve exiting and entering the performance area. The first of these (Solo 32) simply indicates that the performer should leave and then return hurriedly. Later variants call for the performer to exit and return by going up or down (e.g., by using a ladder or a

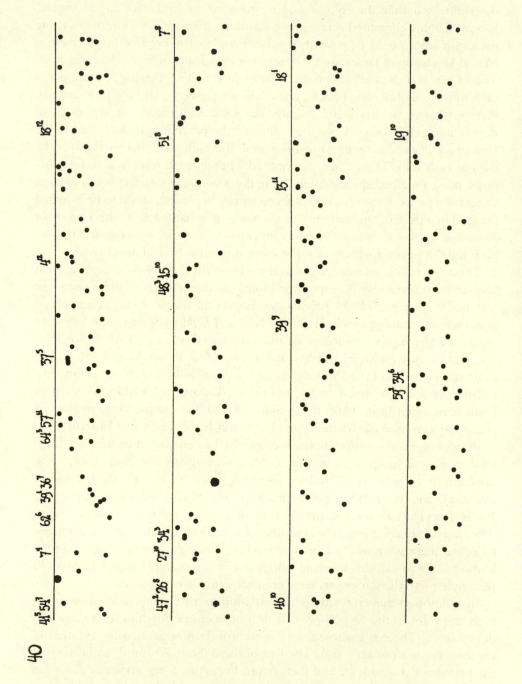

Example 6–3 *Song Books*: Solo 11 (excerpt)

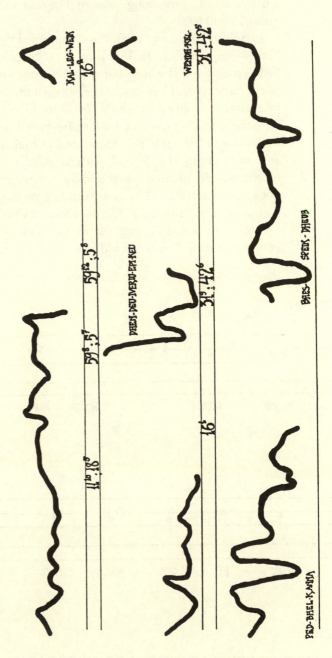

Example 6-4 *Song Books*: Solo 40 (excerpt)

134

trapdoor), by going through the audience, by means of some sort of wheeled conveyance, or wearing an animal's head. Other theatrical solos involve such simple actions as eating or drinking (in Solos 36, 38, 46, 82, and 89), putting on a hat (Solo 78), projecting slides of Thoreau and Satie (Solo 81), and typing (in Solos 15 and 69).

In Solo 85 (Example 6–5), Cage continued the idea of making "imitations" of Satie's music, in this case by making "rubbings" of Satie chorales. Here he used Satie's music as if it were a star map. Superimposing a larger musical staff on top of the Satie score, Cage traced the notes of the Satie, thus generating a different, microtonal, "rubbed" melody. In Solo 35 – one of the least Cagean of the set – the singer is presented with thirty-two different pairs of musical fragments, each marked "A" and "B". These are to be taken as the halves of a binary piece, and sung using the formal pattern AABA. The music (Example 6–6) is conventionally notated, rhythmically square, and melodically limited to a six-note range; the text ("The best form of government is no government at all") is a paraphrase of Thoreau's "On the Duty of Civil Disobedience." Cage indicates that this solo should be sung "in an optimistic spirit as though you believe what you are singing," and should "be used as an irregular 'refrain' in a given

Example 6–5 *Song Books*: Solo 85 (excerpt)

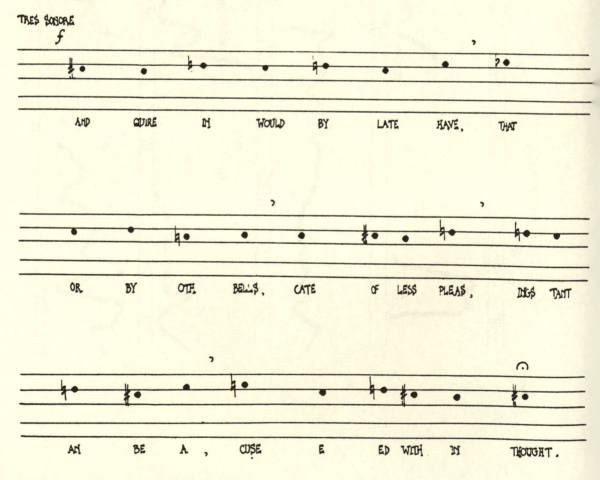

Example 6–6 *Song Books*: Solo 35 (excerpt)

A'S

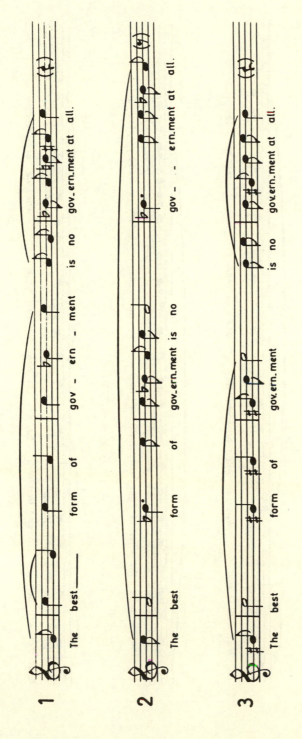

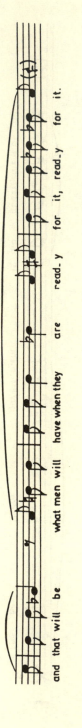

performance." Before singing it, the performer is instructed by Cage to "raise either the black flag of Anarchy or the flag of the Whole Earth."

This is just part of the diversity found in the *Song Books*. It is a piece that is impossible to characterize in any brief description – a piece which juxtaposes the old and the new, determinacy and indeterminacy, the subtly-crafted melodies of *The Wonderful Widow of Eighteen Springs* and the galumphing cheers of the "Best Form" songs. The theatrical parts of the piece range from the ordinary to the inexplicable. Cage's description is as good as any: "To consider the *Song Books* as a work of art is nearly impossible. Who would dare? It resembles a brothel, doesn't it?"[8] One really has to study the score and to witness a performance of the *Song Books* to begin to get a picture of it, and even then it stays just beyond one's ability to grasp it entirely.[9]

Thus, the *Song Books* is a work that ignores history: old and new styles exist all at once. That Cage could create such a piece demonstrates his abandonment of the idea that his work should necessarily develop in one direction. This was perhaps the most important turn of events in his music after 1970: if *Cheap Imitation* and the *Song Books* are rejections in any way at all, if they mark a change of course, then it is in their rejection of the idea of stylistic progression. In all Cage's work up to this point, if there was one constant, it was his need to embrace new ideas and new techniques. In the 1960s, his objection to being famous was that people wanted him to repeat himself, to keep him from moving on. After 1970, this attitude seems to fade somewhat; rather than move ever forward, Cage takes as his goal to "do so many things no one will know what you're going to do next."[10]

The change of attitude can be dramatically illustrated by comparing the two essays titled "The Future of Music," one written in 1937 (and cited in chapter one) and the other in 1974. In 1937, Cage predicted that, as a result of new electronic instruments, the increased use of noises would be the predominant development in future music. As a result, the old methods of writing music based on pitches (such as tonal harmony) would be found to be "inadequate" and would be replaced. What is most characteristic about this 1937 essay is that it envisions a *single* music of the future, a point to which the then-current use of percussion was heading. In 1974, when Cage writes about the future of music, he seems to go out of his way to mention as many completely contradictory styles as possible. The essay is an optimistic description of the possibility of open-mindedness; in it, Cage says approving things about composers as disparate as Elliott Carter, Philip Glass, Frederic Rzewski, Charles Dodge, Nam June Paik, and Pierre Boulez. Cage defines music as being "work," and sees a myriad of composers and performers working to develop new technologies and other new musical resources; to change the relationship of composers, performers, and audiences; to change society at large; to change people's minds and spirits. Where in the 1930s Cage saw artistic change as moving in a single direction, and as being concerned primarily with matters of compositional technique, in the 1970s he saw change as taking place in many directions and many domains simultaneously. The situation, in his view, no longer resembled a stream or river, but now resembled the ocean, limitless and full of currents and cross-currents.

It is this attitude that makes Cage's later work so difficult to describe historically; like the *Song Books*, his activity after 1970 is impossible to summarize. Any blanket statement one might make about these pieces is surely doomed to fail. In *Cheap Imitation*, *Hymns and Variations*, and *Ryoanji* his work is simpler and sparser; but what about the complexities of *Song Books*, *Roaratorio*, and the *Europeras*? Beginning with *Mureau*, he seems to be more interested in writing and poetry-based compositions (such as *Roaratorio* or *Essay*); but what about the various sets of etudes or the "number" pieces? Styles appear, disappear, and reappear in Cage's work without any apparent connections. One cannot even say he goes through periods – a technique might be used at intervals of several years, during which intervals there occur three or four other types of composition. The most that one can say about any given compositional technique or style is that it is the one that Cage used to make some particular piece or group of pieces; one cannot say that it has a privileged position over other techniques or styles that he may have been using at the same time in other works. It is as if he had fulfilled the promise of "Lecture on Something":

> There is not one of the somethings that is not acceptable. When this is meant one is in accord with life, and paradoxically free to pick and choose again . . . New picking and choosing is just like the old picking and choosing except that one takes as just another one of the somethings any consequence of having picked and chosen.

I feel that Cage's ability to pick and choose among disparate styles in his work after 1970 was due at least in part to his getting older. In 1972 he turned sixty; he had been composing, experimenting with new media and new techniques for almost forty years. In surveying his later compositions, writings, and visual artworks, I sense that, at age sixty, Cage realized that he need do nothing more than what he felt like doing. His work, although inconsistent and beyond characterization, was that of an artist completely at ease with his various personae: the lover of Satie and the lover of technology, McLuhan, and Fuller; the explorer of new sonic frontiers and the hunter of mushrooms; the anarchist who wants to change society and the Zen devotee who wants only to change his mind. On top of all this, Cage continued to possess an overwhelming urge to do things he had not done before – not necessarily to do the *next* thing, but always a *different* thing.

After devoting himself to new ideas for four decades, Cage may have decided that this was no longer necessary. A particular exchange with Daniel Charles in *For the Birds* demonstrates this clearly, and suggests the diversity of Cage's work to come. Cage mentions the work of a molecular biologist who had asserted that all the important work in the arts and sciences had been completed; "that doesn't mean that we don't need to compose new music," Cage says, "but new ideas on music are no longer necessary." Cage continues, pointing out that "in a sense, everything is finished, everything has been discovered and tested." When Charles connects such stasis with "impoverishment," Cage objects, claiming that what he has been referring to is a state of *abundance*, not poverty. The situation he foresees – and in which he obviously takes great pleasure – is one in which the various arts and styles "intermingle in a climate very rich with joy and – I am purposely using an expression frequent in Japanese texts – bewilderment."[11]

Work in other media

In speaking of "joy and bewilderment" in the passage above, Cage is referring specifically to the mingling of different arts and disciplines. In this respect, he is speaking of his own work, in which he not only embraces multiple styles and methods, but branches out into other media – specifically, writing and visual arts. Of course, Cage had always had a strong interest and reputation in these fields: by 1970, two volumes of his writings had been published, and his musical manuscripts had been exhibited as graphic art works in galleries. But after 1970, his interest in these areas intensified, and he began to make writings, etchings, and paintings that were totally unrelated to music – works whose origins were not in musical works, whose techniques were not derived from his compositional practice, and were not designed to be musical in any sense. However, because the bulk of Cage's work was musical – because he was primarily a composer – his work in poetry and art inevitably came back into his music, providing him with ideas and themes for new compositions. My concern here is with Cage's music more than his writing or art: I will deal only briefly with these other media, particularly with the transactions between literary and visual media and music.

Writing

Before 1970, Cage was inclined to apply his compositional techniques to the task of making lectures or essays, so that these might thus become not only writings about his work, but demonstrations of it. Thus, one finds him using rhythmic structure in "Lecture on Nothing," chance in the "Juilliard Lecture" and "45' for a Speaker," simultaneity in "Where Are We Going? and What Are We Doing?" and amplification in *Talk I*. In these lectures, Cage applied his approach to music: in particular, he substituted the *subjects* of his writings for the *sounds* of his music. Thus the structure of "Lecture on Nothing" controls which aspect of music he will discuss, and the chance procedures of "45' for a Speaker" determine which topic to write about and for how long. After 1970, Cage felt the need to do more than this; as he told Daniel Charles: "I must say that I have not yet carried language to the point to which I have taken musical sounds. I have not made noise with it."[12] As a result, he began to pursue writing with more purely artistic goals – he began to write poetry, not communicative or demonstrative prose.

Cage saw the solution to this problem as lying in the approach to the materials of language: sentences, words, letters. In particular, he saw his failure to create "noise" with language as being the result of dealing solely at the level of sentences or phrases – i.e., larger units of meaning:

> As soon as you surpass the level of the word, everything changes; my essays in [*Silence* and *A Year From Monday*] didn't deal with the question of the impossibility or possibility of *meaning*. They took for granted that meaning exists.[13]

Cage experimented with manipulating smaller units of language in creating the texts for some of the solos in the *Song Books*. In Solo 5, for example, the text was made from a chance-determined mix of letters and syllables taken from a single page of Thoreau's journal, producing lines such as "a e whis not m ct th t s for e eat."

Immediately after the *Song Books*, Cage began work on a large-scale text that employed similar procedures: *Mureau*. Once again, Cage drew upon Thoreau's journals. In this case, he made a listing of all the references in the journal to sounds, silence, and music, and used only these portions as the source material for the new text. The title reflects this selective use of the journals, being a combination of the words "music" and "Thoreau." Cage identified five types of material in the journal: sentences, phrases, words, syllables, and letters. As he wrote *Mureau*, he used the *I Ching* to select the type and amount of material to use, and to select the precise element from the journal passages he had listed. Elements could then be connected to one another (thus forming nonsense words) or not, and the typeface was selected at random as well. The text occasionally makes sense, but mostly does not, as in the following excerpt:

> They hear muttering, crashing in muggy air mid-heaven Sound travels round, invades, advancing at grand pace rkI heard it vibrating high overhead She hears a snoring, praying soundsand, etc. eLedum hourafaspiringlifeblack mio ina singlyraisedthe but thehear ndng sthat toh fa nothingisef withintermittentp sofhear.

The theme of sound and music comes through clearly throughout, owing to Cage's having chosen only certain related passages of the journal as source material.

The text *Empty Words*, written in 1974, is a continuation of the *Mureau* idea on a larger scale. It was written using a similar method, but drawing on the entire fourteen volumes of Thoreau's journal, not just selected passages. Rather than present the text in blocks, as he had done with *Mureau*, in *Empty Words* Cage divided the text at random into lines and stanzas, based on the punctuation marks found in the original journal. The work as a whole is divided into four parts, which form a progression in terms of the kinds of materials used: the first part uses phrases, words, syllables, and letters; the second uses words, syllables, and letters; the third uses syllables and letters, and the fourth is made up solely of letters drawn at random from the journal. The effect of this is that the text makes less and less sense – it changes from something that is recognizably drawn from a work of literature to a pure vocalise with more and more empty space around each event. In the publication of the text, Cage included reproductions of drawings from Thoreau's journal, as well; these were chosen at random and distributed among the columns of text.

Both *Mureau* and *Empty Words* have a dual musical–poetic nature: these are poems that are meant to be read aloud, not silently. In this regard, as well as in his use of chance to manipulate language, Cage drew upon the work of poets such as Jackson MacLow. Cage performed *Mureau* and *Empty Words* on various occasions. In *Empty Words*, his idea was to time the reading so that it would last all night long; at dawn, the fourth and final part was to commence and the windows were to be opened, allowing the morning sounds into the performance hall. During the performance, slides of Thoreau's drawings were projected.

Mureau and *Empty Words* thus straddle the line between poetry and music. Later texts by Cage are more fully literary, and are based on a technique that has no musical parallels at all: the mesostic. The principle of a mesostic is simple: a name, word, or phrase serves as a "key" for the text to be written. This key is embedded in the poem, and Cage points out its letters by capitalizing them and aligning the lines of the poem so that they run down the middle. As an example, here is a mesostic poem titled "July 13, 1972," written for an airline hostess and using her name (Verena) as the key:

> aViary without birds
> (airplanE
>   fRom frankfurt
>   to basEl), hostess
>   recogNized me,
>   Asked for a poem.

Thus, the basic rule of a mesostic is to capitalize the first instance one comes across of each key letter in order. Cage originally called these poems "acrostics," but later used the term "mesostic" at the suggestion of Norman O. Brown, who pointed out that in an acrostic, the key word is spelled out down the left side, not the middle.[14]

Cage found the mesostic technique a useful discipline for his writing. The earliest mesostics were simply gifts to friends, occasional pieces written freely on the spot. In the later 1960s, he began writing groups of mesostics on a particular subject ("mesostic Re"), or groups in which some mesostics pertain to a given subject, while others are irrelevant to that subject ("mesostics Re and not Re"). The earliest examples of this are the "36 Mesostics Re and not Re Marcel Duchamp" of 1970, followed by mesostic sets about Mark Tobey (1972), Norman O. Brown (1977), and others.

These mesostics are all consciously-written poems; in the 1970s Cage began using mesostics as a way of rearranging an existing text, much as he had in *Mureau* and *Empty Words*. The first such use was in his "Writing Through *Finnegans Wake*" (1977). Cage realized that he could start at any point in Joyce's novel and use its words to make mesostics on any key he chose. In this case, he used

"JAMES JOYCE" as the key, and "wrote through" the entire novel from front to back. He included not just the words necessary to spell out the key, but also a certain amount of their original context, the exact amount chosen according to his tastes, but within the restrictions of the mesostic form. Thus this passage from page 627 of *Finnegans Wake*:

> Just a whisk brisk sly spry spink spank sprint of a thing theresomere, saultering. Saltarella come to her own. I pity your oldself I was used to. Now a younger's there. Try not to part! Be happy, dear ones! May I be wrong! For she'll be sweet for you as I was sweet when I came down out of me mother. My great blue bedroom, the air so quiet, scarce a cloud. In peace and silence.

Becomes the following mesostic:

> Just a whisk
> Of
> pitY
> a Cloud
> in pEace and silence.[15]

After the first "Writing Through *Finnegans Wake*." Cage wrote three more, using slightly different rules for finding mesostics.[16] Later, Cage applied the same procedure to the Cantos of Ezra Pound (1982), Kafka's *Die Verwandlung* (1983), Duchamp's *Notes* (1984), and Thoreau's "On the Duty of Civil Disobedience" (1985). He also developed a kind of "global" form of "writing through," in which the words of the source text are not used in their original order to form the mesostics. Instead, words fulfilling the mesostic rules are chosen at random from the entire text. Cage's "62 Mesostics Re Merce Cunningham" (1971) is a precursor to this method, with its words drawn at random from Cunningham's writings and other books. Texts written in this fashion include a number of shorter poems, such as "Mirakus[2]" (1984, based on Duchamp's notes) and "Sonnekus[2]" (1985, based on the Book of Genesis), as well as longer writings such as "Anarchy" (1988, based on the writings of various anarchist writers) and the book-length *I–VI* (1988, based on a wide range of literature including Wittgenstein and *The New York Times*). Cage's overall goal in such "writings through" was "to explore a way of writing which though coming from ideas is not about them, or is not about ideas but produces them." By following the mesostic key strings through his chosen source materials, Cage saw himself as being "in a forest hunting for ideas."[17]

While some of his writings (particularly the later mesostic-based texts such as *I–VI*) have no strong connection to Cage's musical works, many contributed in some way or another to his music. Most public performances by Cage in his later years, for example, consisted of his reading from his poetry. In some cases these readings were quite straightforward, but others involved a sort of enhanced or musical form of recitation. In reading *Mureau* or *Empty Words*, for example, Cage would change the pitch, tempo, and timbre of his reading; the result bordered on singing. Given such performance circumstances, it is difficult to say whether *Mureau* and *Empty Words* are musical compositions or poetry. Neither work is listed in the catalog of his music publisher, although the *62 Mesostics Re Merce Cunningham*, a text that Cage also performed with a very musical style of reading, is published as a musical score.

Cage also used his texts in a more traditional musical fashion: he set them as songs. It will be recalled that his first experiments in poetry had as their objective the production of texts for certain of the solos in the *Song Books*. While some of these texts were set in rather unusual ways (in Solo 65, a tracing of the profile of Marcel Duchamp is to be used to generate a vocal line for the text), others are quite tame. In Solo 91, fifteen of the "26 Mesostics Re and not Re Marcel Duchamp" are set using a simple four-note collection of pitches, the results being quite similar to *The Wonderful Widow of Eighteen Springs*. Later vocal works to draw upon Cage's texts include *Eight Whiskus* (1984), *Mirakus²* (1984), *Selkus²* (1984), and *Sonnekus²* (1985). In pieces such as these, Cage attempted to make a musical version of the mesostic. Different series of all twelve tones form the "keys" to *Mirakus²*, and a passage from Satie's *Socrate* is the key to the *Sonnekus²*. The notes of these musical mesostic keys are used to set the syllables of the text that contain the literary mesostic key, so that the two keys both run down the middle of the scores.

In two instances, Cage's writings served as the basis for musical compositions in a more unusual way. In *Roaratorio* (1979), the second "writing through" *Finnegans Wake* served as both musical material and as structural guide. The work, a composition for magnetic tape, is a translation of Joyce's 628-page novel into sound. Making use of the abundant indices, gazetteers, and other specialized inventories for *Finnegans Wake*, Cage listed all the references to sounds and music in the book, then grouped them into various categories and made chance-determined selections from these. Similarly, a random selection was made from the huge number of place-names found in the book. With the help of others world-wide, Cage then collected all these sounds on tape, finding instances of all the specific sounds mentioned (such as bells, dogs barking, water running, etc.), and recording ambient noises at all the places mentioned.

The tapes were then assembled and mixed. The first step was to record Cage reading the entire text of "Writing for the Second Time Through *Finnegans Wake*." This tape served as the template for the placement of the other recorded sounds. Since Cage's text goes through the entire book from start to finish, and includes running page references to the original, the recorded sounds could be easily superimposed upon the reading of Cage's text at the exact point that they are referred to in Joyce's book. Thus, the piece opens with the sound of a viola d'amore ("Sir Tristram, violer d'amores, fr'over the short sea") and closes with the cries of gulls ("Whish! A gull. Gulls. Far calls. Coming, far!"). Chance controlled the duration of sounds, their relative loudnesses, and other aspects of the mixing process. Several multi-track tapes were made in this fashion and then mixed together, along with recordings of Irish folk musics, to form a single two-track tape. The effect of this is a thick, joyous collage of sounds, music, and reading – as the subtitle explains, this is "An Irish Circus on *Finnegans Wake.*" Although Cage later published an "*a posteriori*" score for the work which generalizes the process so that it could be applied to any book at all, it is hard to imagine any novel that would be as perfectly set by such an incomprehensible, phantasmagoric soundscape as this.

A more austere musical work, also based on Cage's reading of his own poetry, is *Essay* (1985–86), realized at the computer music studio directed by Charles Dodge at Brooklyn College. In this case, the literary work in question is Cage's writing through Thoreau's "On the Duty of Civil Disobedience"; this text is actually a set of eighteen different "writings through" of various lengths, using *Messe des Pauvres* (the title of a work by Satie) as the mesostic key. Recordings were made of Cage reading all eighteen of these texts at a normal, constant rate of delivery; since the texts themselves are of different lengths, the recordings ranged from thirty seconds to twenty minutes in duration. These tapes were taken to the Brooklyn College studios where a team of young computer musicians (composer Frances White, audio engineer Victor Friedberg, and computer technician Kenneth Worthy) used the speech analysis-synthesis technique of linear predictive coding to expand or contract each of the eighteen sections in time (but without altering the pitch) so that they all had the identical duration of sixteen minutes and forty-seven seconds (this duration having been arrived at by chance). Thus in the tracks based on shorter segments, single words can drone on for minutes, while the speech of the longest segment is clipped and hurried. These eighteen tracks of tape were used in a number of different works. In *Essay*, they were simply mixed together to form an almost impenetrable wall of sound. In the work *Voiceless Essay*, only the consonant sounds – the "unvoiced" vocal sounds – were used; the silent spaces where the vowels had been make the result much lighter, sparse, and airy. Finally, the tapes of individual tracks of *Essay* were used for an installation in a church in Kassel in 1987.

Visual art

The other artistic field Cage became involved in was the visual arts, especially printmaking and etching, but also drawings and watercolors. His visual sense was always acute, and he had strong connections with artists of various sorts. But although he lectured at the Artists' Club, befriended Robert Rauschenberg and Jasper Johns, and played chess daily with Marcel Duchamp, Cage did very little work himself in the visual art field until the late 1970s.

This is not to say that there is no purely visual interest in Cage's musical scores or his poetic texts; quite to the contrary, these works have themselves been

Example 6–7   *Song Books*: Solo 43 (excerpt)

et tout cela m'est advenu par la faute de la musique .

exhibited as works of art in their own right. Even in his earliest scores, the layout and calligraphy was meticulous and considered. The *Seven Haiku* of 1952 are a particularly striking example of this: the decision to use an unusual oblong format with a single line of music taking up just the very bottom of each page has nothing at all to do with the music, but everything to do with a sense of visual style and effect. The later graphic notations, such as those in the *Concert for Piano and Orchestra*, have an obvious visual appeal, even though they were not necessarily designed with visual impact as a prime consideration. These notations, along with other Cage scores, were exhibited in a New York art gallery in 1958 (in conjunction with the twenty-five-year retrospective concert), and exhibits of Cage scores have taken place at various times since then.

Cage's texts, too, have features designed for purely visual interest. Many writers have noted the unusual typography and layout of his lectures and essays. In some cases, such as "Lecture on Nothing" or "45′ for a Speaker," the unusual graphic features reflect performance considerations. In other cases, however, visual interest is pursued for its own sake. In the 1957 "2 Pages, 122 Words on Music and Dance" a random layout of the text fragments was made, and in the "world improvement" diaries, the line lengths and typefaces are constantly changing. The use of different typefaces in Cage's texts reaches an extreme in some of the solos from the *Song Books* and in the *62 Mesostics Re Merce Cunningham*. Example 6–7 is an excerpt from Solo 43 of the *Song Books*, with text by Erik Satie. The accompanying performance note for this solo gives no indication as to the meaning of the changing typefaces, but in other solos, Cage

Example 6–8   *62 Mesostics Re Merce Cunningham* (excerpt)

has used changes in typeface to suggest changes in sound – the typeface becomes another aspect of the notation. In the *62 Mesostics Re Merce Cunningham* (one of which is shown in Example 6–8), each *letter* is set in a different typeface, making even more of a visual impact – to the point of being nearly illegible (a key, given as part of the score, is necessary to read the texts). Cage described these poems as being less "texts" than they are "waterfalls" or "ideograms."[18]

The *62 Mesostics Re Merce Cunningham* were meant to be considered as poetry (or, in their electronically amplified declamation, as music); a similar project, *Not Wanting to Say Anything About Marcel* (1969) was the first work that Cage intended as a visual art object from the very beginning. Made with the assistance of Calvin Sumsion, *Not Wanting to Say Anything About Marcel* is made up of randomly-chosen text fragments set in randomly-chosen typefaces. In addition, Cage used chance to decide whether letters would remain whole or would be partially or completely erased. The resulting fragments were arranged at random on sheets of plexiglas; eight of these plexiglas sheets mounted parallel to one another constituted the work (four different constructions of eight sheets were made and produced in limited edition). The extreme complexity of the visual elements, especially when eight layers are viewed simultaneously, pushes the graphic element of the text to its limit – from poetry into visual art.

Empty Words contains drawings as accompaniments to the text; this is a more direct approach to making visual art than any seen thus far, since it does not derive from some visual heightening of text or music. The drawings are all taken, like the text of *Empty Words*, from the journals of Henry David Thoreau. Thoreau's journals are full of little sketches of various things that interested him: bird and animal tracks, plants, patterns of cracks in ice. In designing the layout of *Empty Words*, each two-page opening was divided into four columns, two with text, and two with drawings. Which columns would contain drawings, how many, which ones, and their locations were all determined by chance. Few of the Thoreau drawings are recognizable when presented out of the context of the journal. The result of their random selection and placement in *Empty Words* is what Cage described as a trip "through a museum on roller skates" – they *suggest* rather than illustrate.

Inspired by his discovery of Thoreau's drawings, Cage went on to use them in his musical works. *Score (40 Drawings by Thoreau) and 23 Parts: 12 Haiku* (1974) was made by arranging Thoreau drawings randomly. This score consists of twelve lines subdivided into seventeen segments (Example 6–9); these are grouped into three sections of five, seven, and five segments, thus following the syllable structure of Japanese *haiku* poetry. The Thoreau drawings superimposed on this score are then parceled out among the twenty-three parts: when the ensemble plays together, all the drawings are fully realized in sound. A similar procedure was used to make *Renga* (1976), this time using the 5–7–5–7–7 structure of *renga* poetry, filled with 361 drawings, and distributed among 78 instruments. Finally, Thoreau drawings, printed in negative as white-on-black, make the images seen on the "lightning" film that accompanies *Lecture on the Weather* (1975).

Example 6–9   *Score (40 Drawings by Thoreau) and 23 Parts: 12 Haiku*, score (excerpt)

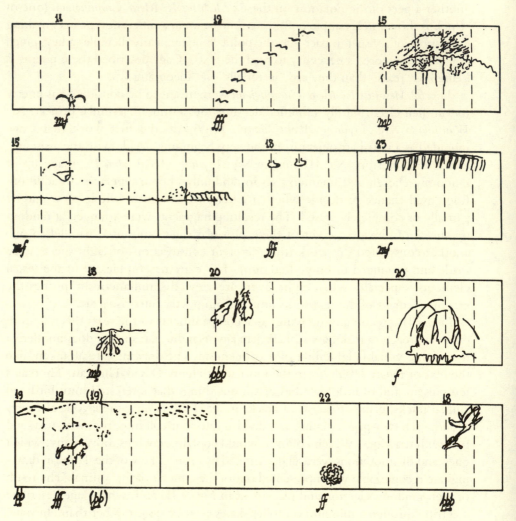

In 1978, Cage was invited by Kathan Brown to work at Crown Point Press in California. In this way Cage began his career as a printmaker, working with etchings and monotypes; he returned regularly for the rest of his life. In the beginning of his work at Crown Point Press, Cage relied heavily on the drawings of Thoreau. His first project was simply to make a colored print of the score of *Score (40 Drawings by Thoreau)*. In *17 Drawings by Thoreau* (1978), the drawings were enlarged and arranged randomly on the page. Twenty-five different prints were made by changing the colors (also selected by chance) of these images. In *Signals* (1978), the same procedures were followed, except that circles and straight lines are added to the drawings as possible elements, and the thirty-six prints are all of different images. Cage added more and different elements to his prints over the next few years, continuing to rely on random placement of the images – they float over the available space – and randomly-chosen colors.

With *On the Surface* (1980–82), Cage made his first prints that did not use Thoreau drawings as their source. Here, randomly-cut plates of scrap copper were used. For each of the thirty-six etchings he used the *I Ching* to determine how many and which of the sixty-four plates would be used, where and at what angle they would be placed. There is an imaginary horizon line in each print; it lies at the top of the page in the first etching, and moves down gradually to the golden mean point by the last. No plates were allowed to extend above this horizon. If, by its random placement, a plate would extend above the horizon, that plate was cut at that point, thus creating more and smaller plates. No images were engraved on the plates at all, but any random scratches that happened to occur during the printmaking process were accepted. The results are very subtle: only the pale outlines of the plates show up in the prints, along with the tiny scratches and imperfections. The near-invisibility of the images and the use of a gradually falling horizon suggest the inspiration for this piece, a quotation from Thoreau: "All sound is nearly akin to silence, it is a bubble on the surface which straightaway bursts."

Although etchings dominated his work in the visual arts, Cage pursued many other projects; I can only indicate a few here. In the series *Where R = Ryoanji* (1983) he began drawing. His method of drawing was automatic: he took smooth stones, placed them on paper, and then drew around their outlines. He used this method, with placement and densities of rocks controlled by chance, to make both etchings and pencil drawings. In 1985, he made the series of monotypes *Fire*, using a hot iron teapot to scorch the paper, thus making circles of differing intensities. In 1988, he was invited by Ray Kass of the Virginia Polytechnic Institute for a residency to produce watercolor paintings. Cage made fifty-two paintings, the *New River Watercolors*, using his rock-drawing technique in conjunction with watercolor washes.

Just as his poetry had done, Cage's work in the visual arts had its effect on his musical works. An early and direct example of this is *Thirty Pieces for Five Orchestras* (1981). The compositional process here was derived from the method used in the *On the Surface* etchings. A piece of cardboard the size of one score page was cut up at random, producing a large number of unique templates, much like the copper plates of *On the Surface*. Holes were then punched at chance-determined locations in these templates. A different set of templates was made for each of the five independent orchestral groups. For each of the thirty pieces, the *I Ching* was used, as it was in the etchings, to determine which of these templates would be used and in what positions. The notes of the piece were then inscribed through the holes of the templates. No "horizon" line was used here – such a purely visual element would be inappropriate – but a similar effect was produced by distinguishing between those templates that lay wholly within the space of the page and those that extended outside it. The notes of these latter templates were added together to form a single chord, and this chord was then repeated in a randomly-derived ostinato pattern. The notes produced by the other templates were given randomly-chosen durations, pitch inflections, dynamics, vibrato, and so forth. The result of this is that within each piece, there are free curves and outbursts, distinctive and unique, set against the grid of the irregularly repeated sonorities.

Each of the thirty pieces for each orchestra is placed within a flexible time bracket. For each piece, an earliest and latest time is given for its start and end: for example, the first piece can begin anywhere from zero and forty-five seconds elapsed time, and must end at any time between thirty and seventy-five seconds. The unused portion of the time bracket is left silent. Thus the pieces have no fixed locations in time, and can "float" in the brackets allotted them. The overall effect of the five spatially-separated orchestral groups playing both repeated patterns and spontaneous outbursts of sound, all of these overlapping and drifting freely in time, is very similar to the visual effects of some of Cage's prints – the flexible time brackets emulate the freely-moving engraving plates.

The time bracket technique is found in other works. Similar music with time brackets and ostinatos appear in *Dance/4 Orchestras* (1982) and *Thirty Pieces for String Quartet* (1983), but it is *Music for* (1984–87) that extends the principle of the *Thirty Pieces for Five Orchestras* to its fullest extent. Cage envisaged *Music for* as a continual work-in-progress, never to be completed. It was composed one solo part at a time; any number of these parts could be performed simultaneously, the title of the work changing to include the number of performers in a given performance (e.g., *Music for Five*, *Music for Four*, etc.). Each part was written using the same basic method, this method having been computerized so as to speed up the process of composing the pieces. Each part consisted of a number of individual pieces placed within flexible time brackets. These are of two types, designated by Cage as "pieces" and "interludes." Pieces consist of: a single, quiet sustained tone, preceded and followed by silence, and repeated any number of times; or a more complex passage of many notes (chosen from within a limited range of notes), all with different durations (notated in space-equals-time notation) and dynamics; or both of these types of music in succession. The interludes – which, in contrast to the flexible "pieces," are placed within fixed time brackets – consist of phrases which present varying patterns made up of only a handful of notes or sonorities. Example 6–10 is taken from one of the piano solos of *Music for* , and shows the different types of music.

While *Music for* has no immediately apparent connection with Cage's graphic works, the effect of these floating fragments of well-defined and distinctive music – the way they overlap with each other and interact with each other – is, I believe, indebted to his work with etchings. Looking at a series of prints like his *Déreau* (1982), in which five different types of image (a circle, a horizon line, blocks of parallel lines, patches of aquatint, and random curves)

Example 6–10   *Music for*   : Piano I (excerpt)

Example 6–11 *Ryoanji* for oboe (excerpt)

move freely from print to print against a backdrop of Thoreau drawings, one's understanding of *Music for* is enhanced. In hearing the repeated tones, the recurring patterns of the interludes, and the free virtuoso articulations of pitch bands, one can almost *see* these elements as they drift across the space.

These compositions, then, are ones in which we find echoes of the techniques of Cage's graphic works. The results, however, are more or less traditionally notated – the works are not in themselves graphic, as many of Cage's earlier compositions had been. In fact, after *Renga*, almost none of Cage's compositions have graphic elements in their notation. The one exception is *Ryoanji* (1983–85), a series of pieces which stem from his stone drawings and etchings. In the parts for oboe, voice, flute, contrabass, and trombone, the method of drawing around rocks was used to create pitch curves, notated just as they were drawn (see Example 6–11). In some places, these contours overlap, thus rendering them impossible to play on such melody instruments. In these cases, tape recordings are used to allow a single performer to play duets or trios. This music – curves derived from rock contours – is combined with the parts for percussion or a twenty-member instrumental ensemble. These parts consist solely of metrically-notated rhythms, completely irregular in their patterns of beats and rests. In all cases, whether this music is played by a single percussionist or by twenty different instruments in rhythmic unison, the timbre and dynamic of the sound are constant throughout, so that this music is pure rhythm. Once again we have the effect of free material set against a metrical grid, this time in a very stark way.

Program music

Thematic use of musical materials

I have described the compositional techniques used in *Ryoanji*, and this is sufficient to understand the source of part of its musical effectiveness. What I have not explained are Cage's reasons for choosing the materials and techniques that he did. Through his chance compositions, Cage had opened himself and his art to the entire world of sound. Why would he then so limit the possibilities in a piece like *Ryoanji*? And why those *particular* choices – the metrical percussion and the undulating oboe?

The title *Ryoanji* gives the key to understanding Cage's purpose in putting together so limited a sound world. Ryoanji is a famous stone garden in Kyoto, Japan; it consists of fifteen irregularly-shaped rocks placed in a rectangular bed of raked sand. The garden is attached to a Zen temple, and was designed as an object of contemplation, as described by Heinrich Dumoulin:

> Void of all animal life and nearly all vegetation, this stone garden is a symbol of the pure mind purged of all forms – of nothingness or of what Meister Eckhart calls the "desert of the godhead." . . . When the silver moon glides over the white sand, the mind of the contemplative pilgrim is carried to the world

beyond, where there are no opposites and the nothingness of pure divinity dwells in impenetrable light.[19]

It is not hard to imagine the importance of such a place for Cage. The placement of stones within an empty space begs the comparison with Cage's own conception of music as "sounds thrown into silence." Cage visited the garden when he toured Japan, and mentioned it in his writings from the 1950s onwards.[20]

Cage's selection of materials and his choice of compositional methods serve an overall purpose, then: to embody musically his understanding of the Japanese stone garden. The percussion music, dry and metrical, stands for the raked sand; the oboe (or other instrument), irregular and alive, stands for the stones – its contours are even derived from real stones. There is no escaping the deliberation of Cage's choices here, choices made to articulate perfectly the analogy to the garden. This is music with a specific content, that is not just "pure sound." To appropriate a term from a different era, this is a kind of "program music" – music that carries connotations from a world outside of sound and music.

It certainly goes against the predominant view of Cage to have him choosing materials and designing compositional techniques based on ideas, images, or tastes – that is, deliberately. Wasn't Cage the one who declared that he wanted an art that was free of memory and taste, that sounds should be "just sounds" and not tokens for other things? In considering this apparent contradiction, one must keep in mind that these statements, like most of the writings that have been used to define Cage's aesthetic, were made during a particular period in his career – the 1950s. It would be foolish and unreasonable to expect his ideas to remain unchanged over the years, or to assume that he would allow a purism of aesthetics to dictate his compositional work. But even in the 1950s, Cage exerted control over his materials, although he did not control their ultimate arrangement within the compositions. In *Music of Changes*, the contents of the sound charts were entirely the product of Cage's taste: he simply sat at the piano and invented sounds that he liked. This control of materials was hidden in the mid-1950s in works like "The Ten Thousand Things" by his goal of inclusion. However, his choice was still present – it was just more wide-ranging than before. In his later music, Cage continued to choose his materials deliberately. Here, however, his reasons were not solely acoustic ones, but, as we have seen in *Ryoanji*, involved references that the sounds made to things outside themselves. The musical materials that he used, in other words, carried meanings in one way or another.

This is not to say, however, that Cage practiced the sort of romantic story-telling we have come to associate with some program music of the nineteenth and early twentieth centuries. Cage's programmaticism – if I may call it that – is uniquely his own; not just in the kinds of themes that he pursues, nor in the kinds of sounds that he uses, it is in the *way* in which the expressive and meaningful sounds are presented that the resulting music is distinctly "Cagean." Just as he allowed his sounds to speak for themselves in his chance works, so in his later programmatic works, he allowed his expressive materials to speak for *themselves*. He simply presents the situation unadorned, without comment; he remains silent about his message. This understated approach to making a music that refers to the non-musical world is one of Cage's most exciting achievements as a composer.

Ryoanji is a perfect example of this approach. I can summarize Cage's image of the Ryoanji garden as follows: the sand represents an empty space, while the stones are concrete things that can inhabit that empty space at any points within it. To use the language of Cage's 1950s writings, the sand is the Nothing that supports the Somethings of the rocks. In *Ryoanji*, Cage's music does not so much comment *about* this model of the garden as it *embodies* it. Cage has taken the Ryoanji garden — taken his understanding of its fundamental nature — and transformed it into music by finding two musical elements (percussion and oboe) which act in the same way as the sand and stones of the garden act.

This was the procedure for other works: Cage began by fixing an image in his mind, and then made a piece which neither communicates nor expresses the image, but which *is* the image — it acts in the way that the image acts. In short, this is an example of "imitating Nature in her manner of operation" in the sense that Coomaraswamy spoke of in his writings. This music has, as a result, an air of both abstraction and precision. M. C. Richards, noting that "the union of mystery and sensory exactitude makes music a possible metaphor of reality," has remarked on Cage's unique abilities as a composer of music of this sort:

> Cage is invigorated by what is enigmatic, untranslatable, vitally itself. He is also masterful at elucidation. The dialogue in his being, between the one who understands and he who experiences, is striking.[21]

"The one who understands" creates and understands an image, a theme; "he who experiences" finds a perfectly concrete sonic embodiment of that image. The combination of abstract and concrete, "of mystery and sensory exactitude," is the source of Cage's poetry; it is what the Japanese poet Bashō means when he commands the poet to keep the mind in both the world of "true understanding" and "daily experience."

An awareness of the sorts of themes about which Cage wrote his music can help explain compositional choices that would otherwise seem peculiar, arbitrary, or bizarre. In the *Song Books*, for example, the "relevant" solos all have Thoreau or Satie standing behind them. In Solo 82, the performer is instructed as follows: "Using a Paris café cognac glass, serve yourself the amount above the line" — a reference to Satie's habit of frequenting Parisian cafés. Solo 3 is a particularly beautiful case of a solo being full of Thoreau. The text here is not a rearranging of Thoreau, but is a coherent passage selected at random from his journal, in which he describes his observations of a circling hawk. The singer uses this as the text for a melody derived from a map of Concord, Massachusetts — another Thoreau reference (the route the singer is to trace on the map is derived from places Thoreau mentions in the journals). Cage has also added the following poetic touch: the solo is to be accompanied by a recording of hawk sounds. The wandering over the map, the text, and the recorded hawk, all come *from* Thoreau, but do not say anything *about* him. Instead they create a musical experience that is *like* Thoreau's observation of the hawk.

Another case in which understanding the theme of the music is essential to understanding the means used to compose it is *Sonnekus²* (1985). The text consists of nine mesostics: "writings through" the biblical Book of Genesis using the word *Sonneries* as a key.[22] The key-word is taken from the title of one of Satie's Rosicrucian pieces, *Sonneries de la Rose + Croix*. The musical "key" that runs down the middle of the musical settings of the poems is also from Satie: a passage from *Socrate*. The settings of the mesostics are simple, diatonic, chant-like. Their performance is to be somewhat theatrical, however. Cage indicates:

> The theatrical character of the performance is to suggest (not heavily) both church and cabaret. The singer will make a program including silences of any lengths (and changes of dress) that presents all nine of these songs in the auditorium space. Elsewhere with accompaniment any cabaret songs by Satie may be performed (at a distance from the audience).

This note reveals the theme of the piece: the contradiction of sacred and secular ("church and cabaret") in Satie's music and character. Here the sacred is represented by the choice of a biblical text, the character of the vocal lines, the Rosicrucian mesostic key; the secular appears in the form of the cabaret songs, sung at a distance. The *Sonnekus²* do not comment on Satie's combination of sacred and secular, they embody that contradiction.

Political themes

In Solo 35 of the *Song Books*, it will be recalled, Cage has the performers raise the black flag of Anarchy while proclaiming that "the best form of government is no government at all." Cage's belief in individualist anarchy as the "best form of government" was in keeping with his artistic goals – in a sense, one can think of his politics as being an extension of his art. Cage believed that the best arrangement of people and sounds was to have them free to be themselves, "unimpeded and interpenetrating." He felt that such an individualist anarchy was possible because of the ability via technology to meet everyone's material needs – Buckminster Fuller's plans for global utilities would make government obsolete and allow all individuals to live freely and independently.

Cage's commitment to anarchy was firm, and statements against the evils of government appeared regularly in his writings and music. One particularly strong example is *Lecture on the Weather* (1975). The work, commissioned by the Canadian Broadcasting Corporation, consists mainly of twelve men reading collages of Thoreau texts.[23] The piece is in three parts, and each part is accompanied by a tape of weather-related sounds. In the first part, there is the sound of wind, in the second the sound of rain, and in the final part the sound of thunder. During this last part, the lights are dimmed and a film is shown in which drawings from Thoreau's journals flash as lightning, white on a black background.

Lecture on the Weather is dark and powerful: the twelve men reading together make the text incomprehensible, and the brewing storm of the weather sounds suggests an impending disaster. Cage's preface to the piece, which is to be read at each performance, makes the meaning even more explicit. In it, he expresses his disgust with the institutions of American government: "not only aspiration but intelligence (as in the work of Buckminster Fuller) and conscience (as in the thought of Thoreau) are missing in our leadership."

Lecture on the Weather is exceptional in its darkness, its criticism and pessimism. Cage much preferred to make positive statements, to suggest alternatives rather than simply to criticize failures. In "The Future of Music" he describes music's ability to serve as a model for the way in which world society could work:

> We now have many musical examples of the practicality of anarchy. Music with indeterminate parts, no fixed relation of them (no score). Music without notation. . . . Musicians can do without government.
>
> By making musical situations which are analogies to desirable social circumstances which we do not yet have, we make music suggestive and relevant to the serious questions which face Mankind.

Clearly, Cage thought that many, if not all, of his post-1957 works were musical analogies to anarchy in one form or another. Some works seem to have been deliberately designed to embody such a program. In *Etcetera* (1973), the twenty performers play in two different social situations: either as soloists (tapping on a "non-resonant cardboard box") or in conducted groups of two, three, or four players. The unmeasured box-music (occasionally punctuated by sounds from the players' instruments) continues from the start to the finish of the piece. At any point, any player may stop playing this part and decide to become part of a duo, trio, or quartet. Three stations with the appropriate number of chairs and stands are placed at the front of the stage, and a conductor waits at each. When players have, of their own volition, filled the station, the conductor leads them in their ensemble (this music is quite simple, but its structure is controlled by the conductor). This piece thus contains both freedom and control, anarchy and government. It could be seen (although Cage never indicated such) as an embodiment of the kind of possibilities that Benjamin Tucker, an early American anarchist, suggested:

> We [anarchists] offer cooperation. We offer non-compulsive organization. We offer associative combination. We offer every possible method of voluntary social union by which men and women may act together for the furtherance of well-being.[24]

Such political sentiments stand behind other works. *Etcetera 2/4 Orchestras* (1986) reverses the situation of *Etcetera*: the entire ensemble is conducted throughout the work, and the players are free to become soloists at any time. *Les chants de Maldoror pulvérisés par l'assistance même* (1971) consists of 200 pages of text to be read by "a francophone public of no more than 200 persons." The rules for reading these texts are determined by the performers as a group. Finally, in the orchestral version of *Cheap Imitation*, Cage insists on there being no conductor for the ensemble: the players must work together without imposed leadership.

Nature imagery

Another favorite theme of Cage's that connects his work to Henry David Thoreau is the world of nature. The use of nature imagery in Cage's writing and music begins to appear around the mid-1950s. According to Cage, when he moved from New York City to the rural setting of Stony Point in 1954, he realized that he was "starved for nature." He began wandering in the woods, and it was at this time that his devotion to mushrooms and mycology began. In essays such as the 1958 "Experimental Music" he began using the world of nature as a model for his own musical ideas. The connection to nature diminished in the 1960s as Cage traveled heavily, but it returned to the fore with his discovery of Thoreau in the 1970s. Even after his move from Stony Point back to New York City, Cage surrounded himself with natural things: he had an enormous collection of houseplants which filled his home, with smooth river stones distributed around them.

Recorded sounds drawn from nature appear in a number of pieces in the 1970s, particularly in connection with Thoreau. In the *Song Books*, there are the recorded hawk and other bird songs that accompany the Thoreau texts in Solos 3 and 4. In *Score (40 Drawings by Thoreau) and 23 Parts: 12 Haiku*, the orchestral music derived from the Thoreau drawings is followed by a tape recording made at Stony Point at dawn one morning. The effect is to let the outside world of nature into the concert hall, much as when, in all-night performances of *Empty Words*, the windows are to be opened at dawn, at the start of the fourth and final part of the text. In *Etcetera*, a recording of the ambient sound in Stony Point accompanies the instrumental music, but for somewhat different reasons. Here, Cage wished to use sound to give a sense of a particular place: the place where he composed the piece. The recording transforms the sound of the space where the piece is performed into the sound of the space where it was written. *Etcetera 2/4 Orchestras* does the same thing, with the recording this time of the ambient sounds of Cage's Sixth Avenue apartment.

Cage's involvement with natural subjects also afforded him the opportunity to reconcile himself to musical improvisation, to which he had a long-standing aversion. His dislike of improvisation is not hard to understand: given Cage's devotion to discipline and the silencing of his own voice, improvisation, when concerned with self-expression, was bound to appear as self-indulgent and decadent. In *Child of Tree* (1975) and *Inlets* (1977), however, Cage moved into the realm of improvisation in his own work. In *Child of Tree*, a single player performs using amplified plant materials. Cage specifies two of the ten "instruments" to be used: a pod from a poinciana tree and a cactus, this latter being played by plucking the spines with a toothpick or needle.[25] Cage provides elaborate instructions to the performer on how, via chance operations, to divide the eight-minute length of the piece into parts, and subsequently how to divide the ten instruments among the various parts of the performance. This is all done ahead of time, and in performance the player improvises on the plant instruments, changing instruments according to the time structure. *Inlets* is similar, although there is no fixed time structure. Here, three players each have four conch shells of gradated sizes, each filled with water. These are played by tipping the shells "this way or that," an operation which will produce audible gurgles (these are amplified in performance). Cage indicates no overall performance time, nor any particular division of that time, only that each shell should be played only once, and that each successive shell should be played for a longer time as the piece progresses. Two other elements enter the work: halfway through the performance, the players should become silent for a time, during which time a tape recording of burning pine cones is faded in. At any point after this, a single note is played by a fourth performer on a conch shell trumpet; the note is to last as long as possible.

Cage's problems with the self-expressive quality of improvisation are solved in *Child of Tree* and *Inlets* by using instruments that can not be controlled. In an interview, Cage explained his choice of instruments in these works:

> In the case of the plant materials, you don't know them; you're discovering them. So the instrument is unfamiliar. If you become very familiar with a piece of cactus, it very shortly disintegrates, and you have to replace it with another one which you don't know. So the whole thing remains fascinating, and free of your memory as a matter of course.
>
> In the case of *Inlets*, you have no control whatsoever over the conch shell when it's filled with water. You tip it and you get a gurgle, sometimes; not always. So the rhythm belongs to the instruments, and not to you.[26]

Cage's choice of natural objects as instruments in this context is not arbitrary: the world of nature could provide that uncontrollability that he needed. Thus pieces like *Child of Tree* or *Inlets* embody the kind of relationship between people and nature that Cage favored: working *with* the unpredictability of nature and not *against* it. Improvisation, when conducted with natural objects, becomes an act of discovery and not of expression; it is like a walk in the woods, a mushroom hunt.

The choice of sounds in *Inlets* is not just for the purposes of insuring an uncontrolled improvisation. The three sounds of the piece are related thematically, in their "elemental" nature – water, fire, air. The piece thus presents a very simple tableau: first the sound of water, then the sound of fire, then the two together with the blown conch shell tone, the sound of air. In *Inlets*, the combination of the concrete and the universal, together with the model interaction of people and nature, gets at the heart of Cage's use of sounds to embody some message or image. The resulting music works at various levels – simple nature imagery, social paradigm, and, of course, as exquisite sound.

Music using other music

It is not just Cage's music that carries various meanings via the materials chosen; his writings are full of references to his favorite authors, such as Thoreau or James Joyce. In *Mureau* or *Empty Words*, in the various *Writings Through Finnegans Wake*, Cage wrote about other writers simply by using their books as source materials. Other texts were made from collections of different materials that were tied together thematically. In *Anarchy* (1988), the sources include Emma Goldman, Buckminster Fuller, Cage – all represented by quotations that in some way refer to the need to abolish governments of all kinds. *I–VI* (1988), a series of lectures given at Harvard University, draws on a huge repertory of source texts (487 different quotations, to be exact). Some of these texts relate to a list of fifteen different subjects that Cage felt were important aspects of his work (method, structure, intention, discipline, notation, indeterminacy, interpenetration, imitation, devotion, circumstances, variable structure, nonunderstanding, contingency, inconsistency, and performance), while others were drawn at random from the daily newspapers, the writings of Ludwig Wittgenstein, or other sources. The Harvard lectures, being about Cage's own work, were an extension of two earlier texts based on the same idea, *Themes & Variations* (1980) and "Composition in Retrospect" (1981), both of which draw upon his own words as source materials. Cage thought of these writings as a search "to find a way of writing which though coming from ideas is not about them" – in short, these are more examples of the sort of programmaticism I have been exploring here.

That Cage could use other texts as the source for his own writing suggests that he could also use other compositions as the source for his own music. *Cheap Imitation* is the first example of this: the notes of Satie's music have been used to construct a new composition, a composition that is thus "from Satie" but not "about" him. Here, Cage has used Satie's music in a way parallel to his use in his writings of *Finnegans Wake* or Thoreau's journal. Other works in the 1970s and 1980s use this method of music made from other music. Cage turned to it when the thematic requirements of a work uniquely demanded it – he never arbitrarily rearranged other music.

A cluster of these pieces were written around 1976, the year of the bicentennial of the American Revolution. Orchestras, particularly in the United States, wished to program new American music, and hence commissioned many new works. Cage received commissions from the orchestras in Boston, Chicago, Cleveland, Los Angeles, New York, and Philadelphia. Cage felt that such a piece needed to be "American" – eighteenth-century American, to be exact – and hence he used distinctly American materials. *Renga* (1975–76), the orchestral work that he created for the bicentennial, was based on drawings from Thoreau's journal. It is to be performed with *Apartment House 1776* (1976), which is a collection of music to be played by any number of musicians as a "musicircus."[27] These pieces are all drawn from eighteenth-century sources: popular melodies, drum solos, Moravian church music, and choral music by composers such as William Billings, Andrew Law, Supply Belcher, and Jacob French. The choral music was subjected to a method of "subtraction," in which only a few of the notes of the originals were maintained (this was described in the Introduction to this book). These notes were then extended to fill the space resulting from the deleted notes. The result is music that retains its eighteenth-century flavor, but which has become quite Cagean in its aimlessness and unpredictability. Cage was fond of these pieces, and used the same method in a number of other "Americana" pieces during the years following the bicentennial: *Quartets* for various ensembles (1976–78), *Some of "The Harmony of Maine" (Supply Belcher)* for organ (1978), and *Hymns and Variations* for chorus (1979).

A commission from the Frankfurt Opera resulted in another series of works drawing on existing music: the *Europeras*. Opera is a medium that is closely tied to its history and tradition: as a result, Cage made his opera out of the materials of other operas. This is an opera about Opera, not based on any one work or composer, but on the genre as a whole. In *Europeras 1 & 2* (1985–87), Cage took the components of opera, assembled collections of materials relevant to each, and subjected them to chance operations. The singers select arias from eighteenth- and nineteenth-century operas and sing them within given time frames. Their costumes, taken from the opera repertory, are chosen at random. The sets, lighting, props, and stage directions were all designed using chance. The orchestral musicians play excerpts from the orchestral music of other operas, and so on. Even the synopses printed in the program books (there are twelve different synopses of the two operas) are chance-derived:

> Dressed as an Irish princess, he gives birth; they plot to overthrow the French. He arranges to be kidnapped by her; rejuvenated, they desert: to him she has borne two children. He prays for help. Since they have decided she shall marry no one outside, he has himself crowned Emperor. She, told he is dead, begs him to look at her. First, before the young couple come to a climax, he agrees. Accidentally, she drowns them.

The turns of phrase, the character-types, the plot twists are all reminiscent of nineteenth-century opera stories, but transformed. The result here, and in the work as a whole, is an homage to the genre. The *Europeras 1 & 2* are extravagant spectacles in which anything, no matter how far-fetched, seems possible (towards the end of the second opera, a radio-controlled Zeppelin flies out into the audience). Cage went on to make *Europeras 3 & 4* (1990) and *Europera 5* (1991) using similar collage techniques, but with an eye towards concert performances, using piano accompaniments and no costumes or props.

Instrumental music

Etudes

By the time of his sixtieth birthday in 1972, John Cage had become a respected figure not just in avant-garde musical circles, but in the musical world at large. As a result, he began to receive more and more commissions and requests for pieces from groups specializing in new music and also from more conservative performers. Cage endeavored to fulfill as many of these commissions as possible, so that he produced a rather large number of purely instrumental works in his later years.

Prominent among the works made in response to performers' requests are the three sets of etudes composed during the 1970s. All of these etudes were composed using star charts, following the practice of *Atlas Eclipticalis*, but to a different end. In these etudes, there is very little left indeterminate beyond the durations of the individual pieces. Indeed, Cage often remarked upon the very detailed instructions given in the *Freeman Etudes*: practically every aspect of sound and sound-production is specified. These pieces are all fiendishly difficult to play, and deliberately so. Cage saw in musical virtuosity a chance for optimism. He explains the social implications of his etudes in an interview:

> These [the etudes] are intentionally as difficult as I can make them, because I think we're now surrounded by very serious problems in the society, and we tend to think that the situation is hopeless and that it's just impossible to do something that will make everything turn out properly. So I think that this music, which is almost impossible, gives an instance of the practicality of the impossible.[28]

The first of the etudes were the *Etudes Australes* for piano (1974–75), written for Grete Sultan. The pieces consist of single tones and chords, derived from the star charts of the *Atlas Australis*. In composing the chords, Cage made a table of all the possible chord formations that could be played by a single hand on the piano, and then used these tables in conjunction with his star charts. There are thirty-two etudes, and the number of chords increases through the series: the first is almost entirely single notes, the last is almost entirely chordal. The difficulty of the pieces comes from Cage's decision to write the music for each hand separately and independently, with both the left and right hands having to cover the entire range of the piano. Hence the hands cross constantly, and the pianist must manage tremendous leaps within a single hand's part.

After the piano etudes, Cage went on to write a set of etudes for violinist Paul Zukofsky, the *Freeman Etudes* (1977–80/1989–90). These thirty-two etudes are similar to the *Etudes Australes*, but are even more controlled. Again, pitches and rhythms were determined by means of the start charts. Beyond this, though, Cage went on to use chance operations to determine a multitude of other performance instructions. Staccato and legato, up- and downbows, bowing locations and styles, tremolos, vibratos, a wide variety of martellato attacks, and so forth were all determined individually for every single note in the piece. Even the fingerings were chance-determined by an elaborate process. In the case of a triple stop, for example, Cage would determine by chance operations the first note and which string it would be played upon. He would then determine the second string to be played, and would ask Zukofsky to indicate what range of notes a violinist could play on that string while holding the already-determined note. Cage would then select randomly from this range, choose the third string to be sounded, and Zukofsky would indicate the range of possibilities for this third note. The music is so difficult, that, when Cage reached the eighteenth etude, he ceased composing – the density of notes was so great that he feared the piece would be unplayable. It was only several years later that he decided to add the performance indication that the violinist, when faced with an impossible density of notes, should simply play as many as possible. He then finished the final fourteen etudes.[29]

The final set of etudes is a double set: the *Etudes Boreales* for cello and piano (1978). These were written for Jack and Jeanne Kirstein, the latter having performed and recorded Cage's piano music in the early 1970s. The two sets of etudes were written independently, but can be performed together or as solos. The cello etudes are similar to the *Freeman Etudes*, with the exception that they use only a portion of the total range of the cello at any one time. The size and location of the available pitch range change during the course of the etudes. The piano etudes are really more like percussion pieces, the player using beaters and making noises on the piano construction. Rather than indicate precise pitches, Cage used the star charts to determine *where* on the piano the performer is to play: keyboard, strings, construction. Kirstein found the piece unplayable; it was only Michael Pugliese, a virtuoso percussionist, who found the way to play these "impossible" pieces.

The "number" pieces

During his last years, Cage became almost entirely occupied as a composer with instrumental music, particularly in response to commissions for his eightieth birthday in 1992. Most of this instrumental music forms a single series of compositions I call the "number" pieces – their titles are all simply the number of performers in the particular ensemble. The first such work was *Two* for flute and piano, composed in 1987. A scattering of similar works appeared over the next few years, but by 1991 Cage had become devoted to this series of compositions. Ultimately, there were forty-three such pieces for various ensembles. The convention of giving the pieces titles based on the number of performers continued – for example, *One* for solo piano (1987); *Seven* for flute, clarinet, percussion, piano, violin, viola, and cello (1988); *101* for orchestra (1988). When a particular number of performers was used again in the series, the number title was given a superscript so as to distinguish it from the others. There are six different quartets in the series, for example: *Four* for string quartet (1989); *Four²* for four-part chorus (1990); *Four³* for four performers (1991); *Four⁴* for four percussionists (1991); *Four⁵* for saxophone ensemble (1991); and *Four⁶* for four performers (1992).

All these pieces have a common compositional technique: that of the time bracket, fixed or flexible. Example 6–12 is the flute part from *Two*, which consists of ten such brackets. The principle here is that there is a period of time during which the music of a given bracket must begin, and a period of time during which it must end. The exact placement and duration of the music is free within these limitations. In the notation, the time periods are indicated in terms of elapsed time. Hence, in the first bracket, the note D must begin at some time during the first forty-five seconds of the piece, and end sometime between thirty seconds and one minute fifteen seconds into the piece. As a result, the note could be very short or very long: it might last as long as seventy-five seconds, if it used the entire bracket. All the remaining brackets in the flute part continue in this fashion, with the exception of the eighth bracket. This is a fixed time bracket: the A♭ contained within it must begin at seven minutes fifteen seconds elapsed time and continue until seven minutes forty-five seconds.

All the number pieces consist of several independent parts which are a series of such brackets, one after the other. In *Two*, the piano part also consists of ten brackets with the same time indications, but the two performers do not coordinate their interpretations of the brackets with each other: these are "parts without a score." Since the brackets overlap slightly, it happens at times that two or more sounds follow each other directly, without a break. At other times, a pause of some duration may occur while a performer, having finished a phrase, waits for the next time bracket to begin.

The time bracket idea itself was not new to Cage's work: it first appeared in 1981 in *Thirty Pieces for Five Orchestras*, and was used in a very similar form in *Music for   *. What distinguishes the number pieces from these others is the content of the brackets. In *Two*, the flute has only single notes; this is the pattern for all the other pieces. Usually a bracket will contain only a single note, or a phrase of two to four notes (phrases are particularly common in the pieces with string parts). These notes have certain characteristics: although they can have a range of durations, they tend towards the long (ten seconds or longer). This tendency, inherent in the length of the time brackets themselves, was emphasized in some of the later pieces through the use of even *longer* brackets: in *Four⁴*, they can be a few minutes long, and in *One⁶* for violin (1990), brackets that contain the same note are combined, so that the piece opens with a single F♮ that could last for over four minutes. The dynamics are given by Cage for each individual note in the very early pieces of the series, but later he indicates simply that when the notes are long they should be very quiet and when short they may be somewhat louder. Especially in the early pieces, he indicates that the attacks of the notes should be made unclear: they should be "brushed into existence."

Example 6–12   *Two*: flute part

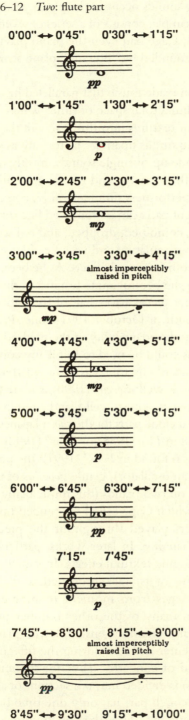

Exceptions to these characteristics of the sounds occur in the piano writing of the early pieces: the piano part of *Two*, for example, consists of a series of several chords in each bracket. But by *Fourteen* (1990), Cage had even the piano playing long, quiet tones: all the notes here are to be sounded by "bowing" piano strings using bundles of horsehair.

Thus in the number pieces Cage again made music that paralleled his visual art works: fragments of sound floating within a total space of time. Where in *Music for* he had thrown a variety of different textures into this space, in the number works the "images" that he has inscribed on his floating "plates" are as simple as they can be. The number pieces are made up of single sounds, mostly quiet and long, with silence surrounding them – they emerge and recede gradually in and out of silence. When played by several performers simultaneously, combinations of notes arise spontaneously. The different parts can be followed like threads in a complex tapestry as they are picked up, combined, dropped, and rediscovered.

Cage found this style of composition stimulating and very flexible, so that he was able to use it as a means to discover other musical effects. As he became more and more involved in the number works, he became quite prolific: in the last year of his life he wrote twenty-three number pieces (over half of the entire series), with seven works appearing in the month of October 1991 alone. Part of the reason for the profusion of these pieces is the adaptability of the method: it could be used for any ensemble at all, and thus could be used to fulfill any commission or request. There are pieces for such standard ensembles as string quartet, chorus, and orchestra. There are odd groupings, as well: *Seven*^{2} (1990) is scored for bass flute, bass clarinet, bass trombone, two percussionists, cello, and contrabass. *One*^{9} (1991), *Two*^{3} (1991), and *Two*^{4} (1991) all include parts for the *shō*, a Japanese mouth organ. No instruments are specified at all in *Five* (1988) or *Four*^{6} (1992). Perhaps one of the most interesting arrangements is found in *Four*^{3} (1991): the performers here play a single note on the violin (or an oscillator), gentle *swooshes* of rainsticks (a kind of rattle), and slow, aimless lines on two pianos (this music being chance-derived variations of Satie's *Vexations*, which Cage called "Extended Lullaby").

In the earliest pieces, all the players played throughout the piece – the instrumentation and texture were unchanging. In later works, particularly the larger ensembles, Cage made use of changing textural effects. In *Twenty-three* for string orchestra (1988), each part has some of its brackets deleted, so that the size and composition of the ensemble changes from moment to moment. This method of omitting brackets is used in many of the other number pieces for various effects. In *Fourteen* for piano and chamber ensemble the piano plays throughout, but the other instruments enter and exit during the fifteen-minute duration of the piece, making it a kind of concerto. *Two*^{3} for shō and conch shells (water-filled and played as in *Inlets*) is divided into ten sections of about ten to fifteen minutes' duration each. The conch part has only one time bracket in each section deliberately placed at its very end. Thus the conch gurgles emerge from the reedy sound of the *shō*.

The three largest pieces are for full orchestra: *101* (1988), *103* (1991), and *108* (1991). Here Cage divided the orchestra in varying ways. In *101* the strings, piano, harp, flutes, and clarinets all play quietly throughout. The rest of the winds and brass play only two short, loud, screeching outbursts – one towards the beginning of the piece, one towards the ending. The percussion instruments play notes that are scattered all over the entire duration of the work. In *103* the orchestra is divided between strings on the one hand and winds and brass on the other. The ninety-minute duration of the piece is divided into seventeen parts; the number of wind and brass instruments playing in each part was determined by chance, so that the orchestral color changes from section to section. *108* consists of four segments of music separated by lengthy silences. It can be played together with *One*[8] for cello (1991) to form a cello concerto.

Towards the end of his life, Cage became increasingly interested in employing the flexible time bracket method within severely limited pitch ranges. This was first done in an early piece, *Four* for string quartet (1989). Cage had the idea here of having all four parts performable by all four string players, hence he limited the pitches in each part to a two-octave range common to violin, viola, and cello. He was delighted with the amount of music that could arise from such a restricted space and began restricting the pitch ranges in other works. In *One*[6] for violin (1990), the three sections of the work are differentiated by their use of different parts of the violin's range: one of these sections draws upon a range of only a minor third.

Cage's interest in exploring such subtle effects within narrow pitch ranges ultimately led him to write microtonal music. In *Two*[4] for violin and *shō* (1991), he settled on a division of the semitone into six parts. His idea here was not that a performer could play such a fine division precisely, but that the differences in intonation would suggest the kind of flexibility in the pitch domain that the time brackets had achieved in the domain of time. In an effort to experience the subtleties of intonation more clearly, he began putting more notes within his brackets. In *Ten* for chamber ensemble (1991), there can be twenty or more notes in a bracket, but the notes within a single bracket always span no more than a major second. Thus in one bracket of the violin part to this piece, there are ten notes, all of which are microtonal inflections of the same C♯. By filling the time brackets full of notes in this way, Cage sought to create the effect of a kind of "florid song."

In his last orchestral works, Cage continued in this vein – a music of minute variations – by having all the players play the same music. In *Eighty* (1992) and *Sixty-eight* (1992) the parts for all instruments are exactly the same: the same fifteen pitches in the same fifteen time brackets. The result is that, although the performers all play the same "melody," each plays it with a slightly different rhythm: this is what Cage called "a unison of differences." As with the microtonal works, he was fascinated here with the small differences in time and color that would arise from the combination of flexible time brackets and unison playing. *Seventy-four* (1992) employs the same idea of unison playing, this time with the orchestra divided between two different melodies, one low and one high. Using two melodies in two different pitch ranges allows the entire resources of the orchestra to be used.

Shortly after John Cage's death (on August 12, 1992) a friend told me that he felt the number pieces would always be a special part of the Cage literature. This is true, I think, in part because of Cage's death. His last works – as with the last works of any composer – will have a certain gravity for us because we know that he will compose no more – they are Cage's last words as a composer. But I also believe that these pieces will have a privileged position in Cage's *œuvre* because they are genuinely some of his very best work. He was in his element – discovery and invention – in these compositions, and was openly delighted and joyful in his last years as he explored the possibilities the time bracket method opened up to him.

These works are so beautiful because they return to John Cage's compositional strengths: concentration, spaciousness, simplicity. Because each bracket contains a single sound, there is an intensity to each and every note, a focused concentration to every event. Nothing here is "filler," every note is meant deeply. The silence surrounding the sounds is crucial: it provides both the floating quality of the time brackets and the spaciousness that Cage loved and had sought out ever since the *Concerto for Prepared Piano*. Finally, because the materials are so simple – single tones – the relationships among them can arise of themselves, can spring forth from silence. The music is effortless and transparent. These are all qualities found in some of Cage's most inspired music over the course of his sixty-year career as a composer: *Music for Marcel Duchamp, Sonatas and Interludes, String Quartet in Four Parts*, the third movement of the *Concerto for Prepared Piano, Variations II, 0' 00"*, *Cheap Imitation, Inlets, Ryoanji* (to name my personal favorites). In these final works we continue to hear John Cage, the composer, speaking with his own unique and marvelous musical voice.

Notes

Introduction

1 Eric Salzman, *Twentieth-Century Music: An Introduction*, 3rd edn. (Englewood Cliffs: Prentice Hall, 1988), p. 160.
2 Donal Henahan, "The Riddle of John Cage," *The New York Times*, 23 August 1981, p. D-17.
3 Kyle Gann, "Philosopher No More," *The Village Voice*, 25 August 1992, p. 77.
4 Paul Griffiths, *Cage*, Oxford Studies of Composers no. 18 (London: Oxford University Press, 1981), p. 28.
5 John Rockwell, *All-American Music: Composition in the Late Twentieth Century* (New York: Alfred A. Knopf, 1983), p. 52.
6 Charles Wuorinen, "The Outlook for Young Composers," *Perspectives of New Music* 1/2 (Spring 1963), p. 60.
7 Salzman, *Twentieth-Century Music*, p. 163.
8 Cope's interview with Cage appeared in *The Composer* 10/11, pp. 6–22. The description of *Apartment House 1776* occurs on p. 8.

1 "For more new sounds" (1933–1948)

1 John Cage, "A Composer's Confessions" (1948), p. 8. All quotations from Cage in this chapter come from this source, unless otherwise noted.
2 The story is recounted in Rita Mead, *Henry Cowell's New Music 1925–1936* (Ann Arbor: UMI Research Press, 1981), p. 228.
3 Calvin Tomkins, *The Bride and the Bachelors: Five Masters of the Avant-Garde*, p. 84.
4 The names of these fifteen men formed the basis for Cage's text *Themes & Variations*.
5 Tomkins, *The Bride and the Bachelors*, pp. 84–85.
6 *Ibid.*, p. 85.
7 Virgil Thomson, "Modernism Today," *New York Herald Tribune*, 2 February 1947, section V, p. 6.
8 Henry Cowell, "Towards Neo-primitivism," p. 153.
9 The dancers' insistence on the primacy of choreography over music is reflected in Cage's comment in 1939 that their music "has not been constructive," since "they have made the music identical with the dance but not cooperative with it." ("Goal: New Music, New Dance" (1939), in *Silence*, p. 88).

10 Henry Cowell, "Drums Along the Pacific," p. 48.

11 Those familiar with Cage's later writings will note that this explanation of his adoption of rhythmic structure omits his oft-quoted statement that duration is the only aspect of sound common to both sound and silence, and hence is the only basis for structure in music. Although Cage states this quite strongly from the 1948 "Defense of Satie" onwards, it never appears in his writing before that lecture. In fact, he does not seem to have given much thought to the matter of silence at all prior to his statement in "A Composer's Confessions" that he wished to compose a piece consisting of four and a half minutes of silence to be called "Silent Prayer" – the origin of his famous *4' 33"*. I believe that it was his interest in the concept of a spiritual silence as expressed in the sermons of Meister Eckhart which led to the inspired thought of a silent piece, and that it was only after this musical application of Eckhart's thought surfaced in his thinking that he began to adapt his compositional beliefs to include silence. I will return to this point in the next chapter.

12 In reality, there is a nine-bar "coda" to the sixteen-by-sixteen structure, thus giving a total of 265 measures. Since my purpose here is to communicate the simple principles of micro-macrocosmic structure, I have ignored the coda in this presentation.

13 It is my practice to notate the number series for Cage's rhythmic structures as a list of numbers, separated by commas, within curled braces. While this may suggest to some a connection with set theory, I only use this format to distinguish more clearly the number series from the accompanying text.

14 John Cage and Robert Dunn, *John Cage* [catalog of works] (New York: C. F. Peters, 1962), p. 39. Although Cage names only two works in which this technique was used, there may have been others.

15 There are some problems with this story, particularly as regards chronology. *Bacchanale* is dated 1940 and, indeed, Syvilla Fort's dance was on a program at the Cornish School on 26 April, 1940. In *Second Construction*, however, the piano is prepared with one or two items. *Second Construction* predates *Bacchanale* by two months, thus suggesting that *it* was the first piece to use the prepared piano. Nevertheless, ever since "A Composer's Confessions" in 1948, Cage has consistently identified *Bacchanale* as the work in which he discovered the prepared piano, and I am disinclined to doubt his memory of this particular event. Perhaps the 1940 dance program was a second performance or revised version of the piece, or perhaps the piano part of *Second Construction* was changed after the composition of *Bacchanale* to take advantage of that work's innovations. None of the possible histories of *Bacchanale* is completely satisfactory; this will perhaps always be a mystery – intriguing, but probably of little real importance.

16 Cage was well aware of this phenomenon which accounts for his scrupulously indicating the use of the *una corda* pedal in his prepared piano scores. A failure of certain contemporary performances of these works is the use of pianos whose *una corda* pedals do not shift the hammers far enough to the right, thus failing to produce the dramatic changes in timbre that Cage desired in the *una corda* passages.

17 Cage had to write a new score for conventional percussion instruments in the week before the broadcast.

18 The last two compositions for prepared piano – *34' 46.776" for a Pianist* and *31' 57.9864" for a Pianist* – were composed in 1954.

19 Cage gives the source for this as Patmore's *Prefatory Study on English Metrical Law* of 1879. Patmore's use of the terms "law" and "freedom" – associated with what Cage refers to as "clarity" and "grace," or structure and content – is perhaps the source of Cage's division of the aspects of music into "Law elements and Freedom elements" in "Defense of Satie" in 1948.

20 A manuscript has recently come to light that suggests that *Tossed As It Is Untroubled* is in fact a portion of a larger work composed in 1943 and entitled *Mediation*. This earlier piece was written as an anniversary gift for Xenia Cage; its use as a dance accompaniment would appear to have been a later development.

21 The silences are not "pure," however, since the pedal is held down throughout the piece – the resonances of the muted tones extend into the measures of rests.

22 This same idea reappears in 1969 as the basis of *HPSCHD*.

23 In some treatments of *rasa*, tranquillity is listed along with the other eight permanent emotions and not as their "common tendency." Coomaraswamy, in *The Dance of Shiva*, lists tranquillity (or, in his words, the "peaceful") along with the other eight in this fashion. Coomaraswamy's list of emotions omits the mirthful (no doubt a typographical error) and uses different wording for some of the other eight. The nine permanent emotions appear elsewhere in Cage's work over the years. For example, they form the theme for Merce Cunningham's *Sixteen Dances* (1950–51), for which Cage wrote the score. A particularly interesting example is this passage from the 1957 essay "Experimental Music" (*Silence*, p. 10), in which the eight emotions (but not tranquillity) are connected with the world of nature: "Hearing sounds which are just sounds immediately sets the theorizing mind to theorizing, and the emotions of human beings are continually aroused by encounters with nature. Does not a mountain unintentionally evoke in us a sense of wonder? otters along a stream a sense of mirth? night in the woods a sense of fear? Do not rain falling and mists rising up suggest the love binding heaven and earth? Is not decaying flesh loathsome? Does not the death of someone we love bring sorrow? And is there a greater hero than the least plant that grows? What is more angry than the flash of lightning and the sound of thunder?"

24 Cecil Smith, "Ajemian Plays Sonatas by John Cage," *Musical America* 69/2 (15 January 1949), p. 9.

25 Peter Yates, "Music," *Arts and Architecture* 64/4 (April 1949), p. 23.

26 Ross Parmenter, *The New York Times*, 13 January 1949, p. 28.

2 "To sober and quiet the mind . . ." (1946–1951)

1 Tomkins, *The Bride and the Bachelors: Five Masters of the Avant-Garde*, p. 97.

2 John Cage, "List No. 2" (1961), *John Cage*, p. 138.

3 Ananda K. Coomaraswamy, *The Transformation of Nature in Art*, p. 62.

4 *Ibid*., pp. 10–11, 13.

5 That Cage was still thinking in essentially dualistic terms is revealed at the end of the lecture where he refers to "the two fundamental and opposed elements" (i.e., structure and form) that are "ornamented by other elements, which may lend support to one or the other" (i.e., method and materials).

6 There are a few irregularities in the realization of this structure at the phrase level. First, the phrase lengths are altered to account for tempo changes: the lengths are increased to {3, 3, 1½, 4½, 3, 6, 1½, 4½, 1½} when the tempo increases from 76 to 112 beats per minute. Second, the nine-part phrase structure is superseded in Prelude I by a binary structure, and in Prelude IV by a ternary structure, these structures being similar to those found in *Sonatas and Interludes*.

7 These piano pieces are actually sketches for parts of *The Seasons*. The first piece contains most of the music that would ultimately become the first Prelude, while the second contains music similar to parts of the Winter movement and the fourth Prelude.

8 The original publication is in *The Tiger's Eye* no. 7 (March 1949), pp. 52–56. The journal had published a profile of Cage in its premiere issue of 1947 (Leon A. Kochnitzky, "The Three Magi of Contemporary Music") and Cage was the only composer to contribute an article during its brief lifespan. The article as printed in *The Tiger's Eye* is nearly identical to the subsequent publication in *Silence*; only minor matters of punctuation were changed, and two diagrams illustrating the four-fold division of music appeared in the original publication.

9 The quotation is taken from Raymond Bernard Blakney, trans., *Meister Eckhart: A Modern Translation*, p. 107.

10 C. de B. Evans, trans., *Meister Eckhart by Franz Pfeiffer*, vol. I, p. 7.

11 Blakney, *Meister Eckhart*, p. 107.

12 Evans, *Meister Eckhart*, vol. I, p. 127.

13 *Ibid.*, p. 22.

14 The film was *Works of Calder*, directed by Herbert Matter. Cage's score for the film (for prepared piano and recorded sounds from Calder's studio) won a prize at the Woodstock Art Film Festival in 1951.

15 John Cage, letter to Pierre Boulez, n.d. [Feb. 1950?], JCA-10.

16 Irving Sandler, *Abstract Expressionism: The Triumph of American Painting* (London: Pall Mall Press, 1970), p. 213. Note that Cage is referring to this lecture on sand painting (and *not* the "Lecture on Something") when he says in "Lecture on Nothing" that "Last year when I talked here I made a short talk. That was because I was talking about something." (*Silence*, p. 114)

17 John Cage, Foreword to *Silence*, p. ix.

18 *Ibid.*

19 Daisetz Teitaro Suzuki, *Mysticism: Christian and Buddhist*, World Perspectives, vol. 12 (New York: Harper and Brothers, 1957), p. 28.

20 The last line is perhaps a reference to the famous definition of Zen: "Eat when you are hungry, sleep when you are tired" (cited, among other places, in Watts, *The Spirit of Zen*, pp. 107–108).

21 The other "absurd" idea that Cage describes is to compose a piece for 12 radios to be called *Imaginary Landscape No. 4* – another piece that would not actually appear until the 1950s.

22 Cage revised *4' 33"* sometime around 1960, creating a wholly different work from the original. The score of the original version appears in *Source* 1/2, pp. 47–54.

23 John Cage, *I–VI* (Cambridge: Harvard University Press, 1990), pp. 20–21.

24 This is exactly the aspect of the piece that Cage removed in his 1960 revision. In the score of the piece as published in 1960 he indicates that the duration of the three parts is free, and thus negates the composed structure altogether. Later he even rejected the idea of dividing the piece into three parts (in an interview with Richard Kostelanetz in 1966, he asserted that "I don't need that piece [the three- part *4′ 33″*] today" because "we don't have to think in terms of movements any more."). Both of these actions reflect the decline in his interest in structure in the late 1950s.

25 Text translated by D. T. Suzuki in *Manual of Zen Buddhism*, p. 171.

26 *Six Melodies* uses not only the same compositional technique as the quartet, but even uses a near-identical gamut of harmonies, here rearranged for solo violin and piano.

27 In an interview with Daniel Charles, Cage makes this connection of inner and musical conflicts explicit: "The *Concerto for Prepared Piano* is an example of the lack of resolution I felt at that time, around 1950 to 1951, between letting the aggregates of sounds emerge by themselves . . . and continuing to experiment with my own personal tastes." (Cage, *For the Birds*, p. 104)

28 Cage, *For the Birds*, p. 41.

29 *Ibid.*, p. 104.

30 Morton Feldman, liner notes to sound recording, Time Records No. S/8007 (1962). Reprinted in Morton Feldman, *Essays* (Kerpen: Beginner Press, 1985), p. 38.

31 Text of the last picture as translated in Suzuki, *Manual of Zen Buddhism*, p. 161.

32 There is another method of obtaining hexagrams using yarrow stalks instead of coins, but Cage always used the coin method. Beginning with *HPSCHD* in 1969, he used a computer simulation of this coin-tossing method as a labor-saving device.

33 John Cage, letter to Pierre Boulez, n.d. [18 Dec. 1950?], JCA-15.

34 Cage, *For the Birds*, p. 104.

35 Quoted in Alan Watts, *The Way of Zen*, (New York: Vintage Books, 1957), p. 132.

3 "Throwing sound into silence" (1951–1956)

1 John Cage, "Composition as Process: Communication" (1958), in *Silence*, pp. 46–47. Although "Communication" was written in 1958, Cage says in the text that the passage in question is taken "from a lecture I gave years ago." Excerpts from this same lecture appear in the "Juilliard Lecture" of 1952, and the content of this lecture (which includes mention of the *I Ching*) places it after the start of 1951. Cage cites a "lecture last winter [presumably 1950–51 or 1951–52] at Columbia" by Suzuki as the source for the concepts of unimpededness and interpenetration.

2 The anechoic chamber story is recounted in various places, most fully in "How to Pass, Kick, Fall, and Run," in *A Year From Monday*, p. 134.

3 John Blofeld, trans., *The Zen Teaching of Huang Po*, p. 44.

4 *Ibid.*, p. 61. This particular passage was clearly of great importance to Cage; he quotes its final lines in two different places: "45′ for a Speaker" (*Silence*, p. 149), and "Composition as Process: Communication" (*Silence*, p. 47).

5 Blofeld, *The Zen Teaching of Huang Po*, p. 48.

6 Cage almost certainly encountered the story in Heinrich Zimmer's *The King and the Corpse: Tales of the Soul's Conquest of Evil* (Princeton: Princeton University Press,

1948), a book that he cited in a footnote to "Forerunners of Modern Music." The story appears in Zimmer's book as the tale of Prince Conn-eda (pp. 26–33); Cage's "shaggy nag" story deviates from Zimmer's only in minor details.

7 Cage, *For the Birds*, p. 178.

8 The charts used in composing *Music of Changes* are in a notebook currently in the possession of David Tudor. In transcribing these charts, I have tried to preserve the character of the originals as much as possible.

9 Cage allowed himself a fair amount of flexibility in the handling of rhythms. All or part of the chart duration could be used, and the individual rhythmic components could be subdivided. The precise treatment of rhythm depended largely on the context: in very dense parts of the piece, the durations tend to become more fragmented.

10 Virgil Thomson, "The Abstract Composers," *The New York Herald Tribune*, 3 February 1952. Reprinted in *The Score* no. 12 (1955), pp. 62–64.

11 Cage even made experiments with applying the chart method to poetry: "I have also tried charts of words based on a gamut of vowels and then made poems by tossing (which means that I can extend the method to include vocal works)." (Cage, in a letter to Pierre Boulez, JCA-14.)

12 See, for example, Henry Cowell's account of the premiere in "Current Chronicle: New York," *The Musical Quarterly* 33/1 (January 1952), pp. 123–36 (reprinted in *John Cage*, pp. 94–105)

13 Quoted in Tomkins, *The Bride and the Bachelors: Five Masters of the Avant-Garde*, p. 114.

14 John Cage, letter to Pierre Boulez, n.d. [July 1952?], JCA-11.

15 Cage intended that the performer should make his own transcription, and, in 1961, he himself prepared transcriptions for two- and three-octave instruments.

16 The remaining piece, *Music for Piano 20* (1953), is a separate piece composed in a manner similar to *Music for Piano 4–19*.

17 Cage, *For the Birds*, p. 44.

18 John Cage, "Composition as Process: Changes" (1958), in *Silence*, p. 27.

19 John Cage, letter to Pierre Boulez, 1 May 1953, JCA-16.

20 "45′ for a Speaker" was written using the same rhythmic structure as "The Ten Thousand Things" pieces, and was designed to be read simultaneously with any of those works. It is based in part on Cage's earlier writings and in part on new material.

21 This explains the apparent inconsistency in Cage's descriptions of the structures of the various pieces, found in "45′ for a Speaker" and in the scores of the works themselves. At times he says the structure is based on 100 units of 100 measures each, and at other times he indicates that the proportions are {3, 7, 2, 5, 11} (which adds up to 28). In the former case, he is referring to the original thirteen-part plan; in the latter, he refers to the incomplete realizations that encompass only the first five sections of that structure.

4 Indeterminacy (1957–1961)

1 Earle Brown, program note for *Music for Cello and Piano*, quoted in "Prefatory Note" to *Folio and 4 Systems* (New York: Associated Music Publishers, 1961).

2 The unusual orchestration (particularly the doubling of bassoon and saxophone) would seem to derive from the makeup of the ensemble Cage was able to gather together for the work's 1958 premiere.

3 In fact, the premiere performance was a disaster for just this reason. The instrumentalists, who had been coached by Cage before the concert, disregarded his instructions at the performance and, in Cage's words, "acted like idiots."

4 Antonín Bečvář, *Atlas eclipticalis 1950.0* (Prague: Czechoslovakian Academy of Sciences, 1958). Cage first used star charts in the composition of *Music for Carillon No. 4* (1961).

5 Tomkins, *The Bride and the Bachelors: Five Masters of the Avant-Garde*, p. 130. The original title of *Performance Mix* appears in Cage's notebooks documenting the composition of the piece.

6 Cage's appearance on *Lascia o raddoppia* made him an instant celebrity in Milan. A full account of his appearance on the show is given in Tomkins, *The Bride and the Bachelors*, pp. 130–32.

7 MacLow, a poet, attended Cage's composition classes at the New School for Social Research in New York in the mid-1950s. *The Marrying Maiden* is based on the *I Ching* and its associated Confucian commentaries, and was written using chance procedures not unlike Cage's.

8 Cage also suggests here that a piano might be treated as four instruments (keyboard, strings, inside construction, and outside construction), or even more "where further distinctions are made (of range, or mode of action)."

5 "Music (not composition)" (1962–1969)

1 Arthur Berger, "Composers are Nostalgic for the Turbulent 1920s," *New York Herald Tribune*, 20 May 1951, section 4, p. 5.

2 Jay Harrison, "New Music Concert," *New York Herald Tribune*, 31 May 1956, p. 15.

3 Michael Kirby and Richard Schechner, "An Interview with John Cage," *Tulane Drama Review* 10/2 (Winter 1965), p. 67.

4 Leonard B. Meyer, "Art by Accident," *Horizon*, September 1960, p. 123.

5 An account of the horrendous circumstances surrounding this performance are given in Tomkins, *The Bride and the Bachelors: Five Masters of the Avant-Garde*, pp. 139–44.

6 John Cage and Morton Feldman, "Radio Happening II," recorded at WBAI, New York, July 1966.

7 John Cage, "Things To Do," *The North American Review* 6/4 (Winter 1969), p. 16.

8 Cage and Feldman, "Radio Happening II." A little later in the radio program, Cage tells an amusing story on this subject:

> I went to San Jose State College, in California. Buckminster Fuller had been there for I think a month, not so long before I arrived. And I gave a talk in which I mentioned both him and Marshall McLuhan a good deal. And during the question period, after the talk, a girl came up and said, "Now, Mr. Fuller . . ."

Cage then notes that he was "very pleased" with this "freedom from being known."

9 Cage and Feldman, "Radio Happening II."

10 John Cage, "Happy New Ears!" in *A Year From Monday*, p. 34.

11 Cage and Feldman, "Radio Happening V," recorded at WBAI, New York, January 1967.

12 John Cage, Foreword to *A Year From Monday*, p. ix.

13 John Cage, "Diary: How to Improve the World (You Will Only Make Matters Worse) Continued 1967," in *A Year From Monday*, p. 157.

14 John Cage, "Interview with Roger Reynolds" (1961), in *John Cage* [catalog of works], p. 49. Cage first mentions Wolff's "zero time" notations and their implication of music as process in "Composition as Process: Indeterminacy," in *Silence*, p. 38.

15 Cage, "Diary: How to Improve the World (You Will Only Make Matters Worse) Continued 1966," in *A Year From Monday*, pp. 58–59.

16 Ross Parmenter, "Avant-Garde Sound Mosaic," *New York Times*, 22 August 1963, p. 20. This performance is also described in Tomkins, *The Bride and the Bachelors*, p. 139. That this performance is similar to *0′ 00″* is attested to by Michael Nyman's confusing of the two in his book *Experimental Music: Cage and Beyond*, pp. 77–78.

17 Richard Kostelanetz, "Conversation with John Cage," in *John Cage*, p. 18.

18 Cage, *For the Birds* (Boston: Marion Boyars, 1981), p. 225.

19 Marshall McLuhan, *Understanding Media: The Extensions of Man*, p. viii.

20 Marshall McLuhan, "The Agenbite of Outwit," p. 43.

21 McLuhan, *Understanding Media*, p. 71.

22 Cage, *For the Birds*, p. 211.

23 *Variations IV* achieved a great notoriety through two recordings, released in 1965, of a performance that took place in an art gallery in California. The sound sources for this performance were drawn mainly from tapes made from fragments of recorded music, radio broadcasts, and so forth. Unfortunately, the content of the sound sources – the one aspect of the recording that is entirely irrelevant to the work itself – has come to be identified by many as the essence of *Variations IV*. Thus, when Daniel Charles spoke to Cage about the piece in the early 1970s, he refers to it as "a quiz" in which the listener "is asked if he recognizes Schumann, or Tchaikovsky, or such and such a tango." Cage's response to Charles makes it clear that the sound content of the performance is totally outside the work: "The original piece dealt with space and space alone. And it didn't have anything to do with the sounds which happen in that space." The recording, Cage felt, completely misrepresented the work, since it was impossible to recreate the spatial differentiation of the sounds that occurred in the performance. (See *For the Birds*, p. 133.)

24 R. Buckminster Fuller, *Utopia or Oblivion: The Prospects for Humanity*, p. 348.

25 Cage and Feldman, "Radio Happening IV," recorded at WBAI, New York, January 1967.

26 John Cage, Lejaren Hiller, and Larry Austin, "*HPSCHD*," *Source* 2/2 (July 1968), p. 13.

27 Cage, "Diary: How to Improve the World (You Will Only Make Matters Worse) Continued 1968," in *M*, pp. 18, 20.

28 Cage wanted to call the exposition "Godamusicday", but university officials objected to the perceived profanity.

29 Cage, "Diary: How to Improve the World" (1968), p. 17.

30 Cage and Feldman, "Radio Happening III," recorded at WBAI, New York, December 1966. Even at this time, however, Cage was not sure about his plans.

He told Feldman the following week (during the "Radio Happening IV"), in regard to "that business with the scales and so forth," that "the more I think of it the more ridiculous it seems."

31 Cage, however, was not pleased with the inordinate length of time necessary to complete the project – a circumstance not uncommon in the earlier days of computer music. As a result, he avoided computer music projects for over fifteen years, until the creation of *Essay* in 1985.

6 "Joy and bewilderment" (1969–1992)

1 The 1969 completion of the two-piano arrangement was made with the assistance of Arthur Maddox, and was premiered at the University of California at Davis as part of *Mewantemooseicday*.

2 Editions Max Eschig has since changed its mind and now publishes Cage's two-piano transcription of *Socrate*.

3 However, note that in the third movement, the distinctive motive of four ascending quarter notes (found at the opening and at various other points) is maintained by choosing a new transposition every measure, and not every half measure.

4 Cage, *For the Birds*, p. 179.

5 *Ibid.*, p. 177.

6 *Ibid.*, p. 183.

7 In Solo 39, Schubert's lied "Die Hoffnung" is the basis of the imitation; in Solo 47, the "Queen of the Night" aria from Mozart's *Die Zauberflöte* is imitated. In the latter solo, the text is drawn from the ten "thunderclaps" of James Joyce's *Finnegans Wake*; Cage called this solo "The Queen of the Thunder."

8 Cage, *For the Birds*, p. 59.

9 The diversity of the *Song Books* creates certain difficulties in staging a performance of it. If it is performed in a straightforward concert-hall setting, with one solo following the other, the juxtapositions of different styles seem too bizarre; if several singers perform simultaneously, the differences among pieces tend to be lost in the resulting blur of activity. Perhaps the best performance I have attended was one that took place in a house, with performers scattered in different rooms, thus affording a balance between the simultaneity of styles and their distinction from one another.

10 Cage, "Diary: How to Improve the World (You Will Only Make Matters Worse) Continued 1969," in *M*, p. 76.

11 Cage, *For the Birds*, pp. 219–20.

12 *Ibid.*, p. 113.

13 *Ibid.*, p. 114.

14 Cage distinguishes between "50% mesostics" and "100% mesostics." In a 50% mesostic, a key letter can occur any number of times before the next one turns up (e.g., in "July 13, 1972", the lines "to basEl), hostess/recogNized me," where the "E" occurs again before the "N"). In a 100% mesostic, a key letter may not appear again before the next.

15 Note that the words "came" and "scarce" cannot be used to set the C, since they also have an E in them.

16 In "Writing for the Second Time Through *Finnegans Wake*" (1977) the same syllable was not to be used twice to set the same key letter. In the third "writing through" (1980), 100% mesostics were used, while in the fourth "writing through" (1980), 100% mesostics were used without allowing syllable repetition.

17 Cage, *I–VI*, p. 2.

18 John Cage, Foreword to *M*, p. *x*.

19 Heinrich Dumoulin, *Zen Buddhism: A History* (New York: Macmillan, 1990), vol. II, p. 230.

20 A photograph of Cage at the Ryoanji temple is reproduced in *John Cage at Seventy-Five*. An early reference to the stone garden is in "Indeterminacy: New Aspect of Form in Instrumental and Electronic Music," in a story where Cage expresses the view that the stones could have been placed at any points in the rectangle of sand and still been harmonious (*A Year From Monday*, p. 137). This statement solidifies the connection between the garden and Cage's musical thinking.

21 M. C. Richards, "John Cage and the Way of the Ear," in *A John Cage Reader*, pp. 38, 45.

22 The "squared" of the title refers to the fact that there are nine letters in the key-word and nine poems in the piece: nine times nine, nine squared.

23 Cage makes – in his typically understated way – an anti-war statement by indicating his preference that the performers be American men who have become Canadian citizens (i.e., draft dodgers).

24 Quoted in James J. Martin, *Men Against the State*, p. 212.

25 The poincianas are trees of the genus *Cæsalpinia*, and are members of the legume family. Although Cage does not say which species he means, he indicates that the tree he has in mind grows in Mexico, suggesting the Mexican poinciana (*Cæsalpinia mexicana*). I would venture that a similar seed pod from some other member of the *Leguminosae* would make an adequate substitute.

26 Cole Gagne and Tracy Caras, *Soundpieces: Interviews with American Composers* (Metuchen: The Scarecrow Press), pp. 76–77.

27 In addition to Cage's music, he indicates that the circus should include "live or recorded, Protestant, Sephardic, and American Indian songs, and Negro calls and hollars."

28 Laura Fletcher and Thomas Moore, "An Interview [John Cage]," *Sonus* 3/2 (Spring 1983), p. 19.

29 I had the pleasure of assisting Cage in the completion of the *Freeman Etudes*. By 1989 he had forgotten the details of his compositional procedures in the work, and so asked me to study his notes and worksheets to determine exactly what needed to be done to complete the remaining etudes.

Sources

General

Cage's writings

In preparing this book, I have relied primarily on the study of Cage's scores, his manuscripts, and his writings. The bulk of his writings have been collected in five volumes, all published by Wesleyan University Press: *Silence* (1961), *A Year From Monday* (1967), *M* (1973), *Empty Words* (1979), and *X* (1983). I gleaned much information about the early pieces from the descriptive catalog of compositions that Cage prepared with the assistance of Robert Dunn (New York: C. F. Peters Corp., 1962).

Some of Cage's later poetic texts have been published on their own. Of particular interest in this regard are *Themes & Variations* (Barrytown, NY: Station Hill, 1982) and *I–VI* (Cambridge, Mass.: Harvard University Press, 1990). The latter is the publication of his 1988–89 lectures at Harvard University, and includes transcriptions of the question and answer sessions held after the lectures.

Collections, correspondence, and interviews

A few collections of critical essays, reviews, and so forth relating to Cage's music have been important to my own work. The first and most important of these is *John Cage*, edited by Richard Kostelanetz (New York: Praeger Publishers, 1970), which is referred to here simply as *John Cage*. *A John Cage Reader*, edited by Peter Gena and Jonathan Brent (New York: C. F. Peters Corp., 1982), and *John Cage at Seventy-Five*, edited by Richard Fleming and William Duckworth (*Bucknell Review* 32/2, 1989) were both birthday tributes to Cage.

The letters between Cage and Pierre Boulez, written in the years around 1950, were of great importance to me in understanding that most important period in Cage's work. Excerpts were published in *John Cage at Seventy-Five* (with commentary by Deborah Campana) as "A Chance Encounter: The Correspondence between John Cage and Pierre Boulez, 1949–1954" (pp. 209–48). These letters are currently housed at the John Cage Archive of the Northwestern University Music Library.

Cage gave a huge number of interviews. The ones from 1970 with Daniel Charles, collected under the title *For the Birds* (Boston: Marion Boyars, 1981), have revealed a great deal to me about Cage's music.

Bibliography

I have literally worn the covers off my copy of Paul van Emmerik's "A Cage Documentary" (unpublished thesis, University of Amsterdam, 1988). It contains a chronology of Cage's life, a complete catalog of his musical, literary, and visual art works, and a thorough bibliography. It is currently being revised and expanded with additional work by Herbert Henck and András Wilheim.

1 "For more new sounds"

The following biographical sources were used to piece together the story of Cage's early years: Calvin Tomkins' profile of Cage in *The Bride and the Bachelors: Five Masters of the Avant-Garde* (New York: The Viking Press, 1965); Robert Stevenson, "John Cage on his 70th Birthday: West Coast Background," *Inter-American Music Review*, 5/1 (Fall 1982), pp. 3–17; Deborah Campana's doctoral dissertation, "Form and Structure in the Music of John Cage" (Northwestern University, 1985); and Cage's largely-autobiographical lecture "A Composer's Confessions" (1948), *Musicworks* no. 52 (Spring 1992), pp. 6–15. Other Cage essays cited in this chapter: "Future of Music: Credo" (1937), in *Silence*, pp. 3–6; "For More New Sounds" (1942), in *John Cage*, pp. 64–66; "Grace and Clarity" (1944), in *Silence*, pp. 89–93; "Composition as Process: Changes" (1958), in *Silence*, pp. 18–34; "How the Piano Came to be Prepared" (1979), in *Empty Words*, pp. 7–9.

The early music (up to *Double Music* and *Third Construction*) is analyzed in some depth in David Nicholls' *American Experimental Music, 1890–1940* (Cambridge: Cambridge University Press, 1990).

Two articles by Henry Cowell gave me a sense of the West Coast percussion movement: "Towards Neo-primitivism," *Modern Music* 10 (1933), pp. 149–53; and "Drums Along the Pacific," *Modern Music* 18 (1940), pp. 46–49.

Ananda K. Coomaraswamy's discussion of *rasa* – the basis for Cage's program in the *Sonatas and Interludes* – is found in the essay "Hindu View of Art: Theory of Beauty," in his *The Dance of Shiva: Essays on Indian Art and Culture* (London: Simpkin, Marshall, Hamilton, Kent, and Co., 1924), pp. 30–37. A similar discussion of *rasa* is in Coomaraswamy's *The Transformation of Nature in Art* (Cambridge, Mass.: Harvard University Press, 1934), pp. 47–55.

2 "To sober and quiet the mind . . ."

To follow Cage's journey through Eastern philosophy, I read the same books that he did, starting with *The Gospel of Sri Ramakrishna* by Mahendranath Gupta (New York: Ramakrishna-Vivekananda Center, 1942), and Aldous Huxley's *The Perennial Philosophy* (New York: Harper and Brothers, 1945). The writings of Ananda Coomaraswamy were listed among the sources for the previous chapter. Cage always cited the two-volume translation of Meister Eckhart's writings as the one he read (*Meister Eckhart by Franz Pfeiffer*, C. de B. Evans, trans.; London: John M. Watkins, 1924–31). However, at least some of the quotations in "Forerunners of Modern Music" (including the pivotal "Interlude" quotation) are from the shorter, more readable translation by Raymond

Bernard Blakney (*Meister Eckhart: A Modern Translation*; New York: Harper and Brothers, 1941). The *I Ching* is available in various translations. The standard one in English (and the one that Cage owned) is Cary F. Baynes' translation of Richard Wilhelm's *The I Ching or Book of Changes* (Princeton: Princeton University Press, 1967). Although I don't know if Cage read it, my own understanding of *4' 33"*, the "Lecture on Nothing," and the "Lecture on Something" was helped greatly by Daisetz Teitaro Suzuki's account of the Zen ox-herding pictures in *Manual of Zen Buddhism* (Kyoto: The Eastern Buddhist Society, 1935).

The major Cage writings from this period are: "The East in the West" (1946), *Modern Music* 23, pp. 111–15; "Defense of Satie" (1948), in *John Cage*, pp. 77–84; "Forerunners of Modern Music" (1949), in *Silence*, pp. 62–66; "Lecture on Nothing" (1950), in *Silence*, pp. 109–26; "Lecture on Something" (1951), in *Silence*, pp. 128–45.

The details of the compositional process of the *Concerto for Prepared Piano and Chamber Orchestra* are presented in my own article "From Choice to Chance: John Cage's Concerto for Prepared Piano," *Perspectives of New Music* 26/1 (Winter 1988), pp. 50–81. The score of the original 1952 version of *4' 33"*, together with historical commentary, was published in *Source* no. 2 (July 1967), pp. 46–55.

3 "Throwing sound into silence"

To understand Cage's interest in Zen Buddhism, I again went to the same sources that he did. Cage first mentions Zen in the "Lecture on Something," although only briefly (*Silence*, p. 143). His initial sources of information on the subject seem to have been the lectures and writings of Alan Watts (whose *Spirit of Zen* first appeared in 1936) and R. H. Blyth's *Zen in English Literature and Oriental Classics* (Tokyo: The Hokuseido Press, 1948). The various *Essays in Zen Buddhism* of Daisetz Teitaro Suzuki (3 vols.; London: Rider and Co., 1949) and his *Introduction to Zen Buddhism* (New York: The Philosophical Library, 1949) gave me a sense of what Cage must have heard in Suzuki's lectures at Columbia University. Suzuki's discussion of interpenetration in the third series of *Essays* (pp. 58–59, 66–67, and 127–28) is the source of much of my presentation here. The only book about Zen that Cage ever named as being of importance to his work was *The Huang-Po Doctrine of Universal Mind* (John Blofeld, trans.; London: Buddhist Society, 1947). This has since been reprinted and slightly revised as *The Zen Teaching of Huang Po* (New York: Grove Press, 1958); note, however, that only the first part of the new edition (pp. 29–66) was available in the 1947 edition that Cage knew.

The Cage essays cited in this chapter: "Juilliard Lecture" (1952), in *A Year From Monday*, pp. 95–111; "Experimental Music: Doctrine" (1953), in *Silence*, pp. 13–17; "45' for a Speaker" (1954), in *Silence*, pp. 146–92.

The details of the compositional procedures used in all the chance works of the early 1950s were the subject of my 1988 doctoral dissertation, 'The Development of Chance Techniques in the Music of John Cage, 1950–1956' (University Microfilms International, No. DA8910602). Cage's own description of the *Music of Changes* and the *Music for Piano* are found in *Silence*, pp. 57–59 and 60–61, respectively.

4 Indeterminacy

Cage's distinction between chance and indeterminacy is made clear in his essay "Composition as Process: Indeterminacy," in *Silence*, pp. 35–40. The text of part of Jackson MacLow's play *The Marrying Maiden*, along with an illuminating description of its premiere (and Cage's music), appears in his *Representative Works: 1938–1985* (New York: Roof Books, 1986).

5 "Music (not composition)"

My descriptions of the performances of Cage's pieces during the 1960s come from various sources. For *0' 00"* and *Rozart Mix*: Alvin Lucier, "Notes in the Margins" (unpublished, 1988). For the Black Mountain "event": Rose Lee Goldberg, *Performance Art: From Futurism to the Present*, rev. edn (London: Thames and Hudson, 1988), pp. 126–27. For *Variations III*: Cage's comments in an interview with Michael Kirby and Richard Schechner, *The Tulane Drama Review* 10/2 (Winter 1965), pp. 50–72. For *Variations IV*: Cage's comments in *For the Birds*, pp. 133–34. For *Variations V*: the score of the piece itself (which is simply a set of descriptive comments about the first performance) and Merce Cunningham, "A Collaborative Process Between Music and Dance," in *A John Cage Reader*, pp. 114–15. For *Variations VII*: Billy Klüver, "9 Evenings: Theatre and Engineering," in *Für Augen und Ohren: Von der Spieluhr zum akustischen Environment* (Berlin: Akademie der Künste, 1980), p. 97. For *Reunion*: Cage's comments in *For the Birds*, p. 168. For *Musicircus*: Cage's "Re Musicircus," in *John Cage*, pp. 171–72; also Stephen Husarik, "John Cage and Lejaren Hiller: *HPSCHD*, 1969," *American Music* 1/2 (Summer 1983), pp. 1–21. For *Mewantemooseicday* and *33⅓*: "MEWANTEMOOSEICDAY: John Cage in Davis, 1969," *Source* 4/1 (January 1970), pp. 21–26. For *HPSCHD*: John Cage, Lejaren Hiller, Larry Austin, "*HPSCHD*," *Source* 2/2 (July 1968), pp. 11–19; also the Husarik article cited above for *Musicircus*.

I read both of Marshall McLuhan's important books, *The Gutenberg Galaxy* (Toronto: University of Toronto Press, 1962) and *Understanding Media: The Extensions of Man* (New York: The New American Library, 1964), but his article "The Agenbite of Outwit" (*Location* 1/1 [Spring 1963], pp. 41–44) was Cage's favorite of McLuhan's writings. I personally find his *The Medium is the Message*, co-authored with Quentin Fiore (New York: Random House, 1967), to be the best and most concise summary of his thought (this book also has a reference to Cage, on page 119). Cage's own interpretation of McLuhan is in his article "McLuhan's Influence," in *John Cage*, pp. 170–71. R. Buckminster Fuller was the author of quite a number of books; I relied on *Ideas and Integrities* (New York: Macmillan, 1963) and *Utopia or Oblivion: The Prospects for Humanity* (New York: Bantam Books, 1969). Edgar Kaufmann's article "Design sans peur et sans resources" (*Architectural Forum* 125/2 [September 1966], pp. 68–70) was much liked by Cage.

Cage's contacts in the art and performance art world are recounted in Calvin Tomkins' book *Off the Wall* (New York: Doubleday, 1980) and in Al Hansen and Dick Higgins, "On Cage's Classes," in *John Cage*, pp. 120–24. James Klosty's compilation *Merce Cunningham* (New York: Saturday Review Press, 1975) includes reminiscences by various members of the company, and many wonderful photos. It gives a sense of the atmosphere surrounding Cage's touring activities in the 1960s.

Cage's day-to-day thoughts are captured in his various diaries. First, the yearly installments of "Diary: How to Improve the World (You Will Only Make Matters Worse)": the 1965, 1966, and 1967 diaries are in *A Year From Monday*, pp. 3–20, 52–69, and 145–62; the 1968 and 1969 diaries are in *M*, pp. 3–25 and 57–84. "Diary: Emma Lake Workshop 1965" and "Diary: Audience 1966" are both in *A Year From Monday*, pp. 21–25 and 50–51. Other Cage writings cited in this chapter (all published in *A Year From Monday*) are: "26 Statements Re Marcel Duchamp" (1963), pp. 70–72; "Where Do We Go From Here?" (1963), pp. 91–94; "Rhythm, etc." (1962), pp. 120–32.

6 "Joy and bewilderment"

Sources for my accounts of various pieces are as follows: for the history of *Cheap Imitation/ Second Hand*, Merce Cunningham's account in "A Collaborative Process Between Music and Dance," in *A John Cage Reader*, pp. 115–16; for the composition of *Thirty Pieces for Five Orchestras*, András Wilheim's description in the liner notes to the recording on Hungaroton LP SLPD 12893. William Brooks has written about the composition of the *Song Books* ("Choice and Change in Cage's Recent Music," in *A John Cage Reader*, pp. 82–100). Information on the process of assembling *Roaratorio* is to be found in *Roaratorio: An Irish Circus on* Finnegans Wake (Klaus Schönig, ed.; Königstein/ Taunus: Athenäum Verlag, 1982). Cage's "Preface to *Lecture on the Weather*" (*Empty Words*, pp. 3–5) makes his political intent for that piece unmistakable. Cage's descriptions of the compositional processes of the *Etudes Boreales* and *Ryoanji* are in his liner notes to Mode LP 1/2. Paul Zukofsky's "John Cage's Recent Violin Music" (*A John Cage Reader*, pp. 101–106) includes an account of the composition of the *Freeman Etudes*. And, although I have not yet read it, Cage thought highly of Laura Kuhn's recent dissertation on the *Europeras* ("John Cage's *Europeras*: The Musical Means of Revolution," University of California, Los Angeles, 1992).

Cage's major poetic efforts mentioned in the text are as follows: *Mureau*, in *M*, pp. 35–56; *Empty Words*, in the collection of that title, pp. 11–77; "Writing for the Second Time Through *Finnegans Wake*," in *Empty Words*, pp. 133–76. This last-named includes a clear description of Cage's mesostic technique. My descriptions of Cage's visual art come from Barbara Rose's description of "Not Wanting to Say Anything About Marcel" in *Source* no. 7 (January 1970), pp. 18–20, and two catalogs: *John Cage: Etchings 1978–1982* (Oakland: Crown Point Press, 1982) and *John Cage: The New River Watercolors* (Richmond: Virginia Museum of Fine Arts, 1988).

Reading any part of the journals of Henry David Thoreau reveals immediately how close his interests were to Cage's. The complete journal, in fourteen volumes edited by Bradford Torrey, is part of *The Writings of Henry David Thoreau* (Boston: Houghton Mifflin, 1906). Cage read the works of various anarchists, but a book that he mentioned on several occasions was James J. Martin's *Men Against the State* (De Kalb, Ill.: The Adrian Allen Associates, 1953), an account of early American individualist anarchists such as Josiah Warren, Ezra Heywood, Lysander Spooner, and Benjamin Tucker.

Cage continued his diaries on world improvement into the 1970s: the 1970–71 and 1971–72 entries are published in *M*, pp. 96–116 and 195–217; the final section, covering the years 1973–82, is in *X*, pp. 155–69. His essay on "The Future of Music" appears in *Empty Words*, pp. 177–87.

Index

anarchism, 156, 158–59, 178, 192, 193–94, 196
Antheil, George, 12

Berio, Luciano, 128
Black Mountain College, 38, 139
Boulez, Pierre, 48
Brecht, George, 139
Brown, Earle, 105, 107, 108, 140
Buhlig, Richard, 7, 8

Cage, John and artists, 55, 140–41; attitude
  towards music and composition of, 143–44,
  145, 174–75, 194, 195; critical reception
  of, 1–3, 11, 35, 36, 140–41; in Europe, 6,
  47–48, 128, 132, 141; and other composers,
  105–106, 139; performances and
  commissions, 141, 142, 149, 155, 157,
  178–79, 182, 196, 198; as philosopher, 1,
  2–3, 4; university positions held by, 139,
  142, 158; visual art works, 175, 180–85
compositions
  Amores, 22, 24, 27
  Apartment House 1776, 3–4, 165, 197
  Aria, 132, 167
  Atlas Eclipticalis, 124, 139, 142, 155–56,
    198
  Bacchanale, 22–23, 25, 26, 27, 206 n15
  A Book of Music, 28, 29, 159
  Cartridge Music, 134–35, 137, 139
  *Les chants de Maldoror pulvérisés par
    l'assistance même*, 194
  Cheap Imitation, 164–66, 167, 173, 174,
    196;
  for orchestra, 165, 194; for piano, 2,
    162–64; for violin, 165
  Child of Tree, 195
  The City Wears a Slouch Hat, 20, 24
  Composition for Three Voices, 7, 8
  Concert for Piano and Orchestra, 112–13,
    154, 166, 167, 182; conductor's
    part, 113; instrumental solos, 113,

123; *Solo for Flute*, 113; *Solo for
Piano*, 113–23, 130, 135–36, 141;
and other works, 123–24, 126, 130,
132, 135–36
*Concerto for Prepared Piano and Chamber
Orchestra*: first movement, 63;
second movement, 63–66; third
movement, 70–71; chance in, 76,
79; chart technique of, 62–66, 74,
75, 78; history and program of, 62
Constructions, 16–18, 27; *First
Construction (in Metal)*, 15–16,
18–19, 24, 28; *Second Construction*,
19, 206 n15; *Third Construction*,
19–20
Credo in Us, 22
Dance/4 Orchestras, 186
Double Music, 21, 154
Dream, 29
Eight Whiskus, 179
Essay, 174, 180, 213 n31
Etcetera, 193, 194
Etcetera 2/4 Orchestras, 193–94
etudes, 174, 198; *Etudes Australes*, 198;
Etudes Boreales, 199; *Freeman Etudes*,
198–99
Europeras: 1 & 2, 174, 197; *3 & 4*, 197;
5, 197
Five Songs for Contralto, 10, 14
Fontana Mix, 124, 128–34, 137, 141,
149, 167
For MC and DT, 89
Forever and Sunsmell, 22
4' 33", 2, 25, 59–60, 69, 145, 206 n11
4' 33" No. 2; see 0' 00"
HPSCHD, 146, 159–61, 164, 209 n32
Hymns and Variations, 174, 197
Imaginary Landscapes, 20; *No. 1*, 14, 20;
  No. 2, 20, 22; *No. 3*, 20; *No. 4*,
  89–90, 140, 208 n21
In a Landscape, 29

Inlets, 195–96
Lecture on the Weather, 183, 192–93
Living Room Music, 20
Metamorphosis, 10, 14
Mewantemoosicday, 158
Mirakus², 179
Musicircus, 144, 150, 157–58
Music for , 186–89, 200, 202
Music for Amplified Toy Pianos, 134
Music for Carillon: No. 1, 92, 95, 109;
 Nos. 2 and 3, 94; *No. 4*, 211 n4
Music for Marcel Duchamp, 26–27
Music for "The Marrying Maiden", 134
Music for Piano, 2, 94, 95, 104, 109–10,
 210 n16
Music for Wind Instruments, 10
Music of Changes, 78–88; chance in,
 108, 109, 190; chart technique of,
 78–83, 92; and other works, 89,
 102–104; style of, 88, 94–95
Music Walk, 126–28
Mysterious Adventure, 27
"number" pieces, 174, 199, 200–202,
 203; *One*, 2, 199; *One⁶*, 200, 202;
 One⁸, 202; *One⁹*, 202; *Two*, 199,
 200, 202; *Two³*, 202; *Two⁴*, 202;
 Four, 200, 202; *Four²*, 200; *Four³*,
 200, 202; *Four⁴*, 200; *Four⁵*, 200;
 Four⁶, 200, 202; *Five*, 202; *Seven*,
 199; *Seven²*, 202; *Ten*, 203; *Fourteen*,
 202; *Twenty-three*, 202; *Sixty-eight*,
 203; *Seventy-four*, 204; *Eighty*, 203;
 1O1, 199, 203; *103*, 203; *108*, 203
The Perilous Night, 24, 27–28, 36
Quartet for Percussion, 12, 16, 20
Quartets, 197
Renga, 183, 189, 196–97
Reunion, 144, 153–54, 155, 157
Roaratorio, 174, 179–80
Root of an Unfocus, 26
Rozart Mix, 144, 149–50, 152
Ryoanji, 174, 189, 191
*Score (40 Drawings by Thoreau) and 23
 Parts: 12 Haiku*, 183, 194
The Seasons, 39, 40–45, 48–50, 50–51,
 55, 208 n7
Selkus², 179
Seven Haiku, 89, 182
She is Asleep, 22
"Silent Prayer"; *see 4' 33"*
Six Melodies for Violin and Keyboard, 61
Sixteen Dances, 207 n23
62 Mesostics Re Merce Cunningham, 178,
 179, 183
Solos for Voice, 166; *1*, 123–24, 167; *2*,
 134, 166; *3–92* (see *Song Books*)

*Solo with Obbligato Accompaniment of Two
 Voices in Canon, and Six Short
 Inventions on the Subject of the Solo*, 7, 8
Some of 'The Harmony of Maine' (Supply
 Belcher), 197
Sonata for Clarinet, 7, 8, 13
Sonata for Two Voices, 7
Sonatas and Interludes, 5, 27, 29–35, 38,
 63
Song Books, 174; music of, 165, 166–73,
 194; programmaticism of, 191–92;
 texts of, 176, 179, 182
Sonnekus², 179, 192
Sounds of Venice, 132–33, 134, 147
String Quartet in Four Parts, 47–55; effect
 on Cage's aesthetic of, 60–61; gamut
 technique of, 48–50, 62; history of,
 47–48; and "Lecture on Nothing",
 57, 59; style of, 58, 66; mentioned,
 25, 39, 63
Suite for Toy Piano, 29
"The Ten Thousand Things", 95–97,
 102–104, 109, 137, 154, 190; Six
 pieces for a string player, 97–100,
 102; *59½" for a String Player*, 97;
 34' 46.776" for a Pianist, 100–102,
 109; *31' 57.9864" for a Pianist* (see
 34' 46.776" for a Pianist); "45' for a
 Speaker", 210 n20; *26' 1.1499" for a
 String Player*, 97, 102; *27' 10.554"
 for a Percussionist*, 102, 109;
 unfinished pieces for magnetic tape
 and voice, 100
Theatre Piece, 133–34, 139, 147
Thirty Pieces for Five Orchestras, 185–86,
 200
Thirty Pieces for String Quartet, 186
33⅓, 158
Three Dances, 28–29
Tossed As It Is Untroubled, 26, 27
Totem Ancestor, 25
Trio for percussion, 12, 16, 27
TV Köln, 126–28
Two Pastorales, 89
Two Pieces for Piano (1935), 10
Two Pieces for Piano (1946), 41
Variations: I, 119, 124, 135–36, 137; *II*,
 119, 124, 136–37, 139, 145, 154,
 155; *III*, 148–49, 150, 155; *IV*,
 155–56, 212 n23; *V*, 144, 152–53;
 VI, 146, 154; *VII*, 150, 153
Waiting, 89
Water Music, 89, 147
Water Walk, 132–33, 134
Williams Mix, 90–91, 96, 100, 105, 109,
 130, 149

Index

Winter Music, 2, 110–12, 118, 123, 124, 167
The Wonderful Widow of Eighteen Springs, 26, 167, 179
Works of Calder, 208 n14
0′ 00″, 138–40, 144, 146–49, 150, 153, 155–56, 167
writings, 142, 144, 175–78, 178–79, 208 n8
"Anarchy," 178, 196
"A Composer's Confessions," 13–14, 16, 37, 39, 59, 206 n11
"Composition in Retrospect," 196
"Defense of Satie," 16, 38–39, 39–40, 45, 56, 206 n11, 207 n19
"Diary: How to Improve the World (You'll Only Make Matters Worse)," 144
"The East in the West," 38, 39
Empty Words, 176–77, 178, 179, 183, 194
"Experimental Music," 194, 207 n23
"Experimental Music: Doctrine," 76–77
"Forerunners of Modern Music," 40, 45–47, 55, 60; form discussed in, 57, 61; harmony discussed in, 48–49; structure discussed in, 46–47, 56
"For More New Sounds," 11, 16
"45′ for a Speaker," 76, 96, 175, 182, 210 n20
"The Future of Music" (1974), 173–74, 193
"The Future of Music: Credo" (1937), 10, 13, 173–74
"Grace and Clarity," 16, 25, 33, 39, 47
"Indeterminacy," 108–109
"Indeterminacy: New Aspect of Form in Instrumental and Electronic Music," 141
I–VI, 178, 196
"Jasper Johns: Stories and Ideas," 135
"Juilliard Lecture," 75, 76, 175
"Lecture on Nothing," 55–59; form discussed in, 56–57, 66; and "Lecture on Something," 66, 69; materials discussed in, 57–58, 76; silence discussed in, 58–59; structure discussed in, 56; style of, 56, 58, 175; mentioned, 40, 61, 182, 208 n16
"Lecture on Something," 40, 55, 66–69, 76, 174
mesostics, 177–79, 192
"Mirakus^2," 178
Mureau, 174, 176, 177, 178, 179
"Rhythm, Etc.," 135
Silence, 142

"Sonnekus^2," 178
"Talk I," 175
Themes and Variations, 196, 205 n4
"26 Mesostics Re and Not Re Marcel Duchamp," 179
"2 Pages, 122 Words on Music and Dance," 182
"Where are We Going? and What Are We Doing?," 135
"Writings Through *Finnegans Wake*," 177–79
Calder, Alexander, 48, 107
chance composition: chart technique, 62, 92, 95, 190, 210 n11 (*see also* Compositions: *Concerto for Prepared Piano and Chamber Orchestra*; Compositions: *Music of Changes*); critical reception of, 1–3, 140; point-drawing technique, 92, 94–95 (*see also* Compositions: *Music for Piano*); principles and implications of, 4, 76–77, 105, 108, 139; star charts, 124, 167, 198; *see also* I Ching
compositional techniques: attack-control method, 22; cellular method, 10, 12, 18, 40; gamut technique, 40, 41–45, 57, 61, 62–63, 66, 74 (*see also* Compositions: *String Quartet in Four Parts*); serial method, 10, 7, 8; twenty-five note method, 7–8, 40; *see also* chance composition
Coomaraswamy, Ananda K., 29, 36–38, 45, 207 n23
Cornish School, 9, 11, 13, 20, 22
Cowell, Henry, 11, 12, 13, 23; Cage's relationship to, 8, 9, 13; reviews Cage's music, 36, 140
Cunningham, Merce, 11, 48, 105, 139, 142; Cage's collaborations with, 154–55; mentioned as dancer or choreographer, 22, 25, 40, 94, 152, 162, 207 n23

dance, 12–13, 13–14, 22, 25, 205 n9
Duchamp, Marcel, 26–27, 145, 153, 166, 167, 178

Eckhart, Meister, 36, 45–46, 47, 58, 60, 206 n11
electronics, 20, 139, 148, 150, 152–54
experimental music, 10–11, 11, 77

Feldman, Morton, 67, 78, 105, 106, 108, 140
Fischinger, Oskar, 12
form (continuity), 39, 56–57, 61, 66–67, 76
Fort, Syvilla, 22, 206 n15
four-fold division of music, 38–39, 45, 56, 61, 75–76
Fuller, Buckminster, 145, 156–57, 158, 192, 193, 196

harmony, 4, 39, 45, 48–50
Harrison, Lou, 11, 16, 21
Hiller, Lejaren, 159, 160
Huang Po, 36, 77
Huxley, Aldous, 36, 45, 56

I Ching, 70, 209 n32; use of, in *Cheap Imitation*, 163;—*Concert for Piano and Orchestra*, 113;—*Concerto for Prepared Piano and Chamber Orchestra*, 70;—*Mureau*, 176;—*Music for Piano*, 94;—*Music of Changes*, 78, 82, 83;—*On the Surface*, 185;—*Song Books*, 167;—"The Ten Thousand Things," 95, 99;—*Thirty Pieces for Five Orchestras*, 185;—"Diary: How to Improve the World," 144
indeterminacy: Cage's early use of, 109; principles and definitions of, 107–108, 139; "tools," 126, 128; in works of other composers, 106–107, 108
Indian aesthetics, 36, 40, 48; permanent emotions (*rasa*), 29, 30, 38, 207 n23
interpenetration, 74–76

Johns, Jasper, 141
Joyce, James, 26, 167, 178–79, 179–80

Lucier, Alvin, 138, 144, 149

MacLow, Jackson, 134, 178, 212 n7
MacLuhan, Marshall, 145, 150–52, 157
Mozart, Wolfgang Amadeus, 28, 159, 160

nature, 37–38, 147, 194–96

performance art, 139
Project for Music for Magnetic Tape, 90, 105

Ramakrishna, Sri, 36
Rauschenberg, Robert, 139, 141
rhythmic structure, 76; discussed in Cage's writings, 25, 46–47, 56; emptiness of, 47, 55, 56, 57, 60, 67, 69; micro-macrocosmic structures, 14–16, 28; necessity of, 39, 45; origins of, 13–14

Richards, M. C., 139, 191
Russolo, Luigi, 11, 12, 13, 17

Sarabhai, Gita, 36, 37
Satie, Erik: and *Cheap Imitation*, 196; and *The Seasons*, 44; Cage's interest in music of, 38, 165; *Socrate*, 162, 179, 192; and *Song Books*, 166–67, 168, 182, 191; and *Sonnekus²*, 192; *Vexations*, 157, 158, 202; mentioned, 51, 180
Schoenberg, Arnold, 7, 8, 9–10
silence: and *4' 33"*, 60, 148; and interpenetration, 75; in Meister Eckhart, 46; as non-intention, 75, 148; as nothingness, 58–59, 69; and rhythmic structure, 47, 206 n11; use of in Cage's compositions, 4, 26–27, 70–71, 79, 203
Suzuki, Daisetz Teitaro, 74, 209 n1

theatre, 146–47, 167–68
Thomson, Virgil, 11, 36, 88, 140
Thoreau, Henry David, 193, 194; drawings used in Cage's works, 177–78, 183, 184, 189, 193, 197; as theme of *Song Books*, 166–67, 191–92, 194; writings used in Cage's works, 167, 169, 176, 177, 178, 180, 192
Tudor, David: as influence on Cage's work, 78, 102, 123; and the Project for Music for Magnetic Tape, 90; mentioned as performer, 100, 105, 139, 141, 153, 155, 157

Varèse, Edgard, 11, 12, 13, 17

Weiss, Adolph, 8–9
Wolff, Christian, 70, 105, 106–7, 108, 140, 147

Zen Buddhism, 74–75, 77, 189–90; ox-herding pictures, 60, 69; Cage's interest in, 36, 74; and "Lecture on Nothing," 56, 208 n20
Zukofsky, Paul, 165, 198